Chris Austin

DISCONNECTED!

Broken Links in Britain's Rail Policy

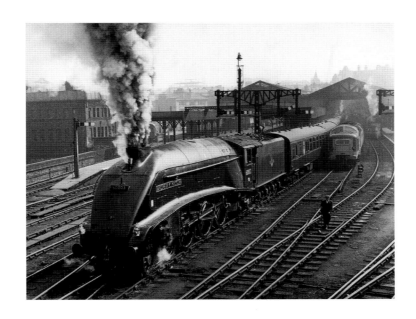

DISCONNECTED!

Broken Links in Britain's Rail Policy

CHRIS AUSTIN & RICHARD FAULKNER

An imprint of
Ian Allan Publishing

First published 2015

ISBN 978 0 86093 664 0

Published by Oxford Publishing Co
an imprint of Ian Allan Publishing Ltd, Addlestone, Surrey KT15 2SF

Printed in Bulgaria

Visit the Ian Allan Publishing website at www.ianallanpublishing.com

FRONT COVER: DISCONNECTED!
The demolition train passes Ashley Heath Halt on the Brockenhurst-Ringwood-Poole line with materials from the lifted down line. The up line became a siding before complete closure in 1969. The locomotive is BR Standard Class 4 No 75077. *John H. Bird*

BACK COVER
Not far from the front cover picture, Ringwood station is seen on 25 April 1964 with the 11.04am Brockenhurst to Bournemouth Central train via Wimborne leaving behind Standard 2-6-2T No 82026 of Bournemouth shed. This route would have been so valuable in serving the expanded Bournemouth/Poole conurbation and relieving the chronically crowded A31. *Michael J. Fox*

FRONTISPIECE: CHANGING TIMES
'A4' Pacific No 60003 *Andrew K. McCosh* of King's Cross shed leaves Leeds Central while a 'Deltic' waits on the engine release road. Trains were later transferred to the nearby Leeds City, and this station and the viaduct on which it was built were demolished. After almost 50 years it has now been redeveloped with offices, shops and restaurants. *Ian Allan Library*

TITLE PAGE: A COMPLEX WEB OF LINES
A Class 9F 2-10-0 crosses Harringworth Viaduct with a northbound freight train on the Midland route via Corby. In the foreground is the locomotive of the Uppingham branch push-pull train waiting in the bay platform at Seaton Junction. Seaton (Rutland) was on the LNWR Rugby-Peterborough (East) line. *Chris Austin*

RCH JUNCTION DIAGRAMS The junction diagram maps on pages 23, 87, 89, 99, 103, 107 and 117 were originally produced by the Railway Clearing House and have been reproduced from the *Pre-Grouping Atlas and RCH Junction Diagrams* published by Ian Allan Publishing Ltd, 2014.

CONTENTS

PREFACE

LIFELINE LOST
Closure of the 'Waverley Route' in 1969 removed a large piece of the railway jigsaw and left the Borders isolated for 45 years, reducing the options when one of the Anglo-Scottish routes was closed. Other diversionary routes had already been lost, to Tweedmouth Junction in 1964 and to Newcastle via Hexham in 1956. Here 'D49' 'Hunt' Class No 62747 *The Percy* waits at Hawick at the head of the 4.32pm train to Newcastle via the Border Counties line on 13 August 1955. *I. S. Carr*

This is our second book about the political and social history of Britain's railways. We were touched and heartened by how well our first offering – *Holding the Line: How Britain's Railways Were Saved*[1] – was received, particularly by those who worked in the industry during the period on which we concentrated (the 1970s and 1980s). Scores of them wrote to us to say how pleased they were that we had managed to uncover so many of the dark goings-on that they suspected, but never really knew about. Every review of the book we saw was generous and well-informed, and we were delighted to be awarded the Railway & Canal Historical Society's 'Popular Transport Book of the Year' prize for 2014.

We were encouraged to write a sequel, but hesitated before we agreed, as we needed to be sure that there was sufficient new material to make such a task justifiable. Those doubts were dispelled in three ways: first, because our further researches at the National Archives at Kew and elsewhere unearthed a mine of previously unpublished information that we believe our readers would wish to see.

Second, a number of people were prompted by reading *Holding the Line* to contact us with fresh insights and, in one particular case,

sensational new material on an incident we covered earlier but, as it has turned out, incompletely.

The third reason was because we wish to set off a 'what if' debate on lines that were closed after the Beeching Report, but should have been retained because of the role they would have been able to play in today's modern, popular and expanding railway. The choice of routes we write about is entirely our own, and we take responsibility for them, though we acknowledge with gratitude the help we have received from members of Railfuture, whom we encouraged to come forward with their own thoughts and ideas.

INTRODUCTION

*'The only function of economic forecasting
is to make astrology look respectable.'*

JOHN KENNETH GALBRAITH[2]

This book looks at the contraction of the British railway network over a 50-year period and its subsequent expansion and development from the mid-1990s onwards. In particular, it reviews lines that were lost and that today would have formed a valuable part of the national rail network. It includes some positive stories where lines have been restored, and some unhappy stories where lines have been lost for ever. It chronicles the seismic changes in the approach to rail planning in Britain over the last 60 years and draws some lessons for the future.

It is not a criticism of Dr Beeching[3] or his report, which we subjected to detailed analysis in our first book, *Holding the Line.* Indeed, it draws on some of his prescient words reflecting a clear view on his part of the railway's strengths and weaknesses. Its purpose is to set out the facts on some of the most significant examples of disinvestment in transport infrastructure from the 1950s to the 1980s. We then move on to record the steps taken to reinstate the routes or the capacity destroyed, and readers may draw their own conclusions on the merits or otherwise of the original closures. We also identify those routes and stations that would have brought real benefits to passengers, freight customers and to the British economy today, and, perhaps more controversially, identify a few key routes that we believe fail the test and would not justify reinstatement.

In general, our aim here is not to criticise those railway managers who brought forward the proposals for retrenchment, for they could not foresee the subsequent revival in the fortunes of the railway or the huge latent demand that would develop for rail travel. Criticism could rightly be levelled at some of the decisions made, notably those on the closure of Birmingham Snow Hill, which had to be recreated at huge expense just 16 years after closure. We should also criticise the lack of strategic direction that was a failing by ministers, civil servants and the British Transport Commission. Perhaps the most significant failure throughout the period of British Railways' existence was that of civil servants and ministers who never identified the role of the industry that had been nationalised in 1948. Throughout the period we review the railwaymen were working in something of a policy vacuum. The main point though is to learn the lessons of history, the most significant of which is that it is impossible to forecast the long-term future with any degree of accuracy, and that this leads inevitably to the conclusion that the only tenable strategy is to keep options open to deal with change that may be unexpected, or contrary to the trend of previous years. One example is the way in which smaller market towns lost their self

sufficiency from the 1960s onwards, and became ever more dependent on a nearby major town or city. Supermarkets replaced local shops, schools and hospitals were concentrated in ever larger units and local manufacturing was lost as Britain moved to import its basic requirements. The story of the Minsters' Line in chapter five is an illustration of this phenomenon and the significance of this change is that it creates the need for more trips between towns which, in the absence of a railway, tend to be made by car on increasingly inadequate roads.

We also pay tribute to the whistleblowers, the courageous people who put their careers on the line or risked prosecution to bring the secret plans on clandestine rail closures to the attention of the press and the public. Without them, we would have a smaller network to develop today.

One of the surprises in researching the material for this book has been the large number of lines that would today form a valuable part of the national network. They might add access points to the network in areas currently remote from a station. They might provide a useful alternative route during engineering work or train or infrastructure failures. They might provide relief for a busy route that can then accommodate more services itself. Or they might serve two or even all three of these functions.

The national network run by Network Rail was 10,625 miles in 2014, of which 780 miles were freight only.[4] The conclusions of our study, described in this book, would increase that mileage only by 530 (5%), and is a modest aspiration that would deliver a big improvement in accessibility and resilience for the current network. Our analysis also suggests that a further 680 miles would have formed a useful part of today's network but are probably not capable of restoration. If the 330 miles of high-speed route are added, that brings the total of new mileage to be built to 860, which would increase the network size by just 8% to 11,485 route miles, an entirely achievable figure. Adding in those that are beyond recall would have made the ideal network size just under 12,200 miles. The actual list of lines we think would have value today is set out in Appendix A.

In saying this, we know (from past experience) that our figure will be wrong, and that the requirement may be for more or less than this. We therefore conclude that action needs to be taken to safeguard the routes that will be required, and plans drawn up for their protection. For tomorrow's planners, the rail link has to become the basic building block for today's development and regeneration, just as the 'spine road' or trunk road junction improvement was seen as essential in the past.

It is significant too that most of the lines that would be useful today are those that were excluded from Dr Beeching's first report, and their closure came later, after Beeching had left BRB. In some cases they were put forward when the Department declined to pay support for the lines concerned, and in others by BR managers who were desperately trying to shed costs to meet Government financing limits.

It is also significant that the decline of the network and its rapid reduction in size took place under BR, while the growth has taken place since privatisation. Latterly BR, to its credit, did reopen many stations and lines, the greatest number being through the initiative and funding of the PTEs[5]. The great surge in demand, however, and the more ambitious expansion programmes to deal with growth have come with the privatised railway, and this too has changed the attitude of Government to the industry. This is not so much a political polemic as an observed fact, and is discussed in more detail later.

MEMENTOES
So many towns still have a Station Road although they have not seen a train for 50 years. This example is at Clevedon, which had two stations.
Chris Austin

Our conclusion has to be that Beeching's 'Reshaping' report was less damaging than is sometimes claimed. The real damage came from the second report, which identified selected lines for development and condemned the rest of the network to a twilight period of no investment or development, and during the dark days of the decade after Beeching's departure in 1965 many withered and died.

It is also worth noting that a number of these later closures were of lines that have subsequently become successful heritage railways for at least part of their length.

1

THE POLICY GAP

*'Small boys play trains, but grown-ups have
a better game; they call it reorganisation.'*

EDITORIAL COMMENT IN *THE ECONOMIST*, ALSO ATTRIBUTED
TO MICHAEL BONAVIA[6]

The mindset of the 1960s and 1970s: contraction and decline

At a time when the growth in demand for rail travel has been running at record levels, with the number of passengers increasing year on year by up to 5%, it is difficult to appreciate how negatively people felt about the railways leading up to the publication of the Beeching Report in 1963, and even more so during the two succeeding decades when most of the closures proposed – and many more besides – were implemented.

One of Beeching's team at BR, Fred Margetts[7], had very clear views on why the commercial approach had to be adopted. Moving from General Manager of the North Eastern Region to the Board with responsibility for operations in 1962, Margetts was respected as a practical railwayman and had immense energy and drive[8]. His view of what was needed was set out in an inspired paper to the BR Officers' Conference at York held between 6 and 9 April 1962. The talk was an encouragement to colleagues to seize the opportunities offered by the new Transport Act, which freed the railway from a lot of historic obligations, and turn it into a commercial success. He encapsulates the view of the position of the railway at the time as untenable:

> 'We have tried everything except running the concern on a purely commercial basis untrammelled by political interference and by monopolistic restrictions. And where have we got to? To a position where dwindling traffics, immense financial losses, a staff dissatisfied with wages and working conditions, and services regarded as unreliable by public and trading standards combine to cause our detractors to prophesy our demise and our protagonists to wonder if their faith is misplaced.'[9]

While the paper was not primarily concerned with closures, he saw them as an essential prerequisite to a commercial railway, and 'speedy elimination of the redundant parts of the system' was needed, so that management attention could focus on the development of the rest of the network. His conclusion was that salvation lay in the hands of railway managers themselves, and not 'upon any presumptive right to a living or upon political change leading to direction and to survival unrelated to contribution ... and perhaps, in working out our own salvation, we shall unravel the conflicting strands of public thought.'

This was an entirely understandable (if ambitious) objective at the time, but subsequent history has proved how unattainable such an objective was. Railways are not commercial undertakings in a conventional sense. They are a social service and highly political with public and political aspirations for the highest standards and quality coupled with an unwillingness to pay either through fares or taxation for the extent and standard of network required. Forty years after Margetts's speech, many railway managers harboured similar aspirations at the time of privatisation and believed it would take railways out of the political arena. In fact, the opposite turned out to be true and the railway is more tightly controlled by Government now than when Margetts was speaking to the York conference. The difference 50 years on is that ministers and civil servants have at last realised the value of a properly invested railway and how essential it is to the long-term economic needs of the country. The greatest change in thinking is at the Treasury, which is now prepared to view railway investment as producing an economic rate of return.

The processes that led up to the Beeching Report have been widely described elsewhere (including in our own *Holding the Line*), and there is no need to repeat them here. What is remarkable – and shocking – is the discovery of just how determined the railway managers and civil servants of particularly the 1970s, and also of the 1980s, were to reduce the size of the network with which they were entrusted, even after public opinion had turned against further major closures, and politicians had wisely followed them.

Beeching had provided the Government with a clear plan for the railway if they wished it to be run on commercial lines, but they had rowed back from that because such a policy proved to be politically unacceptable. The concept of the 'social' railway with support for individual lines required for social and economic reasons had been taken forward under the Transport Act, 1968. But by 1971 the direction of the industry was still unclear. 'The Government does not yet have a transport policy because it has not made its mind up on the railways,' said a young Jim Coates in the minister's private office in a memorandum to colleagues in October 1971.[10] True, but

incredible given that the Ministry was forging ahead with plans for further closures (eventually exposed in the *Sunday Times* leak of 1972[11]). Joe Peeler[12], an Under-Secretary at the Ministry, invited ideas from colleagues on whether it would be better to deal with some 60 anticipated line closures to be put forward in 1971 on the basis of 'dribbling out' information, taking the 'plunge' and publishing the full list, or a 'two-pronged' approach announcing half immediately and the remainder in six months' time. None of these approaches was acceptable, but in the memo[13] he did recognise the underlying truth that while closure proposals were for BR to propose, the fact that the minister could terminate support for any line effectively forced BR's hand in putting the line up for closure.

In October 1971 a secret memorandum from the Board with a very limited circulation set out the problem succinctly.[14] Financial reconstruction following the 1968 Act had left the finances of the railway very finely balanced, with a need for significant levels of investment both to replace assets and to expand services with a good market potential.

> 'The future of the Railway business depends very much on the Government's view of the contribution Railways can make to the country's total transport needs. If it is judged as a purely commercial business, the system will certainly decline, reducing the total transport potential of the country, a loss which will be, effectively, irreversible.'

The value of the railway was not seen as a nebulous social concept, but in hard figures for reductions in road congestion and reduction of accidents, for example.

The Board was very concerned that the continued erosion of the network as more and more grant-aided services went into the closure process would shift more of the overhead to the commercial railway and affect its profitability. At that stage, the Board saw closures as minor pruning rather than root and branch reductions. 'The removal of grant aid, except in a few obvious cases on which the Board and the Department would agree, must inevitably harm the whole structure of the railway business.' Reduction in grant aid would mean an increase in the external financing limit.

To sum up, 'The 'commercial' and 'social' railway services are interdependent and each benefits from the other. It is not just a matter of subsidy – it is symbiosis.'

The question of what the nation required of its railway was one constantly asked by the Board but never answered by Government. The paper pressed the case for national transport planning. 'At the moment, we have the impression that BR is ahead of planning by the Department, and also ahead of the NFC, the NBC, etc, whose plans would also be elements of a National Transport Plan.'

The National Archives contains scores of papers from the British Railways Board that demonstrated that line closures were not just a sought-for objective, but an obsession, despite the fact that shortly before the Conservatives lost office early in 1974 the Transport Minister, John Peyton[15], had announced that the Government had disowned the more extreme proposals contained in the infamous 'Blue Book' (see Chapter 2), and said that the network should remain at broadly its 1974 level.

Supporters of a smaller network were, however, encouraged by Labour ministers such as Anthony Crosland[16], who made no secret of his belief that rail subsidies were regressive and disproportionately benefited the middle classes; he saw bus travel as the best way of encouraging mobility for poorer people and supported suggestions for a much smaller railway.

With remarkable naivety the BR Board appeared prepared to go along with the Crosland approach, up to the point that the transport policy consultation paper was published on 13 April 1976; it then dawned on the Board that it was faced with an ideological enemy from the centre-left, who, left to his own devices, would have inflicted immense damage on Britain's railways as a whole.

Largely thanks to the 'No Rail Cuts' campaign spearheaded by the National Union of Railwaymen's General Secretary, Sidney Weighell[17] (aided and abetted by insiders at the BRB – see Chapter 2), and supported by an impressive myriad of environmentalists and transport campaigners, the mood of the public turned against the Labour Government's anti-rail policy, and by the time Crosland had been succeeded by William Rodgers[18] (as Secretary of State in a re-established Department of Transport), the political appetite for a new round of closures had been significantly reduced.

Relationships between the BR Board and the Department of the Environment were poor during this period, and the lack of trust between the two sides inhibited the sharing of information and the development of a proper railway strategy. Surprisingly, in view of what we have said above, some officials in the Department thought that BR was not sufficiently robust in pursuing closure cases. A good overview of this broken relationship is given in a memorandum written by Joe Peeler dated 8 February 1973.[19] It was written against a background assumption in the supporting strategy studies of the need for withdrawal of 73 unremunerative passenger rail services (URPS) and an upper limit of 123, which the Board accepted was politically unattainable.

In his view BR was convinced that its task was to meet the 'social need', whereas the Department's view was that there was no absolute 'need' and that BR should look to cut costs where it could. 'BR are often keen to expand or maintain traffic by advertising, keeping fares down, etc, while preserving a comparatively high level of frequency of service. The DoE on the other hand are usually keener to make economies as a more effective way of saving grant and real resources.'

Peeler went on to accuse BR of 'grantmanship', or adjusting services to maximise the grant payable or the profitability of its commercial services. He was concerned that blurring the distinction between commercial and social passenger services would make it more difficult for the Department to keep control of the burgeoning deficit. The figure of £75 million a year might have to be increased by 130% unless the losses could be stemmed.

Peeler was right on this. The problem with setting objectives and targets is that people will strive to meet them, even if they produce consequences that were not wished for. It is a penalty of the shadow management practised by the Department over many years, and also demonstrates the problems inherent in trying to allocate costs for components of what is an integrated national network. Ian Campbell[20] described the position he was faced with when managing closures on the London Midland Region in 1969[21]:

'We must make strenuous efforts to improve the commercial worth of the grant aided services. In many cases this will mean a reduction in grant payable but if the alternative is the closure of a grant service and the transfer of all fixed charges to the commercial railway, then the short term loss of grant ought to be accepted.'

Peeler's memorandum also revealed a wish to see more lines closed to save the cost of renewing the Mark 1 diesel multiple units, which was exercising minds at the time, although it was to be another decade before the investment was made.

A section of the paper was also given over to downplaying the economic benefits brought by the railway, a somewhat disingenuous claim as it was evident that no research had been done to demonstrate or disprove the proposition. There was no evidence that reprieving railway lines in Assisted Areas had any appreciable effect on their development 'as far as one can judge,' the paper opined. 'In general, road communications are much more important than rail for the development of new industry in these areas.' 'No instance is known of where URPS [unremunerative rail passenger services] are necessary for travel to work in order to maintain employment in the area.' This latter is perhaps a little surprising as the list of lines planned for closure included significant commuter routes such as Liverpool-Southport, Leeds-Ilkley and the North Warwickshire line from Stratford-upon-Avon to Birmingham. This is a classic example of how the Department operated in the 1970s. An unsupported assertion was made in line with the received wisdom of opinion-formers at the time. Safe in the knowledge that such assertions would not be challenged, they became self-reinforcing and self-fulfilling. Today, such assertions would be challenged and empirical evidence would be required before they could be made. We have come a long way over 40 years.

At the same time as Peeler was writing his fiercely anti-rail memos, other officials were worried about what to do regarding the small number of lines for which ministerial consent to closure had been granted, but not – for a variety of reasons – implemented. This was a particularly hot topic in the late 1960s and early 1970s, as one of the most notorious incidents immediately following Beeching was the refusal of the then Transport Minister, Tom Fraser[22], in the new Labour Government, to reverse any of the closure consents given by his predecessor, Ernest Marples[23], but not yet implemented by the BR Board.

Papers uncovered in the National Archives confirm an official's view that

'Neither section 56 of the Transport Act 1962 nor the amendments made by section 54 of the Transport Act 1968 to that section confer on the Secretary of State a power to revoke a consent under section 56, once it has been given.'

He went on to say that in addition the minister did not have the power 'to attach conditions to a consent which has previously been given without conditions', neither could the Secretary of State 'substitute a radically different set of conditions'.

There was, however, a way out, as the following paragraph in this remarkable memorandum made clear:

'Whilst it is true that a consent under section 56 of the 1962 Act once given, cannot be revoked, there is nothing in section 56 which *obliges* [our emphasis] the Railways Board to implement the closure when it has been granted. This is so even in cases where any conditions attached to the consent have been satisfied. It seems to me, therefore, that there is nothing in law to prevent the Railways Board agreeing with the Department not to implement a closure consent. If such agreement were given and publicised, it would clearly be impracticable for the Board then to close the service in reliance on that consent. I do not see how it is legally possible for the Railways Board to withdraw their application for a consent when the consent has in fact been given, but, as I have indicated above, I do not see why the Board and the Department should not agree that the consent should not be implemented. If you have cases where you are now anxious that a service, to which a closure consent has been given, should continue to operate indefinitely, I would think that these cases are best dealt with in this way. This, of course, assumes that the Railways Board are willing to play.'[24]

Three services were the immediate subject of this memorandum:

Inverness-Kyle of Lochalsh
Ashford-Hastings
Bedford-Bletchley

None had closed because the conditions attached had not been fulfilled, and they can indeed be said to have operated 'indefinitely' and are still very much part of the modern railway. In addition, there was an agreement between the then minister, Fred Mulley[25], and the BR Chairman, Richard Marsh[26], that attempts to close these three lines, and three more – the Cambrian Coast, Wimbledon to West Croydon, and Stockport to Stalybridge – should be abandoned.

The Department's policy on replacement bus services was not progressing because of an unwillingness by the National Bus Company to take over rail services that local authorities wanted to see retained, not least because rural bus services were themselves now subsidised, and the NBC looked to local authorities for this support. Finally, the paper revealed the Department's somewhat disdainful view of the capabilities of local authorities. They were not generally geared up to deal with the complexities of rail closures and managing bus replacement, which meant that the Department had to deal with this detail, instead of concentrating on broader strategy.

As we now know, the Board was assiduously pursuing a policy of retrenchment at the time, and in January 1977 David Bowick[27] produced a paper entitled 'Points We Would Like The Minister To Include' in a forthcoming speech, which was jokily headed 'The Diet of Crewe'. The number of 'points' was 16, and number 6 was 'Bus/Rail'. It read as follows:

'Recognises two-way deal. Recognises the parties (on time-frame) to work up jointly proposition for bus substitution in two specified areas of the country – bringing out feasability (*sic*)/economic/labour issues. Spell out what implications it has for the traveller/the size of the P.S.O. Requires also proposition following study of prospects for rail substitution on defined routes where parallel competitive services exist.'

Although by May 1978 Crosland had gone and been replaced by Rodgers, the BRB still tried to get local line closures back on the political agenda. Bob Reid[28], widely acknowledged by railway managers as the best Chairman BR ever had, observed that in a world of continuous change, the PSO requirement was that BR should stand still. This is reflected in a Board minute from that time:

'The Board discussed Mr Reid's memorandum dated 2nd May 1978, setting out proposals for establishing a policy for local rail services in view of the apparent present lack of urgency on the part of Government to develop the proposals set out in the Transport Policy White Paper (Cmnd. 6836).

The following principal points were made in discussion:-
1. Exercises undertaken on routes in Lincolnshire, and in two areas in Scotland, had indicated the overall financial advantages of the proposed policy.
2. In view of the Government's apparent disinterest (*sic*), it could be questioned whether the Board needed to, or should, take the initiative in this area, particularly as the proposals could give rise to problems with the Government, Local Authorities, and Trades Unions as well as place at risk contributory revenues. To take no action, however, was to have no policy at all, and it was important to strive to take a grasp of the problem and to provide a solution. The exercise in Lincolnshire had shown that the substituted bus feeder services could be run as part of the railway system and provide a better service than the present DMUs. This could increase the contributory revenue.
3. Following the recent rejection of the Ashford-Hastings closure there were no further cases arising in the near future where the reinvestment justified confrontation with the Government. The Board were, in any case, seeking to establish a future policy.
4. The passenger studies now being undertaken would emerge in the form of options to be presented to the Government and one of the options would undoubtedly be related to the question of bus/rail substitution.
5. Even though the Government might not wish to move in this area, it was felt that further action needed to be taken to expose the problem with the Department of Transport and probably with the Trades Unions as a 'green paper' at the BR Joint Consultative Council. The case should be made that this was about a rural transport policy and not a national transport policy.

The Board AGREED that:-
1. Ideas should be developed about the conflict between P.S.O. reduction and freight business implications.

2. Suitable cases should be developed where bus alternative services could be attractive and replacement of train services could make a positive effect on the Board's finances.

3. Discussion should continue with N.B.C., S.T.G. and the Department on this basis.

It was also agreed that care needed to be exercised to ensure that control was maintained over the debate with the various interested parties, in particular as to the timing of the opening of discussions on a firm basis with the Trades Unions and Local Authority associations.

The Board NOTED that a further submission would be made before any proposals for closures were developed.

(ACTION – R.B.REID)'

Despite a lack of enthusiasm from ministers for a closure programme, the Board did not give up – in private at least.

On 31 October 1978 the BRB's Deputy Chairman, Michael Bosworth[29], wrote to the Chairman, Peter Parker[30], a memo preparing for a visit by Rodgers to the Board on 20 November. In a paragraph headed 'Rural Services', we find this:

'Discussions on bus/rail and the possible closure of low value services (40 have been identified) will be the main feature. Changes in this area are difficult politically and the savings on PSO[31] may well not appear very significant – £5/20m. Nevertheless, sums of this order are vital to us if we are to live within the contract.'[32]

The memo also included paragraphs on Freight, Inter-City and London & South East. It said

'Briefs will be prepared on each of the above subjects and we have yet to decide who is to be the main spokesman for each item. If the party is to be kept very small then our team is likely to consist of yourself [Peter Parker], JMB [Michael Bosworth], DMB [David Bowick], IMC [Ian Campbell] and DF [Derek Fowler[33]]. In my view the subject matter is so important that it is difficult to leave out RBR [Bob Reid] and CAR [Clifford Rose[34]], in addition JU [James Urquhart[35]] is also deeply involved in the productivity issue.'

The doctrine of irreversibility

The BR Board made a formal approach to the Department on 24 January 1980, presumably hoping that the election of the Thatcher Government would produce a more sympathetic response to its attempt to close some rural services. A Board official, David Cairns, wrote to his opposite number in the Department, Tony Baker, about lines for which consent to closure had been granted, but not implemented. He also asked about the Board being paid grants to subsidise replacement bus services.

An official in the RB3 section, W. Moyes, was asked to advise on how to respond, and wrote this memo to Baker on 31 January:

'RAIL CLOSURES: OUTSTANDING MINISTERIAL CONSENTS

1. Briefly, the background as I have been able to piece it together is as follows. In January 1974 the then minister, Mr Peyton, announced that no closures of substance would be allowed to take place before 1975, by which time the promised Railways Bill would have passed into law. At that time a number of closure proposals were in the pipeline including five for which Ministerial consents had been given although at that time the services were still operating. When Mr Mulley took office he decided that no further closures should take place until after the review of transport policy. The Minister, however, has no power to prevent the withdrawal of services after his consent to their closure has been given. But equally, the granting of Ministerial consent does not oblige the Board to close the service in question. Mr Mulley's policy was therefore given effect through an agreement which he reached with the then Chairman of BR, Mr Marsh, that closure procedures for the following six closures should cease and that they should be brought within the PSO:-

Cambrian Coast
*Inverness-Kyle of Lochalsh
* Ashford-Hastings
* Bedford-Bletchley
Wimbledon-West Croydon
Stockport-Stalybridge

Ministerial consent had already been given for the three services marked *, but the conditions attached had not been fulfilled and the services had not, therefore, been withdrawn. Mr Mulley also announced that the closure of five further services – including Colchester-Sudbury – would be reviewed further and that in the meantime they too would come within the PSO. Four of these have now closed [believed to be Maiden Newton-Bridport (May 1975), Morecambe-Heysham (October 1975), the fire-damaged East Brixton station (January 1976), and Alston-Haltwhistle (May 1976)], but Colchester-Sudbury is still technically under review by the Department. Of the other two services mentioned by Mr Cairns, Ministerial consent to closure has certainly been granted for the Birmingham-Henley-Stratford service [see Chapter 10], but so far as I can tell from our files it was refused for the Oldham-Rochdale service, although I shall look further into this.'

Here there was a handwritten asterisk, and a note at the bottom of the memo that said, 'I have now discovered that the most recent files have been destroyed.'

Moyes's memo continued:

'2. I think that in law the outstanding consents would certainly be valid, but Mr Woodhouse [the Department's lawyer] made the point when Mr Mulley's announcement was being prepared that the longer the delay between the granting of Ministerial consent and the withdrawal of the service in question the more likely the Courts would be to look sympathetically on an application for an injunction restraining the Board from closing the service until the TUCC had had the opportunity to submit a further report on the hardship that this would cause. The consents referred to by Mr Cairns are all at least

8 years old now, and some are much older. I think, therefore, that in replying to Mr Cairns that we should take the line that the Minister has no power to withdraw his consent and point out the possible scope for legal action should the Board now decide to proceed on the basis of the existing consents.

3. There is one further point that we can make. The original PSO was specifically drawn to include the services mentioned by Mr Cairns. If they were now to be closed, presumably we would adjust the PSO accordingly.

4. Finally, I do not follow the logic of Mr Cairns' last paragraph. We have no powers to pay grant to BR to subsidise deficits on bus services except through the use of the Appropriation Act, and that is not now, I think, an option open to us. I do not see on what basis could argue that because consent to closure was given before the PSO was introduced the PSO grant could somehow be expanded to cover any bus services that BR might introduce to replace those particular rail services.

5. I attach a draft reply, which you may wish to show to Mr Palmer[36] and possibly the Minister.'

The National Archives also contain Baker's reply to Cairns, which followed almost exactly the line proposed by Moyes, and was therefore pretty unhelpful to the Board. It was (a) discouraged from implementing ancient closure consents, and warned of possible fresh hardship enquiries and legal injunctions, and (b) told in the clearest terms that there would be no government money to subsidise replacement bus services.

Even though – seven years on – the euphemism had changed from 'unremunerative rail passenger services' to 'cost ineffective passenger services', and the objectives had now been reduced from the 73 closures in Peeler's paper to something more modest, the assumption that the network had to be further shrunk to enable the losses to be contained was still a basic building block in any strategy for the railway.

In 1982, a paper[37] from the Board to the Serpell Inquiry[38] underlined this in the stark message that 'discharging the 1974 Obligations within existing financial limits has become impossible.' The solution? 'A major programme of bus substitution would be necessary to stabilise the support requirement of the sector.'

At the same time, a paper by the Director of Strategic Development of June 1982[39] outlined the characteristics of the future 'commercial railway'. Most London & South East inner suburban services would close. As towns lost their rail services, large car parks would be required and railhead and parkway stations would be constructed. But this was in the context of optioneering for the Serpell Report (see chapter 2), which aimed to present alternative scenarios to Ministers to allow them to decide. So, this 'what if' approach recognised that 'no account has been taken of the strategic value of the railway in energy, planning or other terms.'

The problem was that no one could take leadership on the issue and ministers were poor at leading and directing. BR's approach was to ask Government what sort of railway it wanted, and it would tell them how much it would cost. The Ministry's approach was to indicate the amount of money available and to ask what sort of railway could be had for that money.

The local view

In retrospect, it is perhaps surprising that so little was done to put the wider case for rail during the period of closures in the 1950s and '60s. Beeching had put a cogent case for contraction of the network based on running the railways as a business, but while many objected to this approach, nobody really articulated the need for rail to fulfil its wider economic, environmental and social role. This was recognised by Beeching in relation to suburban services outside London, and he had urged that 'if the services are to be regarded as essential, the municipalities concerned must join with the railways and bus interests to evolve a co-ordinated system of services with due regard to the economies of both forms of transport.' He also recognised that 'In cases of the type under consideration it may be cheaper to subsidise the railways than to bear the other cost burdens which will arise if they are closed.'[40] Five years later, Barbara Castle[41] provided such coordination by creating the PTEs, but it took longer for Beeching's wise words to be embraced by the BR Board.

In considering objections, the Government focussed only on hardship to start with, a very narrow point and one difficult to demonstrate. Objectors generally pointed to more economic ways of providing a rail service. Only rarely did local authorities and local businesses combine to identify the need for the railway to fill this wider role and to defer or avoid the need for massive expenditure on roads.

One very early case was the Isle of Wight, where the costs and effects could perhaps be more specifically identified. In November 1951, faced with plans to close the Ventnor West branch (see later, Chapter 8), the county council and the island's chamber of commerce combined to publish a report[42] calling for an integrated transport plan for the island before any closures were contemplated. Their particular focus was to protect the Ryde to Ventnor line, on which a large part of the island's tourist economy depended, but also to protect the line to the island's capital at Newport and its second ferry port at Cowes as well as the link to Freshwater (and the third port at Yarmouth) in readiness for the development foreseen for West Wight. Surprisingly, the report is complimentary about the island's vintage rolling stock, a proportion of which the authors thought was 'reasonably modern'. The locomotive fleet was by then 60 years old and the carriages around 40 years old, although the most recent was just 27 years. Beautifully panelled in the Edwardian style, their design still clearly traced back to the stagecoach and they looked pretty antiquated compared with the latest Hillman Minx[43].

Following BR's response and further consideration, a second paper was published in April 1953, 'The Case for Retention of the Island Railways'[44]. By this time the Ventnor West branch had closed and the Bembridge branch, the Sandown-Newport line and even the Freshwater line had all been proposed for closure. The report reflected genuine concern for the future:

'The withdrawal of all the railway services would completely alter the life of the Island.

The Closing of the Ryde-Sandown-Shanklin-Ventnor line would be a major disaster for the whole future of the Isle of Wight, which would have repercussions throughout the railway system of the country.

To close a railway which could be improved by reorganisation and careful management would be throwing away needlessly a valuable asset.'

The mismatch between statutory duty and expectation is also clear from the report. The council expected a public service to be continued to support the island's tourist economy. But the comments appended by the Southern's commercial superintendent refer tersely to the Commission's duty under the Act to balance revenue and costs. The council was understandably concerned that the island would be left in the hands of a monopoly bus operator, Southern Vectis, if the trains disappeared, and that this might be privatised. They also worried about the cost of improving the roads, but again the BR comment was that 'they cannot maintain uneconomic services in order to enable other parties to avoid meeting their costs.' But the island council was right, and its comment reflected the fragmented approach to policy making. It should have been possible to carry out a comprehensive assessment of the relative costs of retaining the railway and those of expanding the road system and the ferry terminals.

The other point of general principle made in the report was the inability of buses to carry the amount of luggage required, together with prams, cycles and, in those days, camping equipment, which were readily accommodated on the trains (a theme repeated on numerous other occasions when rail closures were being considered).

In other, later closures local authorities sometimes raised objections, and these are described in the examples that follow. But in many cases no effective arguments were marshalled against closure, and in any event the capacity of local government for strategic planning and accurate long-term forecasting was as limited as that of the civil servants or indeed the railway itself.

Conclusion – private or public sector?

Those who believe that the future salvation of Britain's railways will be accomplished through renationalisation need to consider what happened during the post-Beeching period of public ownership. First, there is no question that the network today would be a great deal smaller than it is, had the British Railways Board been given a free hand in determining which lines should stay open. The principal enthusiasm for closing the lesser-used services, particularly in rural areas, came from senior railway managers themselves, as well as from ideologically driven think-tanks mostly on the right but on the left as well.

Certainly civil servants in the Treasury would not have stopped them, because they erroneously believed that a smaller railway would cost the taxpayer less. The lesson of the last 20 years has been that the best way to improve railway finances – and to contribute to national and regional economic growth – is to encourage more passengers, with more and better services and affordable fares. Endlessly contracting them, by a combination of closures and track singling, has the opposite effect.

It is also evident that had Department of Transport officials found a way of closing lines without involving their ministers in the process, and eliminating their accountability for closure decisions, they would have done so. But by the late 1970s any chance of slipping through service cuts without a public outcry had disappeared, to the point that they went to almost any lengths to avoid formal closure machinery (hence the continued existence of 'parliamentary trains' with minimum levels of service, such as one train a week. A list of Parliamentary trains is set out in Appendix C).

The unexpected consequence of franchising services to the private sector has been to encourage them to offer more than the franchise agreement minimum. There is no financial inducement to pursue a policy of bus substitution, so beloved by the British Railways Board in the late 1970s and '80s, as the franchises specify rail not bus services. Indeed, such is the modern antipathy to herding rail passengers on to buses during times of disruption and engineering works that the more enlightened train operating companies will go to substantial lengths to keep running trains using alternative longer and slower routes, rather than interrupt a journey by an uncomfortable bus ride in the middle.

In parallel with this, concerns over closures expressed at the time of privatisation have led to safeguards in franchise agreements and in the statutory closure process, which makes it very difficult now to remove a service and requires an unprecedented degree of transparency that would rule out the 'closure by stealth' practised in the 1960s and '70s.

There is of course one very considerable public sector player in the current railway game, and that is Network Rail, the infrastructure provider. Following the humiliating collapse of Railtrack in 2002, after a brief and unhappy life of eight years that were marked by injudicious cost-cutting, risk-taking and outsourcing coming to a head in the Hatfield crash on 17 October 2000, it was replaced by a not-for-profit state-controlled company that has benefited from levels of investment in track, signalling and infrastructure on a scale not seen before in modern times. The difference this time is the contractual commitments to train operators which require the agreed track capability to be delivered.

It is too early to say that the British people love their railways and are proud of them – although many are – but the evidence provided by the numbers travelling by rail – higher than at any time since the 1920s – does seem to suggest that the modern formula is working better than the previous state-owned one. To argue, as supporters of the old British Rail do, that today's railway would have been even better if the BRB had received the same levels of support as its modern successors do, is largely to miss the point. So long as the Treasury controlled the purse-strings the chances of any state-owned company being generously treated were remote; instead they would have been seen as the quick and easy target for cuts when times were hard.

2

PULLING BACK
FROM THE BRINK

'Railways have rendered more services, and have received less gratitude, than any other institution in the country.'[45]

JOHN BRIGHT[46]

Blowing the whistle – a postscript

This book is about how the closure of stations and lines in Britain between the 1960s and the 1980s denied parts of the country – and the national economy – a railway system that could have met the demands of a travelling public that has in unprecedented numbers rediscovered the merits of train level. We show how a lack of imagination, mainly on the part of ministers and civil servants – but some senior railway managers too – has made it more difficult and much more expensive to put back infrastructure wantonly destroyed in the aftermath of the Beeching Report.

But it could have been a great deal worse. *Holding the Line* described a series of attempts made in the 1970s and 1980s by influential enemies of the railway drastically to reduce the size of the network, increase fares far beyond what passengers were willing to pay, substitute buses for trains, starve the system of investment, and make the British Railways Board abandon expansion and plan for decline. For a while there was even a debate about whether Britain should convert its railways into roads.

There were a number of reasons why that didn't happen. The ability of BR to 'make do and mend' kept lines open, albeit with the imposition of significant speed restrictions, and the public displayed a remarkable resistance to abandoning rail travel, even though parts of the system were decayed and unattractive. What made a huge difference to the public mood, however, which was passed on to the politicians, was the revelation that there were forces at work that sought, usually surreptitiously, to abandon, or at least seriously damage, the railway.

The public got to hear of these through leaks and unauthorised disclosure, and this chapter describes some of those that occurred in the 1970s and 1980s and contributed significantly to the public debate. Without exception they made it more difficult for enemies of the railway to achieve their objectives.

The 'Blue Paper' leak

In *Holding the Line*[47] we described in some detail the leak to the *Sunday Times* of the 'Rail Policy Review' in 1972 – a 61-page report written by civil servants, which subsequently became known as the 'Blue Paper'. It proposed huge cuts in the network, with mileage reduced from 11,600 to 6,700 and closure of all railways west of Plymouth, everything in Scotland north and west of Perth and Aberdeen, all lines in Wales except main lines to Holyhead and Fishguard, and much, much more besides.

We were unable to report conclusively on who had been responsible for giving the report to the press. We pointed out that Richard Marsh (then Chairman of BR) had denied in his autobiography[48] that the leak had come from within the railway, and he blamed the Department of the Environment, but we could not prove that.

The truth can now be revealed. The person responsible was a Grade Five Assistant Secretary in the DoE called Reg Dawson, and the key figure who was responsible for seeing that the Blue Paper found its way into the *Sunday Times* was the same Richard Hope[49] who was to play such a valuable role in discrediting the Serpell Report 20 years later (see later).

The story finally emerged at the end of 2012, following the deaths of Reg Dawson and his wife Betty at the Dignitas clinic in Zurich on 17 September 2012. As can be seen from the obituary written by Hope in the December 2012 edition of *Talyllyn News*, the crucial link between Dawson and Hope was the Talyllyn Railway, and a major factor in Dawson's deciding to do what he did was his outrage at the proposal by his fellow civil servants to close the Cambrian Coast line.

The obituary is reproduced in full as it sheds light on the level of secrecy surrounding key policy decisions and describes so well the anxiety faced by whistleblowers who had acted according to their conscience:

'Reginald Dawson (1922-2012) by Richard Hope

Reg Dawson became a member of the TRPS [Talyllyn Preservation Society] in 1955 when he was in the RAF. Having volunteered at the outbreak of war he started as a radio mechanic, but was discharged when it ended in 1945 and married Betty in 1946. After training as a teacher, he rejoined the RAF and was based in Jordan and then Hendon until he finally left the RAF as a Flight Lieutenant in 1960.

In August 1960 he secured at 38 a relatively senior position as a Principal Civil Servant in the Ministry of Transport. He was already

interested in railways, although in his unfinished autobiography he describes his early interest in the TR as 'more akin to industrial archaeology than railways'.

When he became responsible for pay policy in the nationalised industries, this brought him into contact with senior railway managers including the Operating Superintendent at Euston, which resulted in an invitation to join him on the first of many rides in the Divisional Manager's saloon. From then on Reg sought all opportunities to be professionally involved with railways, but all too often found himself dealing with other transport modes and increasingly with European Union matters in Brussels.

Meanwhile, Dr Beeching had produced his infamous report in 1963, and the rail network carrying passengers shrank from 12,600 miles in that year to 9,000 miles in 1972, the year in which Reg was to be plunged into the greatest personal and moral crisis of his life, narrowly escaping at best dismissal from a secure and well-paid job and at worst a prison sentence.

In 1965 Barbara Castle became Transport Minister and set about stabilising the shrinking British Rail network through legislation which, among other things, provided a subsidy for loss-making services. In February 1968 Reg was summoned by the Permanent Secretary who told him that he was being promoted to head the division dealing with grants for unremunerative services. 'So I was to do the work I coveted and get more money for doing so,' Reg wrote later.

As luck would have it, the Cambrian Coast Line had already been selected in 1967 as the guinea pig for this process.

Seeking ideas for preserving the Cambrian lines, which in 1968 delivered around 15% of the TR's passengers as well as volunteers,

PARCELS
These were an important traffic in the 1960s, and hardship to traders was an issue for the TUCCs to consider. Here a barrow full of parcels is being loaded into a Nottingham-Sheffield train at Alfreton, precipitately closed but subsequently replaced with Alfreton & Mansfield Parkway (now called Alfreton again). *Chris Austin*

Reg phoned me as Secretary of TR Co and TRPS and recently appointed Editor of *Railway Gazette International*. My office near Waterloo was not far from the Transport Ministry and we met for lunch to discuss tactics.

Dr Stewart Joy[50], an Australian economist, had been recruited to advise the Minister on implementing Barbara Castle's new rail policy and was overseeing a pilot cost/benefit study of the Cambrian Coast Line. Reg was invited to join him on a visit in August 1968, and declaring his interest in railway preservation ensured that Joy got a footplate trip to Abergynolwyn as well. But on the way back to London Joy told Reg he was determined that the study should show a grant was not value for money, and expected the Shrewsbury-Aberystwyth line to close as well when it lost the Coast Line traffic. This opened Reg's eyes to the fact that Barbara Castle's pro-rail policy was being actively opposed by a substantial body of Transport Ministry officials.

These included the Permanent Secretary David Serpell[51] who had persuaded Dr Beeching to be Chairman of British Rail, and went on to write a report on Railway Finances published in January 1983. This included the infamous Option A which would have cut BR's network to an allegedly profitable 1,630 miles.

Sensing correctly that he was likely to be moved out of railways, Reg's final fling was to surreptitiously arrange a modest grant enabling BR to resume Sunday services on the Cambrian from July 5 to September 6 1970. This produced a significant upturn in TR passengers on the 10 Sundays, and was a factor in thwarting the Transport Ministry's efforts to close the Coast Line.

Before that, Reg had briefed me about a secret high-level meeting of about 20 civil servants to produce a case for drastically shrinking the network without telling the Transport Minister or any other politician. I went to Chapman Pincher who duly published this story in the *Daily Express* on May 15 1970.

Matters rested there until June 1972 when Reg wandered into an adjacent office and spotted a blue A4 document called Railway Policy Review. It had a high-security status with numbered copies, but after some soul-searching he decided in late July to let me borrow but not copy it. This was frustrating because I knew Reg wanted to expose what was going on, but without the document the story had no credibility. So I had a choice: copy it or forget it.

Through August and September I explored ways to break the story with maximum impact, and finally got the *Sunday Times* to tackle it. They did a terrific job and it duly appeared on October 8 1972 with massive coverage and a huge map of lines likely to close. (The map is shown on page 59 of *Holding the Line*.)

Reg tells how he was questioned by security staff of what was now the Department of the Environment, which had absorbed transport. By then they knew whose office the copy had come from because the *Sunday Times* Chief Sub-Editor, who had interviewed BR Chairman Richard Marsh on Friday October 6, had handed over a photocopy which Marsh refused to hand back, and it had hand-written notes in it. Reg writes, 'I came as close to panic as I ever have done during my whole life.' He was asked whether he knew me, and explained that we were both involved in the Talyllyn Railway and had lunched together in London on October 2.

After the media had followed up the *Sunday Times* story, where my line was that I had been called in as an expert to help them deal with the policy review (which was true), things quietened down. Reg worried that one of the two journalists who happened to be in the *Railway Gazette* editorial office when he gave me the blue book might give the game away. Around that time Reg and I agreed that there should absolutely no communication whatever between us until this crisis blew over.

On November 14 the *Daily Telegraph* announced that the Director of Public Prosecutions had told Scotland Yard to find the person responsible for stealing the blue book, raising hackles in Fleet Street. Sure enough, on November 29 Detective Superintendent Croucher and Detective Sergeant Whisker from Scotland Yard raided the *Railway Gazette* office looking for this document.

They were in our office for three hours searching for the blue book, but thanks to the *Daily Telegraph* warning it was well hidden. At that time we shared a room with *The Railway Magazine*, and the Editor John Slater courteously pointed out which filing cabinets and book shelves belonged to them and were therefore not covered by their search warrant.

The police action that really brought the national media to boiling point was that they also interviewed the Editor of the *Sunday Times*, Harold Evans, on December 7, and then told him and two of his reporters that they faced prosecution under the Official Secrets Act.

Shortly after that we realised that *Railway Gazette* phones were being tapped, not just in the office but also our homes. One result was that one of my journalists was visited at home twice by police who threatened to expose the fact that he was homosexual and lived with a male partner. They told him what they had found out by listening in to a call to a friend, proving conclusively that they had tapped his phone line.

I then arranged to meet TRPS member Phil Glazebrook at Euston, who worked for the Post Office as a telephone engineer. He knew the engineer responsible for the private telephone exchange in our office block who was able to confirm this, and showed us the bright solder where the wires had been installed.

When after intensive preparation the *Sunday People* broke the phone tapping story on December 18, the press went berserk. Police were tapping press phones without Home Office clearance that was a legal requirement.

Because of a strike there were no national newspapers in the south on Monday, but northern editions did come out so I phoned our legal adviser and TRPS member Jeremy Wilkinson in Manchester, who arranged for furious press reactions to this revelation to be copied and posted to me overnight. Leslie Huckfield MP[52], who we were absolutely certain was recorded in a conversation with me, secured an adjournment debate in the Commons.

All this time Reg was fearful that he would be charged under the Official Secrets Act or the Theft Act. So was I, but the real risk for me was being jailed for contempt of court if Reg was prosecuted and I refused to reveal who had passed the blue book to me. This would be the judge's decision with no protection of a jury vote. Happily, the phone-tapping scandal broke the government's nerve. On January 17 1973 the Attorney-General announced that there was 'insufficient evidence to charge anyone'.

But for Reg the moment of triumph came in July 1973 when the Transport Minister John Peyton assured MPs that 'draconian cuts of the kind at one time rumoured following the escape of a regrettably mobile document are not in the view of the government the answer to the industry's or the nation's problems.'

Since 1972 a few passenger lines have closed but others have reopened. The national network carrying passengers is still almost exactly the same, and successive governments have been so terrified of closing lines that when Sir Roy McNulty[53] was charged in 2010 with carrying out his Value for Money study of the railways he was firmly told not to recommend closing lines or stations. So what Reg and the TRPS team actually achieved was railway preservation big time.

Back in the 1970s Betty and Reg had decided to move to Tywyn when he retired, and bought a plot of land not far from Wharf. Although he retired in 1982, they had to build a house and did not actually occupy it until 1993. Here they regularly hosted the ritual stuffing of the quarterly *Talyllyn News* when they were put into envelopes and pre-printed address labels applied – a task now undertaken by the printer.

In 2003 they sold up and moved to a flat in Llandudno where a warden could keep an eye on them as Betty succumbed to Alzheimer's and Reg to 'Parkinson's plus', to quote from a letter Reg sent me on September 5 2012. He also told me that they had decided to end their lives at Dignitas in Zurich, where they died peacefully together on September 17.

He wrote, 'My lack of skills confined my activity to things like stuffing the *News*, and my most useful action for the TR was probably to grant-aid Sunday trains on the Cambrian. But I love the TR and had a bitter-sweet final ride on it last week. Next time we shall be ashes to Brynglas.' And so it was on October 1 with their four children and their families present.'

Reg Dawson wrote his own account of these events, and intended that they should be published in his autobiography. Time unfortunately ran out for him, and he was unable to complete it before his death. His manuscript has however survived, and the authors possess a copy.

The 'No Rail Cuts' map

In *Holding the Line*[54] we revealed that it was the British Railways Board's own Chief Rail Planning Officer, Michael Harbinson, who supplied the map that formed the basis of the remarkable 'No Rail Cuts' campaign of 1975, which included a mass meeting at Central Hall, Westminster, a lobby of Parliament, angry exchanges in the House of Commons, the distribution of one and a half million leaflets, and 20,000 submissions by the public to the transport minister. The leaflet showed the size of network that would be left by 1981 if investment levels in the railway were frozen at the then level of £281 million a year. When asked whether he had a map of the system that illustrated the consequences, Harbinson replied, 'We have maps depicting every possible size of network.'

The 'No Rail Cuts' campaign was the product of an alliance between the three railway trade unions – the NUR, ASLEF and TSSA – and the wide range of environmental and public transport organisations that made up Transport 2000 (now the Campaign for Better Transport). A crucial part of its success was its ability to convince sympathetic leader writers on national newspapers (Harold Evans[55], editor of the *Sunday Times,* again deserves special mention) to take the campaign's message seriously and participate in the debate about the role the railway should play in the nation's transport and how large its network should be.

One of the campaign's consequences was that civil servants and ministers grew increasingly nervous about the publication of notional network maps and lists of services for closure (including 'bus substitution', which the British Railways Board continued to promote as a 'solution' in the early 1980s).

In *Holding the Line* we describe in detail the discussions that took place at the Civil Service Staff College at Sunningdale Park, Berkshire, in total secrecy over the weekend of 5 and 6 March 1977 between Department of Transport officials and ministers – the British Railways Board was neither advised that the conference was taking place, nor invited to it. A large part of that weekend was spent discussing how a massive programme of closures could be implemented by stealth, bypassing the statutory procedures for public inquiry by Transport Users' Consultative Committees, and taking away from ministers the final decision on what lines closed or were reprieved.[56] Remarkably, none of the Sunningdale conference proceedings were reported at the time or leaked subsequently. They only saw the light of day because the authors were lent a complete set of the papers when researching *Holding the Line* in 2011-12.

The Class 56 saga

As can be seen by the decision to keep the BR Board away from the Sunningdale conference, the relationship between it and the Department in the late 1970s was an uneasy one. Officials particularly, but ministers too, complained that the Board was briefing the media against them. Sometimes they deserved it, as the story of the Class 56 manning dispute in 1977-78 demonstrated.

The background was a familiar one, that of a 'craft' trade union desperately fighting to keep the jobs of its members in the face of technological advance and modernisation, against an employer under immense pressure to reduce the costs of running its services.

The ending of steam on the railways presented a particular challenge. There was no question that every steam locomotive required a driver and a fireman, but there was no reason to have two people in charge of a diesel locomotive, and in 1965 one of a number of single-manning agreements was negotiated between the BR Board and the train drivers' union, ASLEF. The following decade, however, saw an increase in the level of union militancy, and ASLEF dug its heels in, even succeeding in forcing BR to redesign the interior of the drivers' cabs on its new high-speed trains, so that there would be provision for a 'second man' sitting alongside the driver when the trains were running at their top speed of 125mph.

The next dispute concerned the new Class 56 diesel locomotives, ordered in 1974 at the height of a national oil crisis for the purpose of hauling extra quantities of coal to power stations from the South Yorkshire and East Midlands coalfields.

ASLEF argued that as these locomotives were 10% more powerful than the locomotives they were replacing (principally the Class 47s), they were not covered by the 1965 manning agreement, and that a second man should be on the footplate each time they were used. The British Railways Board thought this was nonsense and said that the Class 56s would be single-manned, but didn't press the issue for some time after the locomotives started to be delivered in 1976. By October 1977, however, the Board decided that the situation could not be allowed to continue, and it was obvious that a confrontation with ASLEF was inevitable. An added complication was industrial unrest in the power stations, where a work-to-rule was imposed, and it also looked as if a miners' strike could be about to be called.

BR kept the Government informed and expected ministers to support it, relying on the sentiments expressed in the Department of Transport's white paper, published in June 1977[57]. This had contained the sentence, 'Continuing improvements in productivity are vital to the future of the railways'. The Secretary of State, William Rodgers, had added, 'Concern about manning practices on British Rail' was 'widely shared'.

At this point the narrative gets confused. On 11 January 1978 Richard Hope had an apparently well-informed piece published in *The Times* entitled 'How many men in the train driver's cab?'[58] In it he alleged that the Secretary of State, William Rodgers, had written 'a confidential letter' to Peter Parker 'asking him not to oppose a blatant attempt by the locomotive men's union to put firemen back on to freight trains… Mr Rodgers's *volte face* has demoralised British Rail's negotiators and cast to the winds any idea that the Government would back them if it came to a showdown on overmanning… Pushed by his Cabinet colleagues, Mr Rodgers told Mr Parker to give in to ASLEF's demands and be quick about it.'

Parker responded instantly and had a letter published in *The Times* the following day (12 January), under the headline 'No intervention by the Secretary of State on locomotive manning'. He said, '…the Railways Board has received no letter or *direction of any kind* [our emphasis] from the Secretary of State for Transport relating to the manning of the Class 56 locomotives… The Board has made it clear that the … locomotives should be manned in accordance with the 1965 manning agreement, so that they will be single-manned subject to the limits on mileage and hours as set out in that agreement.'[59]

Hope returned to the charge with his own letter in *The Times* the next day (13 January). He claimed that following publication of his own article on 11 January Parker was asked by Rodgers to call round at his office that afternoon, and asked to 'explain how a confidential exchange of views on industrial relations strategy had reached a wider audience than originally intended.' Giving a clue about the source of his information, Hope commented that 'it is amazing how many people will phone up when there is skulduggery afoot of which they disapprove.' He concluded his letter with a question: 'If indeed there were no interference by the transport department in the Class 56 manning issue, how could there have been a serious breach of security either at Marylebone or Marsham Street?'

Rodgers finally tried to put the matter to bed in his own letter published on 17 January. He said that he had indeed seen Parker during the afternoon of 11 January, but the 'appointment … had been fixed some days before.' He also confirmed that he had not written a letter to Parker. 'What is serious and distressing is that an attempt has been made to cast doubt on the proper exercise of my responsibilities as Minister in relation to a nationalised industry and the proper exercise by a chairman of his managerial responsibilities.'[60]

The National Archives[61] contain a two-page personal hand-written letter from Rodgers to Parker, dated 14 January, written on Department of Transport writing paper. The first page wishes Parker well following some medical treatment, and the second says:

'I thought you might like to have the enclosed, which should be in Monday's *Times*. We can't let Richard Hope get away with his second instalment.'

The 'enclosed' was a carbon copy of the letter that *The Times* duly published on the 17th.

While Hope may have been mistaken that there had been an earlier letter, there seems little doubt that there were discussions between civil servants and board officials about single-manning of Class 56 locomotives. This was not denied by Rodgers in his *Times* letter, nor in an exchange in the House of Commons three weeks later. He was asked by the Conservative MP Peter Fry[62]:

'As the Secretary of State has publicly denied the existence of any letter from himself to the Chairman of British Rail about the manning of type 56 locos, will he confirm that neither he nor his Department has given any advice to the Chairman of British Rail on this subject?'

Rodgers replied:

'I shall rest on what I said previously in public, that there is no question of my giving *directions* [again, our emphasis] of this kind to the Chairman of British Rail.'[63]

It is undoubtedly true that Rodgers had not given 'directions' to the Chairman – these have a quasi-legal status and represented one of the most extreme ways in which ministers could intervene in the affairs of a nationalised industry – but his parliamentary answer did not deny that he had given 'advice' to Parker. To that extent Hope's original story of 11 January was based on fact. There was no letter, but according to Hope there was a note written by Board officials following a meeting with the Department held on 30 November 1977. He had not been given a copy but he had had the contents read to him over the phone by someone at Board headquarters.[64]

Departmental officials took the issue seriously – not least because their efforts to 'nudge' the board to do what they wanted in a potential industrial relations dispute had been revealed – and insisted on a leak inquiry conducted by the British Transport Police. Members of the Board's public affairs team were interviewed, as was Richard Hope, but as was usual in cases of this sort the inquiries went nowhere and were quietly dropped.

The whistleblowers within the Board had achieved their objective in bringing into the open an intervention by the Government in an issue that was properly the concern of nationalised industry management, and one where the national interest lay quite clearly with the railways board.

The Vole, the Ramblers and the 41 services

An equally effective media briefing operation was undertaken in 1979, shortly after the election of the new Thatcher Government, by the Ramblers' Association (a member of Transport 2000 – now the Campaign for Better Transport) and the environmental magazine *The Vole*. The Ramblers had carried out research into the 41 lines that they believed were likely to be closed and replaced by buses – then an official BR policy objective. Assistance with the compilation of the list had been given from within BR headquarters, and it was therefore authoritative and convincing.

The Vole published the list, together with a powerful comment from Alan Mattingley, secretary of the Ramblers' Association.[65] This was then picked up by the *Guardian*, which ran it as its front-page lead on 9 November 1979 – a day carefully chosen to coincide with transport questions in the House of Commons. Instead of equivocating – which is what transport ministers tended to do when faced with hostile questions on rail closures – Secretary of State Norman Fowler[66] made it clear that not only would there never again be 'another Beeching', but he stated in a letter to Peter Parker that 'the option of closing 40 passenger services is one that the government have rejected.'

Discrediting the Serpell Report

Although this promise not to implement a programme of further closures has been kept by Conservative and Labour Governments ever since, there was one further major threat that the railway had to overcome in the early 1980s: that was posed by the Serpell Review of 1982, set up by Secretary of State for Transport David Howell[67] at Sir Peter Parker's request. We describe the background to the review and its outcome in *Holding the Line*[68], including the fact that the contents of the report were leaked to the media by BRB officials and advisers on Parker's express instructions between Boxing Day 1982 and 20 January 1983.

Corroboration of this account finally emerged 30 years later when Richard Hope responded to a three-page analysis of *Holding the Line* by Alan Williams[69] published in the April 2013 issue of *Modern Railways*, describing official attempts to make drastic reductions in the size of Britain's rail network. Hope's letter to the editor was published a month later:

'Alan Williams contributed to your April issue a gripping account of the way certain senior civil servants in the Transport Department strived to close much of Great Britain's rail network, starting with Dr Beeching's report in 1963 right through to Sir David Serpell's report on Railway Finances published on 20 January 1983.

Alan's account was largely based on the recently published book *Holding the Line*, written by Lord Faulkner of Worcester and Chris Austin, which was based on many hours research among the archives at Kew. He describes how just before Serpell published his report, 'Luckily, Sir Peter Parker and his men had been forewarned of this latest attack and this time had been busy taking pre-emptive action.'

I can confirm this from personal experience. On 19 January 1983 the head of one of BR's three Sectors into which the passenger networks were then divided phoned and asked me to come to his office after normal working hours, which I did.

My informant [subsequently revealed as Dr John Prideaux[70]] handed me a copy of the report, which was massive: 178 pages of print and diagrams in two volumes. And the launch was scheduled for 14.00 next day at a press conference at DfT's headquarters in Marsham Street. 'I can't read and digest that overnight,' I said, 'Nor will the media be able to digest it.'

There was no executive summary, and apparently no press release either. 'Tell me,' I pleaded, 'are there any network maps of closure options?' The answer was, 'Yes.' There were six: Options A, B, C1, C2, C3 and D. Incredibly, Option A was only

1,630 route miles – this at a time when the passenger network had already been whittled down to around 9,000 miles (where thankfully it remains today). So I asked for a few dozen photocopies of Option A.

By 10.30 next day I had already done 13 radio and TV interviews finishing up on Jimmy Young's programme.

The press conference was packed tight, but the only person on the platform was John Palmer, a top DfT civil servant. To every question he gave one of two answers: 'That is a matter for the Secretary of State who is making a statement in the Commons shortly,' or 'That is a matter for Sir David Serpell who chaired the report, but unfortunately cannot be with us today.'

After a few minutes of this farce, every journalist in the room stood up as one, and walked out, where they fell on me saying, 'My deadline is five o'clock and there is no press release or summary. What's it all about?' To which I responded by handing out copies of the Option A map, shouting, 'Forget the rest – that's your story.'

And 24 hours after this farce the Serpell Report was a dead duck.'

Despite a number of attempts by the British Railways Board to revive the notion of 'bus substitution' for rural rail lines through the 1980s, ministers were not prepared to sanction rail closures. The policy was finally abandoned with the reprieve of the Settle to Carlisle line in 1989.

Conclusion

There is no doubt that in each of the cases described here the national interest was served by the decision of insiders to share with the public and the media information about what was being plotted in secret by officials, ministers and sometimes BR managers, inconvenient and uncomfortable that may have been for those involved. Neither Harbinson nor Prideaux – or the BRB's advisers – suffered setbacks in their careers as a result of their 'whistleblowing' activities, and Richard Hope's reputation as the outstanding railway investigative journalist of the 1970s and 1980s was secured, and duly recognised with the award of OBE in 1989.

3
THE MISSING MAIN LINES

'Let the country build the railroads,
and the railroads will make the country.'

EDWARD PEASE[71], QUOTED ON THE TITLE PAGE OF *THE MIDLAND RAILWAY,*
ITS RISE AND PROGRESS BY FREDERICK WILLIAMS, 1878

Although most main lines survived, a number of high-profile closures took place in the 1960s and 1970s, while others were reduced in status to secondary routes.

This followed the second Beeching Report, the Trunk Routes report, published in March 1965, following traffic studies across the whole network that examined existing and potential passenger and freight flows between major centres over a 20-year period to 1984.

This was a reasonable approach given the level of duplication of routes and the rapid decline in demand for rail services. Virtually nothing had been done by the 'Big Four'[72] companies to change the trunk networks that they had inherited from their constituent companies, and by 1958, ten years after nationalisation, British Railways had done very little to rationalise the competitive routes it had inherited in 1948. The trunk routes network in 1962, when the British Railways Board was created, was essentially the same as it had been in 1910, with the opening of the Great Western's 'cut-off' line from Ashendon Junction to Aynho Junction, completing the national network of main lines. It is surprising perhaps that after 14 years of nationalisation no action had been taken to change the way this network was used.

The railway had been expanded and developed through the competitive pressures of the 19th century and had not been adapted to the changing markets of the latter half of the 20th century. On the face of it, the solution was simple – remove the duplicate route, concentrate the traffic on a single route, and retain the business while halving the costs of operation and maintenance.

In practice, it was more complicated. The routes tended to serve different catchment areas through their intermediate stations. The Great Western route from London to Exeter, for example, served Reading, Newbury and Taunton, while the Southern route ran via Basingstoke, Salisbury and Yeovil, each with their own distinct local demand. Which would you select, and how would you continue to serve the alternative route's markets while reducing costs?

Removing a complete 'duplicate' route has, with the benefit of hindsight, in almost every case turned out to be too drastic in terms of cutting surplus capacity. Concentrating on a single route may have provided just enough capacity for the 1970s, but has proved to be completely inadequate in the 21st century. As we shall see, too little time was devoted to the strategic requirements of the network

as a whole and, progressively as the programme of rationalisation was implemented, mistakes were made, closing off options prematurely and leaving inadequate alternatives to provide the degree of resilience required of a reliable railway service.

We review four routes below, each with their own distinctive story.

The Great Central: Britain's high-speed line

'The last grand gesture of a century that had given birth to railways.'
The Making of a Railway, L. T. C. Rolt (Hugh Evelyn, London, 1971)

The story of the Great Central is well known and documented by a number of distinguished writers, notably George Dow, and by the photographer S. W. A. Newton, who recorded every aspect of its construction. Our purpose is therefore not to rehearse this in detail, but to consider its role in the national network and to try to understand the background to its closure. In particular, we explore how its unique attributes were overlooked as it was run down, closed and systematically destroyed, and we consider subsequent events leading to the need to replace the capacity it provided, culminating in HS2.

The Great Central's 'London extension' from Annesley in Nottinghamshire to Marylebone in London was built on the grand scale, driven by its autocratic but visionary Chairman, Sir Edward Watkin[73]. He was Chairman also of the Metropolitan Railway, the South Eastern Railway, a director of the East London Railway, Chairman of two Channel Tunnel companies, and a director of the Nord Railway in France. From this biographical note alone, the reader can already see the line of steel stretching from Manchester to Paris.

Victorian NIMBYs

The construction of the Great Central, particularly at the London end of the line, foreshadows the row that erupted over the routing of HS2 through the Chilterns. In the case of the Great Central, it was even more contentious; building the railway to Marylebone involved encroaching on part of Lord's cricket ground. Contemporary press reports left the impression that the sacred turf itself was to be dug up, although it was in fact to remain unscathed. As if that were not bad enough, the artists of St John's Wood under Sir Lawrence Alma-Tadema[74] also objected. In their petition they described it as 'a line for the conveyance not only of passengers, but of coal, manure, fish and other abominations.'[75] England was outraged; the 1891 bill was hotly debated in Parliament, and the case for the railway put strongly by the honourable member for Hythe (Sir Edward Watkin). But the opposition was too strong and the bill was lost.

The company returned with a revised scheme after a lot of careful wicket rolling (an appropriate metaphor in the circumstances) by Watkin. The MCC did rather well out of the deal. The railway undertook to hide the line under a 'covered way', for which they bought the adjacent property and, when work was complete, presented it to the Cricket Club, providing it with the larger ground that it enjoys today. This site had been occupied by the Clergy Orphan School, and the Great Central bought the charity an alternative site at Bushey in Hertfordshire, which was no doubt healthier for the orphans than St John's Wood. The artists were placated with a pledge that excavations should be removed by rail, rather than carted through the local streets, and that the station should be at Marylebone, rather than on Boscobel Gardens. The magnificent Crown Hotel, built to welcome passengers at this first site off the Edgware Road, was renamed 'Crocker's Folly'[76] in 1987 after its owner, and remains to this day as a fine bar and restaurant, recently restored, the main bar being finished with no fewer than 50 kinds of marble.

Building the business
In 1899 the London extension opened, but the Great Central was a latecomer to the scene. This made it an expensive line to build and also meant that it was difficult for the newcomer to break into the markets already established in the towns and cities along the line. It opened in 1899, but its principal stations were in towns that had been served for many years by other railways:

Town	Alternative railway(s)	Date of opening
Rugby	LNWR	1838
Leicester	MR	1840
	GNR	1883
Loughborough	MR	1840
Nottingham	MR	1839
	GNR	1852
Sheffield	MR	1840
	GNR	1857
Manchester	LNWR	1838
	MR	1867
	GNR	1857

The Great Central could never provide journey times from its stations to London as fast as its rivals, although it excelled on some intermediate journeys, such as Rugby to Nottingham. However, it had its loyal customers, attracted by comfortable carriages and by its restaurant car services. It also introduced the first buffet cars in Britain, for trains travelling at times when a full meal was not required.

Despite its best efforts, the demand on the route never really met the expectations of the promoters, even though the line did build up a thriving local traffic between the main stations and from towns like Brackley and Lutterworth, which found themselves on a direct line to London for the first time.

Under its energetic General Manager, Sir Sam Fay[77], who was appointed in 1902, the railway also introduced an imaginative range of cross-country through services jointly with the Great Western and the London & South Western railways to South Coast and West

Country resorts. It carried the 'Ports to Ports' express from Newcastle to Barry via Woodford Halse, Banbury and Chipping Norton to Gloucester and South Wales. For a brief period before the First World War there was even a restaurant car train from Newcastle to Southampton via the Didcot, Newbury & Southampton Railway (see Chapter 7). One Newcastle to Bournemouth train ran until 1966, when it was diverted to run via Birmingham. Fay also encouraged excursion traffic.

Local stations were well served and long-distance stopping trains, locally known as 'Ords', which linked Marylebone with Woodford Halse, Woodford Halse with Leicester, and Leicester with Nottingham, as well as the expresses. Suburban services ran from Marylebone as well as around Nottingham.

The Great Central had the choice of two routes into London. The original line joined the Metropolitan Railway at Quainton Road and operated as the Metropolitan & Great Central Joint, through Aylesbury, Amersham and Harrow-on-the-Hill. Even before the line opened, relations between the two companies had deteriorated to the point where the Great Central decided it wanted its own line into Marylebone that avoided Metropolitan Railway tracks. Consequently, it entered into an agreement with the Great Western for sharing that company's new line from Ashendon Junction, near Haddenham, to Northolt Junction, where the Marylebone line diverged to run via Wembley to Neasden Junction and so into Marylebone. To reach the Great Western, the GC opened its own line from Grendon Underwood Junction, near Calvert, to Ashendon Junction in 1906.

Ironically, as it was laid out for speed the GC was most successful in building up a thriving freight business, including particularly coal from the Nottinghamshire coalfield and fish from Grimsby and Immingham to London, the South West and South Wales. This role was an important one, relieving the East Coast Main Line, and as late as 1957 fast block train workings between Annesley and Woodford Halse were introduced with Class 9F 2-10-0 freight locomotives on tight timings and with very efficient locomotive diagrams and crew rosters. Known as 'Runners' or 'Windcutters', these trains ran until 1965, when they were diverted away from the Great Central as a prelude to closure.

Originally, the withdrawal of express passenger services in 1960 cleared the way for the greater use of the line by freight. A public information pamphlet produced by the Nottingham Division as late as December 1959 quoted the London Midland Region's 1959 freight traffic plan in relation to the GC: '...to concentrate on it a large proportion of the heavy freight traffic between the Midlands and London would give much more freedom of movement, as suggested above, on the Midland route for passenger trains running at the highest permitted speeds.'[78] It went on to point out that a high proportion of the LMR's parcels traffic originated at just four depots – London, Leicester, Nottingham and Manchester – all linked by the GC, and four new parcels depots were proposed to develop this business.

Under the Modernisation Plan, 33 diesel locomotives had been allocated to the Great Central line at a capital cost of £3.04 million, and a diesel maintenance depot was planned for Annesley at a cost of £210,000.[79]

Decline and fall

At the Grouping, the line became part of the LNER, and on nationalisation it went to the Eastern Region of British Railways. But it did not command the same attention as the East Coast Main Line with its huge traffic flows and major stations in Yorkshire, the North East and Scotland. For more than a decade, however, there were two named trains on the line – 'The Master Cutler' and 'The South Yorkshireman'.

The 'Cutler' had been started by the LNER in 1947, and offered a fast morning service from Sheffield to Marylebone, calling only at Nottingham, Leicester and Rugby. Running via Ashendon Junction, it reached London in around 3 hours 40 minutes. It returned north, via the same route, leaving Marylebone at 6.15pm. In 1958 it was replaced by an all-Pullman service running from Sheffield to King's Cross via Worksop and Retford, and later by a train on the Midland main line to St Pancras.

'The South Yorkshireman' was a less glamorous train, but still enjoyed a cult following of admirers (one of the authors remembers being taken as a child to Chorleywood Common by his mother to watch the up train going through at around 2.50pm). It set off from Bradford at 10.00am and wound its way through Halifax, Huddersfield and Penistone, acquired a restaurant car at Sheffield, then stopped at Nottingham, Loughborough, Leicester, Rugby and Aylesbury, before reaching Marylebone at 3.20pm. The return working left Marylebone at 4.50pm, and arrived back in Bradford 5½ hours later.

The Great Central line was transferred from the Eastern to the London Midland Region in 1958, and that hastened its demise as a main-line railway. 'The South Yorkshireman' came off in 1960, as did the through services to and from Manchester. They were replaced by three semi-fast trains each way between Marylebone and Nottingham, the earliest arrival in London being at 11.42am and the last reasonable departure from Marylebone at 4.30pm.

It is true that, as it had been overlaid on the British railway network in 1899, it was fairly easy, in operational terms, to remove it again without significantly affecting the remaining routes. The estimated savings from closure were £3,296,000, although it was noted that this figure would have reduced to £1,224,500 if diesel had replaced steam traction. In all, 2,168 staff were to be displaced, of which 345 (16%) would be required to handle traffic transferred to the Midland lines.

Intermediate stations were closed in 1963, through freight was diverted in 1965, and the last Nottingham to Marylebone semi-fast trains finished in 1966. The line between Rugby Central and Calvert was closed to all traffic. Only between Nottingham Arkwright Street and Rugby did a residual service, operated by diesel multiple units, linger on until it too ended in 1969. Press comment in 1964 credited Ernest Marples with 'saving' this part of the line, and it is not clear whether this was a misunderstanding by the *Daily Telegraph* (as recorded in a handwritten note in the Ministry's file) or a pre-emptive leak by Marples' press officer. A meeting of the Ministry's working party on passenger closure proposals of 8 February 1965 agreed that the Board should proceed with the closure while retaining the Nottingham (Arkwright Street) to Rugby (Central) section, as this would provide for the bulk of the regular passengers using the route. The meeting noted that this would provide for 389 out of the 427 regular daily passengers.[80] Closure of the remaining 73½ miles of line with an estimated annual saving of £539,000 had been approved by Barbara Castle as Minister of Transport.

HEYDAY
The down 'Master Cutler' races through Woodford Halse on 27 May 1957 behind BR Standard Class 4 4-6-0 No 73157, delivered new to Neasden depot just six months before. *M. Mitchell*

That the intention to close the route was permanent and irreversible is evident from the minutes of a meeting at BRHQ in 1964 chaired by Lance Ibbotson[81], the Board's chief operations manager who reported to Fred Margetts, the Board member who pursued the closure programme vigorously. 'Reference was made to the need to ensure that removal of redundant assets did not lag behind the withdrawal of services.'[82]

Opponents of this policy did warn that this would be a mistake as the route was laid out for high speed and, just as important, was said to be built to the Berne gauge, so that larger European rolling stock could operate over it, surely a useful attribute if the Channel Tunnel were ever built.

In fact, the Berne Gauge assertion turns out to be a myth. The line was built in 1899, 13 years before the Berne Gauge dimensions were adopted as a standard for European Railways in 1912. It was, however, built to the latest standards set out by the Board of Trade and to a structure gauge that was more generous than on most British railways. While it could not have accommodated continental rolling stock, it could have been adapted to deal with modern rolling stock and containers rather more easily than some parts of the network that remained.

But in 1969 the railways were at a very low ebb indeed and few thought of expansion and the need for more capacity. The juggernaut of decline was unstoppable, and the recollection of the time, as well as from recent reading of the files, is that whatever was said the line would close. Management was confident in the policy it was

pursuing, and was supported by ministers and civil servants. The mood of the time was completely different from the position a decade later, when closures became much more difficult.

Sins of omission

When consent for the closure of the Great Central was sought, the link with the GW&GC Joint line between Grendon Underwood Junction and Ashendon Junction was overlooked. Consequently the diversion or withdrawal of GC services from 5 September 1966 included the withdrawal of trains on this 6-mile link without authority. In fact, while it was used by parcels trains, empty rolling stock and light engine movements, only one passenger train a week used it prior to the GC closure date, and that was the 22.50 Saturdays-only Manchester Central to Marylebone. A letter from the Ministry just 18 days later, on 23 September, asked the Board to regularise the position by submitting a closure proposal, recognising that this would be carried out 'only as a formal exercise'[83].

This was done and the TUCC met on 6 March 1967 to discuss the case. There were four objectors, but of course no evidence of hardship, as at that stage there were no trains and consequently no passengers who could conceivably suffer hardship. The Great Central Association had a field day, but inevitably ministerial consent to close was given on 14 July 1967, and formal closure took place the following day. The line from Grendon Underwood to Akeman Street was retained as a single-track siding to serve the Ministry of Aviation's depot and the line was transferred from the Board to the MoD on 1 January 1968. Traffic over this line ceased in 1993.

Critics might say that the London Midland should have ensured that the closure of this section of line was properly included in the main closure submission. However, it perhaps illustrates the

WINDCUTTER
Block train working between Annesley and Woodford Halse made very efficient use of wagons, locomotives and train crews. Class 9F 2-10-0 No 92092 of Annesley gets 'into the collar' as she starts to climb Ashby Magna bank with a block coal train for Woodford Halse. *Colin P. Walker*

enormity of the task facing the Region in preparing so many closure cases during 1965 and 1966. It is perhaps not surprising that a few mistakes were made along the way. It also illustrates the transition problems that left some sections of line with virtually no commercial traffic as the retrenchment proceeded.

Passengers on today's Chiltern Railways trains from Marylebone might wonder why the up and down lines diverge just north of Haddenham & Thame Parkway, leaving a vast space and some remains of bridge abutments. This is the site of the great flying junction that took the Birmingham to Paddington line over this Great Central spur used by the crack expresses that once raced north to Sheffield and Manchester.

Lost opportunities

Speed, however, was important, and the policy of the emerging InterCity business was based on reducing journey times to compete effectively with the car. This might have produced second thoughts around this remarkable line with the attributes listed below, but in the event the strategy chosen was the incremental one of progressively raising line speeds, and the use of the 'Deltics' on the ECML, and subsequently the very successful HSTs on both the East Coast and Midland routes. For the West Coast route, the chosen solution was electrification, followed by tilting trains, initially APT and latterly the successful 'Pendolino' trains that are the backbone of today's service.

The Great Central's London extension had a number of significant advantages that would have fitted the line as a suitable high-speed and international link in the chain leading to the Channel Tunnel:

1. The structural clearances were generous compared with other lines in the BR network.
2. It was relatively level, and between Annesley and Ashendon Junction and Quainton Road had a modest ruling gradient of 1 in 176.
3. The minimum radius was 1 mile, except near the principal stations.
4. There was no level crossing on the extension, and indeed only one (at Beighton) on the whole route between Sheffield and Marylebone.
5. There were well-sited central stations in Sheffield, Nottingham, Leicester and Rugby.

6. It was well aligned for high-speed running with 90mph achieved over long sections of the route, even in steam days.

7. It was a relatively new line, with structures and earthworks around half the age of the lines that were retained.

8. It was laid out for growth. The intermediate stations with their single island platforms were designed to be flanked by additional fast tracks should the line be quadrupled in the future.

The reasons for closure of the Great Central when the demand for rail (freight and passenger) was declining, and costs were the principal problem to be addressed, are self-evident. Nevertheless, such a huge disinvestment of assets that were relatively modern, and on a route laid out for high speed, can now be seen as monumentally short-sighted. The exceptional advantages of the route have been enumerated above, but it is mainly the capacity that was sacrificed that appears to us today to be so wasteful.

Today's Great Central

Despite the railway managers' enthusiasm for wiping the Great Central off the railway map, its potential not just as a heritage railway but as a line where steam-hauled trains could be run at relatively high speeds was spotted by enthusiasts very soon after closure. They formed the Main Line Preservation Group with the purpose of first preserving, then restoring the railway.

The task was massive and a variety of trusts and charities were created to acquire and reopen the railway from Loughborough to the outskirts of Leicester. Initially this was a single-track section, but in the 1990s a benefactor, David Clarke[84], provided a substantial part of the funds to double the track from Loughborough to Rothley.

Now there are plans to reinstate a bridge over the Midland main line just north of Loughborough Central station to make possible the reopening of the route from south of Nottingham to north of Leicester.

Various individuals have played crucial roles in the metamorphosis of the railway; in addition to the late David Clarke, Michael Gregory, owner of Cromwell Tools, has been very generous, particularly in funding the restoration of carriages and locomotives, and for a number of years day-to-day management has been provided by the indefatigable Bill Ford, who has held every position from President to Chairman, General Manager and Managing Director (the position he took on in 2011).

The GCR is a remarkable heritage operation: it offers main-line steam running on a double track, through Bill Ford's leadership it is being reconnected to the national network and extended, a former goods branch line has been restored, and a unique agreement has been signed with the elected Mayor of Leicester and the National Railway Museum for it to become effectively the Midlands outstation of the museum.

The planned destruction of this route was almost complete and relatively little would have been left of the London extension had not the

LAST RITES
A week before closure of the rump section to Nottingham (Arkwright Street), two railcars wait at Rugby Central in April 1969. *Ian Allan Library*

THE GRAFFITO SAYS IT ALL!
Brackley should today have been a busy commuter railhead in
Northamptonshire, a large county that today has only six stations. Instead it
is a tyre depot and the railhead is at Banbury, 8 miles away. *Richard Faulkner*

heritage railway taken over the central section based on Loughborough,
with the vision to extend further north in the longer term.

South of Annesley, what remains today is:

- Weekday Cross Junction to Nottingham Midland station
  forms part of NET, Nottingham's tram system. The Clifton
  extension uses the GC formation to Arkwright Street.
- Ruddington to Loughborough is a heritage railway and will
  form part of the GCR's northern extension when the bridge
  over the Midland main line has been replaced.
- Loughborough to Leicester North (the former Belgrave
  & Birstall) is now the GCR heritage line.
- Calvert to Quainton Road is now a freight line used by
  waste trains from Northolt, but will become part of the East
  West Rail project carrying passenger trains from Aylesbury
  to Milton Keynes (see the following section on the 'Varsity
  Line').

Leicester to Whetstone (both exclusive) has become a track for walkers
and cyclists, while Nottingham Victoria has become a shopping centre,
retaining its clock tower. At Woodford Halse the line lies under an
industrial estate, while Brackley Central is now a tyre depot, with its
viaduct demolished to make way for the dualled A43.

Conclusions

Like the Didcot, Newbury & Southampton Railway (page 65), the
Great Central did not thrive under the ownership of a larger company
for which the line was not its first priority. It performed well under the
independent management of Sir Sam Fay, and would have done better
under a management independent of the LNER. Its premature end
came when it was managed as part of British Rail, particularly after the
transfer from the Eastern to the London Midland Region. The success
of the southern end of the line under the leadership of Adrian
Shooter[85] and Chiltern Railways from 1996 onwards shows what
might have been possible under independent management.

It might have lost its intermediate stations, and the famous
'Windcutter' coal trains would eventually have ceased with the

decline in indigenous coal-mining, but the route would have been
ideal as a base for a high-speed line with limited stops, and enjoying
excellent city-centre access along its route. Parkway stations, like
Haddenham & Thame, would have followed as on other main lines.
It would have offered the step change in capacity needed to relieve
the East Coast, West Coast and Midland main lines. It is a great
'might-have-been'.

It would not have been an easy choice, as Chiltern Railways has
proved so successful that capacity south of Princes Risborough
would now be limited and it might have required some four-tracking
or reinstatement of platform loops. There was also the general
problem that connectivity between the GC and the older railways
was poor, particularly at Sheffield. It is also true that closure paved
the way for the magnificent heritage railway that has replaced it
between Belgrave & Birstall (now Leicester North) and
Loughborough, and is due to be extended further north towards
Nottingham.

The loss of such capacity from the rail network in 1966 has had
serious long-term consequences, although at the time it was seen as
reducing surplus capacity for which no profitable use could be
foreseen. That capacity is now having to be replaced and augmented
at great cost by HS2, which will follow the corridor of the Great
Central between Aylesbury and Brackley, and for a short stretch
between Quainton Road and Calvert will use part of the formation.

The 'Varsity Line': Oxford-Cambridge

'Bletchley was on what was then known as the 'Varsity Line' – the trains
ran direct to both Oxford and Cambridge, which was very useful from
the point of view of all the dons who were working there.'[86]
Baroness Trumpington writing in her autobiography *Coming up
Trumps*

Many rail closures went ahead in the decade and a half after the
Beeching Report was published in 1963, but few were as surprising
or short-sighted as that which removed the through route between
England's great university cities of Oxford and Cambridge on
1 January 1968 (the last trains ran on 30 December 1967).

The line had not been listed for closure in the Beeching Report
published in 1963 – this proposed 'modification' of the service, with
the axing of most intermediate stations – but British Railways came
forward on 7 February 1964 with a proposal for the withdrawal of all
passenger services on the line, having made an earlier unsuccessful
attempt to close it in 1959.

The Transport Users' Consultative Committee concluded its
hearings on 21 July 1964 (still during the time of the 1959-64
Conservative Government) and submitted its report to the new
Labour transport minister, Tom Fraser, on 28 October 1964. He gave
his consent to the closure on 8 July 1965, on condition that
replacement bus services were provided.

History

The railway had come to Oxford as early as 1844, when the Great
Western Railway opened its line from Didcot. By 1851 the
Buckinghamshire Railway Company had reached the city from
Bletchley, which was already linked to Bedford, and in 1862 the

through link from Oxford to Cambridge was achieved with the opening of the line from Bedford to Cambridge.

As the Buckinghamshire Railway was worked by the London & North Western Railway, the latter's great rival the GWR refused to allow it to use its Oxford station, so a new terminus was built almost alongside (and nearer to the city) on land that had been owned by Rewley Abbey, a 13th-century Cistercian monastery, destroying much of what was left of the remains of it. With the help of Joseph Paxton[87], the station was constructed by Fox, Henderson, which at the same time was building the Crystal Palace at Hyde Park in London. Both were built out of pre-fabricated cast iron, and Rewley Road station was essentially a miniature version of the other (earning it a Grade 2 listing much later).

Following the public ownership of the railways in 1948 some rationalisation of competing routes and stations was undertaken by British Railways, and it was possible for the London Midland Region to route its passenger trains into the former Great Western station at Oxford in 1951, and close Rewley Road, almost exactly 100 years after it opened.

The goods yard stayed in use until 1984, and the site was eventually cleared in 1998, when it was developed for housing. Paxton's station building with its Grade 2 listing could not be demolished, and it underwent a series of unsatisfactory commercial uses (including a tyre depot) until the University of Oxford succeeded in locating its new Saïd Business School on the site, having first helped to fund the station's removal to the Buckinghamshire Railway Centre at Quainton Road, where it has happily been restored to heritage railway use as a museum. There is a plaque in the pavement at the front of the business school in Frideswide Square, depicting the original station building and commemorating its contribution to Oxford's railway heritage.

Quainton Road is a particularly fitting home for Paxton's station, for although it was not located on the east-west route, it was linked to it by two lines. One was the junction from the Great Central at Calvert, formerly used by freight trains carrying refuse to a local landfill site.

The other was altogether more romantic – a branch line to Verney Junction, which was where passengers on Oxford to Bletchley trains also changed for Banbury. There was – and is – no place called Verney; the station was in the middle of a field and a place only to change trains. Your co-author remembers that when he did so in about 1962 there was a cheerful wishing well on the platform and a well-kept garden. The station was named after Sir Harry Verney[88], who lived at nearby Claydon House and was Chairman of the Aylesbury & Buckingham Railway Company, which had been bought by the Metropolitan Railway in 1891.

Whether the Metropolitan ever imagined that it would be able to cover the acres of green fields and open countryside in deepest Buckinghamshire with the sort of houses that had proved so phenomenally popular in the Middlesex and Hertfordshire suburbs is unclear, but soon after 1933, when the Metropolitan Railway became part of London Transport, its services north of Aylesbury were abandoned and the line to Verney Junction closed.

FREIGHT AT FENNY STRATFORD
A train of empties comes off the Bletchley flyover and passes through the
station on its way to be loaded at Fletton brickworks, Millbrook, in October
1964. The locomotive is BR Standard Class 5 4-6-0 No 73013 from Bletchley.
E. J. S. Gadsden

'The houses of Metroland never got as far as Verney Junction. Grass triumphs, and I must say I'm rather glad,' said John Betjeman[89] at Verney Junction in his 1973 BBC film *Metroland*.

Despite its strategic importance as almost the only east-west route north of London and south of Leicester, the 'Varsity Line' was never really given the opportunity by its owners to develop its potential. Verney had said, 'The cross line was to give railway communication across England via Oxford, Bletchley, Bedford and eastward to Lynn.'

An attempt was made in 1905 to create a commuter service operated by steam railmotors (and later by a prototype petrol railmotor known as the 'Michelin') from Bicester to Oxford, with the opening of a succession of halts in the suburbs – Port Meadow, Wolvercote and Oxford Road – and Oddington, Charlton and Wendlebury between Islip and Bicester. These were closed as an economy measure during the First World War, reinstated in 1919, then closed permanently in 1926 during the General Strike.

The line's heyday was during the Second World War; many trains were run to and from the Bicester Military Railway, carrying troops, munitions and essential supplies, as well as the Oxford and Cambridge dons working at Bletchley Park, to whom Baroness Trumpington referred. A junction with the Great Central main line was constructed between Calvert and Claydon and opened in September 1940.

Extensive use was also made of the Yarnton curve, which had been built by the Buckinghamshire Railway in 1854 to allow through

trains to run from Euston to Worcester and Wolverhampton through Bletchley, avoiding Oxford. There was originally a connection at Hanborough (then known as 'Handborough') for Oxford. The Euston to Worcester trains only lasted until September 1861.

In August 1940 a marshalling yard of nine long sidings came into use at Yarnton Junction for the wartime traffic. It remained after the war to deal with ironstone trains, and eventually closed in 1966. The Yarnton curve had closed earlier in November 1965. There is no record of passenger services over the curve in recent times, but one of the authors travelled over it on a Locomotive Club of Great Britain special train on 3 April 1960[90].

Not fast enough?

One of the arguments put forward for the line's closure was that with the advent of fast trains from London to both Cambridge and Oxford, it was always going to be quicker to get from one university city to the other via London. It is hard to sustain this point of view. Even using the fastest trains to both cities, and moving smartly on the Underground between Paddington and King's Cross, it is impossible to get between Oxford and Cambridge in less than 2½ hours. In the first half of the 20th century through trains were completing the journey in well under 3 hours; in 1938, for example, a service from Oxford to Cambridge (but not in the return direction) had a 2hr 28min journey time, and even in 1911 the 10.50am from Oxford arrived in Cambridge at 1.20pm.

Closure threats

Following the publication of the Beeching Report, the future of the Oxford-Bletchley-Cambridge line had been the subject of an adjournment debate in the House of Commons on 19 December 1963[91], initiated by the MP for Buckingham, Major Sir Frank Markham[92]. Markham protested against the proposed closure of not just the 'Varsity Line', but also those from Verney Junction to Buckingham, Bedford to Northampton, and Wolverton to Newport Pagnell. He based his speech on the area being one of the fastest developing in the country, and complained bitterly about what he saw as the inadequacies of the TUCC inquiry process, which had denied members of the National Union of Railwaymen at Wolverton Works the right to put their case properly; he described the TUCCs as 'rubber stamps of British Railways'.

'The Minister has laid it down in legislation that the TUCC may consider only cases of travelling hardship. Thus local protesters can be heard only on this one subject of travelling hardship. Any protests on any other subjects made either by individual objectors or local authorities must be made in writing to the Minister of Transport, who is already a prejudiced person, as it were, because he is carrying out the legislation that he has introduced by means of an organisation, and individuals which he has created or appointed, and often clashing with other policies which he has enunciated as the principal roads Minister in this country.

This shows that in these broad spheres of finance, transport, stewardship, costs of alternative services and many others we can appeal only to the Minister in writing. We are never allowed to see the replies given by the British Railways Board or another Ministry, and from the moment the Minister receives our letters of protest we are entirely excluded from any further investigation. This is wrong, unjust and does not even give the appearance of justice.

British Railways give us certain figures, but not the lot. We are told some of the costs, but not all of the takings. Not only the NUR, but, I believe, other bodies would like to have an opportunity to challenge the figures. These organisations say that the figures do not contain the accretion of the parcels services, advertisements and vendors. They also say that the railways have not included in the costs the future costs of caretaking of disused stations. There is also the cost, possibly, of subsidising the buses.

Let me refer to the railwaymen again, because theirs is one of the key protests that ought to be considered. Articles 51, 52 and 53 of the Handbook of the Transport Users' Consultative Committees state that if the railwaymen have a protest they can put their protests through the hierarchical channels of the trade unions. Their protests never get up through those channels. They are dead-ended at somewhere like branch level. Railwaymen both at Bletchley and at Wolverton have protested – and I believe them – that their protests got to the local consultative committee, and not a step further.

Many of these railwaymen are not only indignant, perhaps, at losing their jobs, but are more public spirited and are indignant at a good service being closed down, and indignant because there is no channel through which they can make constructive proposals for improving traffics on the railways. These are grave charges against the present system by which these railway closure inquiries are conducted.'

The minister replying to the debate was Tom Galbraith[93]. Brushing aside Markham's criticism of the TUCC process, his response was very revealing:

'The first and most important thing to get clear is that the responsibility for deciding whether or not to propose a closure is a matter for the railway management. Often, Hon Members come to me and say, 'Why are you proposing to close this line?' when what they mean is, 'Why is Dr Beeching proposing to close the line?' Why Dr Beeching should be doing it is, of course, a question which the Minister cannot answer. After all, he does not run the railways; that is the Board's duty, and the Board has, to quote the words of the 1962 Act, to do it with 'due regard' to efficiency, economy and safety of operation.

It was in fulfilment of this duty that, last March, in its Report, the Board gave in outline plans for closing about 330 passenger services involving over 2,000 stations. This was a general proposal, but when it comes to any particular line or station the Board must give formal notice, and this allows users seven weeks in which to object, and, if they do object, then the proposal cannot be effected without the Minister's consent. This is an important restriction on the railway management's discretion which was introduced in the 1962 Act, which my hon and gallant Friend seemed to be complaining about, because it brings in both the TUCC and the Minister.

The new procedure thus gives full opportunity to discuss what really matters to passengers, that is: will there be hardship, and are the alternatives satisfactory? This is the only thing that a passenger is really concerned with – how to get from one place to another if the railway line is closed. The financial matters to which my hon and gallant Friend referred and other wider planning considerations are utterly irrelevant to the passenger. He is concerned only with movement, not with costs, and that is why there is no wide-ranging discussion at the TUCCs and why there is no cross-examination of financial figures, since whether the railways lose £5 or £500,000 does not really affect the hardship issue.'

This was without doubt one of the more frank descriptions of how the closure procedures under the 1962 Transport Act operated, and goes a long way to help us understand how it was possible at that time – when the power of the road lobby was at its height, and it was felt that the railways would shrink and decline – that so many contentious closures would go ahead. It was not until much later

BEDFORD BARED

The 16.15 school train from Bedford St Johns to Bletchley awaits departure on 6 May 1981, formed of a Cravens Class 105 unit. The station buildings have gone and only the most rudimentary facilities remain. The spur to Bedford Midland and the replacement station would be built just behind the signal box three years later. *Brian Morrison*

that the contribution that the railways could make was acknowledged and the policies of decay and contraction reversed.

Less than two months after Markham had secured his adjournment debate, British Railways published the closure notice for the Oxford to Cambridge line.

Eight months after that – in October 1964 – Markham retired from Parliament at the General Election, and the Buckingham constituency was won for the Labour Party by one Robert Maxwell[94], who succeeded in beating every other new MP to make his maiden speech on the first day of the debate on the Queen's Speech. He used the occasion to say this about the threatened closure:

'I hope that the Minister of Transport will confirm soon that he will refuse to sanction the closure of the Oxford-Bletchley-Cambridge line. People in my constituency have already suffered grievously from Beeching closures, and, because of the considerable expansion of population in this part of Buckinghamshire, it would be social as well as economic madness to close this important line.'[95]

This argument cut no ice with the Labour transport minister, Tom Fraser, and he gave his consent to complete closure in July 1965,

subject to the provision of rail replacement bus services. Bus services were provided between Oxford and Bletchley, and between Bedford and Cambridge, but road service licences for the central section were refused because the operators could not provide the necessary crews, and the Bletchley to Bedford section remained open. BR managed to persuade Barbara Castle, who had succeeded Fraser in December 1965, to agree to the closure of the rest of the route, however, and services between Oxford and Bletchley and from Bedford to Cambridge were withdrawn at the end of 1967.[96]

Opposition to closure outside Parliament was widespread, and in the National Archives we came across a letter sent by Mr P. M. Eavis, a member of the public, to the General Manager of BR's London Midland Region on 20 January 1968. We reproduce it here, complete with the General Manager's hand-written notes, because it is the best example of an angry but utterly coherent protest by an individual outraged by the closure of the Oxford to Cambridge line that we have come across. All the arguments he uses are those that should have stayed the minister's hand in allowing the closure; they are also largely those that are being put forward today for its reinstatement nearly 50 years later.

With Oxford to Bletchley and Bedford to Cambridge gone, further attempts were made to close Bletchley to Bedford after 1970, as the junior transport minister, Reginald Eyre[97], explained in an adjournment debate in the House of Commons initiated by the latest MP for Buckingham, William Benyon[98], on 23 November 1972[99]:

'Late in 1970 we were advised by the bus operators that the staffing position was likely to have improved sufficiently by the spring of 1971 to allow provision of a rail replacement bus service between Bedford and Bletchley, without detriment to existing bus services. However, in view of the long interval which had elapsed since consent to the previous closure proposal was given, it seemed inappropriate for that consent to be implemented even if the special rail replacement bus services could be provided. Accordingly, in December 1970, the Railways Board was notified in the usual form that it was unlikely that grant aid would be renewed at the end of 1971 unless a closure proposal had first been refused. The Board published a proposal to discontinue all passenger train services between Bletchley and Bedford involving the closure of Bedford St Johns and nine intermediate stations.

As the rail service crosses the boundary between the East Anglian Transport Users Consultative Committee and the East Midland Transport Users Consultative Committee, objections were received by both. The two committees held a joint hearing to consider these objections, and later reported jointly that the withdrawal of the train service would cause hardship to some passengers and inconvenience to others, but the committees felt that the hardship could in the main be alleviated by the provision of the proposed additional bus services.

Other representations were received, mainly on the grounds that improved east-west transport facilities were needed, rather than a reduction of these facilities. I note that my hon Friend stressed that. This was given the most careful consideration before the eventual decision on the closure proposal, as were the observations of the South Eastern Economic Planning Council.

The Government were of course aware of the fact, which my hon Friend properly stressed, that this area contains rapidly expanding communities which must be provided with adequate public transport facilities. But the evidence was that only some 450 regular travellers were involved each day, although total usage in each direction was about 900. By providing no less [*sic*] than 15 extra buses in each direction from Monday to Saturday it was felt that the needs of these travellers could be met, and at the same time a useful saving made. From all the advice received it did not seem that the future development of the area would be significantly affected by the closure.

In actual cash terms the rail service was being subsidised to the extent of £173,000 per annum from public funds. The costs that would actually be avoided in the future if the rail service was discontinued – as opposed to those assessed for the purposes of grant – are estimated at £82,000 per annum of which £59,000 would be saved in the first year after closure. Additional costs for renewals estimated at £46,000 between 1972 and 1976 would also be saved. So the closure of this rail service would represent a considerable saving in public funds and real resources without imposing hardship on the existing users.'[100]

INTO THE WOODS
A special train was run by Chiltern Railways in 2012 to allow stakeholders to see the line between north of Aylesbury and west to Bicester Town. The train paused at Claydon, and beyond the train the line heads towards Bletchley, but is completely overgrown. *Chris Austin*

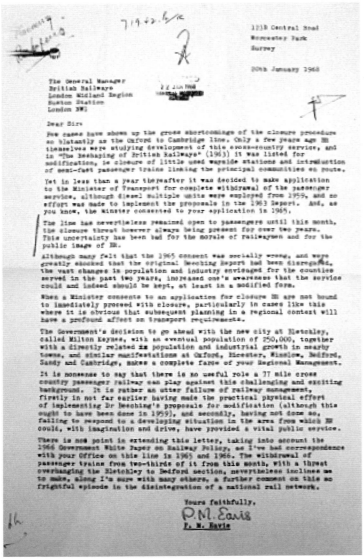

THE ARTICULATE CAMPAIGNER
The letter from P. M. Eavis regarding the 'Varsity Line'.

The minister's speech is interesting for a number of reasons.

First, it demonstrates how much decisions on closures post-Beeching were based on the subsequently discredited Cooper Brothers' formula for assessing railway costs and revenue.

Second, his reference to 'rapidly expanding communities' does scant justice to the plans for and eventual creation of the new city of Milton Keynes. Indeed, the 1968 Interim Report on Milton Keynes had recognised that 'the city of Milton Keynes is at the crossroads of transportation routes giving a setting of great potential' and the 'East-West Rail Lines could represent an important element in future transport services for the City.'

Third, the case for 'improved east-west transport facilities' was given 'the most careful consideration', then utterly dismissed.

Fourth – and this applies to a great many of the closures implemented by Conservative and Labour Governments alike in the 1960s and '70s – there was no consideration whatever to the future growth in demand for passenger and freight rail travel, which by the second decade of the 21st century is threatening to overwhelm significant parts of the nation's railway, and provides the essential justification for the building of new high-speed railway lines linking the North, the Midlands and the South of England.

Benyon had started his speech – at 7 minutes past 3 in the morning – by pointing out that 'British Rail claim to have looked into the future and to have found no substance for the increased viability of the line that many of us consider will occur as a result of the massive development which is taking place in the area.'

Benyon also referred to BR's intention to keep the line open for freight traffic, 'which would seem to indicate that they see a future requirement here.'

The reference to freight services is interesting because back in 1955 BR's Railway Modernisation Plan proposed improvements in cross-country facilities between Oxford and Cambridge with the aim of maintaining a link between the major main-line railways outside the congested Greater London area. This would have allowed freight traffic to be transferred between three railway regions and reduced the pressure on London marshalling yards.

One tangible piece of evidence of the modernisation plan was the construction of a flyover at Bletchley, intended to serve a freight marshalling yard at Swanbourne and finally completed, after many delays, in 1962. The yard, however, closed in 1967 and the flyover's main raison d'être disappeared: a National Union of Railwaymen spokesman described it as a 'white elephant'[101].

Not only did this fail to realise its potential as a vital part of a national freight network, it was also hardly ever used, and stood for decades as a reminder of how well-intentioned plans can go disastrously wrong if investment is embarked upon, then abandoned.

This sad story may be about to have a happy ending, as the flyover appears to have been sufficiently well built to enable it to come back into use as an essential part of a new east-west route.

Campaigning for reinstatement

The Bletchley to Bedford service has not closed and is now operated as part of the London Midland franchise, with trains going into the main Bedford Midland station, rather than terminating at St John's. It is supported by the Marston Vale Community rail partnership and the lively Bedford & Bletchley Rail Users' Association, which help to market the line. One of the unusual cottage orné stations has been well restored by the partnership at Ridgmont, and now includes a tea shop and heritage centre. The trackbed between Bicester and Bletchley has been retained (though much became heavily overgrown), and in May 1989 services were restored between Bicester London Road and Oxford. The section from Bedford to Cambridge, however, was completely abandoned, including the bridge over the East Coast Main Line at Sandy. Other parts of the trackbed were built upon, thus making the feasibility of reinstatement through to Cambridge very difficult and expensive. One section, near Lord's Bridge station, is occupied by the Mullard radio astronomy observatory (part of

Cambridge University) and the telescopes move up and down on 20-foot-wide tracks laid on the formation of the line.

Campaigning for reopening started just five years after the two ends of the line closed. The Oxon and Bucks Rail Action Committee (OBRAC) was formed on 7 March 1987, to press the case for reopening the Oxford and Aylesbury rail lines to Milton Keynes. The Railway Development Society (now Railfuture) and rail user groups formed the basis of OBRAC.

When it began, in its own words, 'OBRAC was to find no national rail reopenings policy, new road proposals dominant, the new towns movement largely ignoring rail, that support from MPs, councils and the public on reopening made limited effect, policies were often just words, changing policies and moving goal posts, privatisation increased costs, few train companies wished to invest in new lines or services while fragmenting of the industry meant negotiations were complex and bureaucratic. In spite of feasibility studies showing the case for reopening, it took 25 years to get Government funding approval (with conditions).'

The full diary of events for the 42 years of campaigning for the reopening of this line that should never have closed is set out in Appendix D. It is an amazing story of dogged determination by a group in the face of overwhelming odds. A huge number of agencies have been involved and a vast number of changes have taken place in organisations and staff since 1973. Over this period BR was reorganised three times, privatised, Railtrack was replaced by Network Rail, then restored to the public sector. The franchise covering the Bedford-Bletchley line has changed hands three times. The Oxford-Bletchley section has been used for freight and parcels trains and moving diesels to Bletchley for maintenance, then was later disused over part of its length and completely overgrown. Part has been restored with a limited passenger service, and now phase 1 of the project that will allow Chiltern trains to run from Marylebone via Bicester to Oxford is well under way.

The diary ends in 2012, and since then there has been a series of announcements and developments. These included confirmation by Network Rail in January 2013 that it had included in its five-year strategic business plan for 2014-19 the construction of the western section as an electrified main line between Bedford and Oxford, Aylesbury and Milton Keynes.

Clearance of vegetation that had swamped the disused rails was started by Network Rail in February 2014, and a month later the identity of the contractors – a joint venture between Carillion and Buckingham Group – was revealed, starting with Oxford to Bicester, and NR said that the date for completion was 2019.

To complete the story, and to mark the transformation of a line that was almost lost for ever, Network Rail said in May 2014 that the line speed – 125mph – will be the same as the maximum for main-line express services elsewhere in Great Britain, with trains being run by Chiltern Railways, CrossCountry and London Midland.

By October 2014 the members of the East West Rail all-party parliamentary group were told by the communications manager of the consortium that

'There has been much progress over the last year. On the Western Section, construction work is progressing well between Oxford and Bicester and early work under way on the Bicester-Bedford and Milton Keynes-Aylesbury-

London (Marylebone) line is under way. A recent forecast of the potential value of the Western Section in terms of regional GDP has doubled since an earlier forecast in 2010. Furthermore, it has been shown that development of the Central Section could unlock sufficient economic benefit to justify further investment to extend the East West Rail line for services to run through Cambridge and on to East Anglia.'[102]

Also that month the Liberal Democrat Party issued a press release headed 'New garden city train link would expand towns'. It began:

'A Liberal Democrat government would re-open the Oxford to Cambridge Rail Link in full as the 'Garden Cities Line'. This would dramatically expand three to five of the towns along the route to enable approximately 50,000 new homes to be built on Garden City principles.'[103]

Presumably the return of this railway to Cambridge would not provoke the same reaction as that of the Master of Magdalene College, George Neville Grenville (1789-1854) in about 1844. He is reported to have said, 'The coming of the railway to Cambridge would be highly displeasing both to God and myself.'[104]

What is remarkable is the length of time that it is taking to restore a crucial line that should never have closed, and the enormous costs involved. Why BR was so keen to abandon it, given that it had not been proposed for closure in the Beeching Report, remains a mystery. When it disappeared in the 1960s there was no east-west line between the North London Line and the Birmingham-Leicester route, 100 miles to the north – a gap that imposed immense operating difficulties on a railway whose popularity had started to grow again in the 1990s after three decades of decline and contraction.

The 'Withered Arm': Exeter-Plymouth via Okehampton

Brunel's[105] railway provides the only link west of Exeter to Plymouth, Torbay and Cornwall today. It is a difficult section of railway, with steep gradients between Newton Abbot and Plymouth over the notorious South Devon banks, and there is a vulnerable coastal stretch of line between Dawlish Warren and Teignmouth, which is periodically breached by incursion of the sea, or rock falls. Indeed, since its opening 169 years ago the line has been closed on 19 occasions, varying from part of a day to eight weeks. The average closure period for these interruptions is six days, although on 13 occasions out of the 19 the closure has been for three days or fewer[106]. It is also true that, as a result of both the gradients and the speed restrictions resulting from the alignment of the railway, it is possible to travel more quickly by coach from Plymouth to Tiverton Parkway than it is by train, a point not lost on travellers when the line was closed for two months in 2014 following an incursion by the sea at Dawlish.

The steep gradients required to lift the line over the southern fringe of Dartmoor resulted from the decision to build the line as an atmospheric railway where gradients were of less concern than on a line worked by steam locomotives. In fact, atmospheric trains never ran further west than Newton Abbot, but the gradients remain to this day.

The vulnerability of the sea wall near Teignmouth was first demonstrated in 1847, a year after the line opened, and the engineer charged with rebuilding this section was Brunel.

ACE
The Plymouth portion of the 'Atlantic Coast Express' climbs from Bere Alston towards Tavistock on 12 May 1961 behind 'T9' 4-4-0 No 30709 two months before the locomotive was withdrawn. Calstock Viaduct on the Callington branch can be seen crossing the Tamar in the background. *S. C. Nash*

An alternative inland route, the Teign Valley line, from Exeter via Heathfield to Newton Abbot, existed until 1958. However, this was single track with low speeds, steep gradients and limited capacity, but was maintained by the GWR and BR's Western Region as a 'red' route (for heavier locomotives) to allow diversions to take place when the coastal main line was blocked.

Despite its difficult physical characteristics, the existing line serves the communities along the route effectively with well-sited stations and stunning views for rail passengers.

Competition between the Great Western and the London & South Western companies had resulted in an agreement as early as 1845 that the LSWR would not seek to promote new lines west of Salisbury or Dorchester, while the Great Western relinquished its lease of the Southampton & Dorchester Railway (known as 'Castleman's Corkscrew'[107]), which was then taken up by the South Western. The agreement was soon challenged when the Great Western promoted a direct line to Exeter via Westbury and Yeovil the following year. Berkshire, Wiltshire, Somerset, Devon and Cornwall were to remain disputed territory for the next 40 years, and one of these later skirmishes we examine in Chapter 7 on the Didcot, Newbury & Southampton line.

So, competitive pressures meant that the LSWR did build its line west, and it reached Exeter in 1860. The broad gauge confederacy was not, as we shall see at Gloucester (Chapter 10), quick to defend its interests, so missed a trick when the LSWR purchased a controlling interest in the Exeter & Crediton Railway in 1847. Beyond Crediton, the North Devon Railway was opened to Barnstaple in 1854. The Okehampton Railway (later the Devon & Cornwall Railway) took the line from Coleford Junction to Lydford in 1874, where it joined the Great Western branch from Launceston to Plymouth. The London & South Western competed for traffic to Plymouth from that date. Its separate route via Bere Alston (built by the Plymouth, Devonport & South Western Junction Railway) was opened in 1890, and its own terminus at Plymouth Friary the following year.

The railway from Salisbury to Exeter was laid out as a fast line with balancing gradients, but west of Exeter it was a more sedate affair. While Great Western trains had to travel the 'great way round' via Box, the LSWR had the upper hand, but with the upgrading of the Berks & Hants line and the opening of the cut-off lines, completed in 1906 (the Westbury and Frome avoiding lines were not opened until 1933), the competition became intense, particularly for the ocean mails traffic from the transatlantic liners offloading at Plymouth. The amazing exploits of locomotives and crews on both railways are well known and sadly culminated with the derailment of one of the ocean mail expresses at Salisbury in 1906 with the loss of 25 lives, after which a working agreement was made between the two companies in 1910. A further consequence of the accident was that all trains had to stop at Salisbury.

In later years the LSWR route never quite managed the same fast timings as the Great Western. The mileage from Paddington to Plymouth North Road was 225.75, while that from Waterloo to North Road was 5 miles longer. From Exeter to North Road it is 52 miles by the GWR, and was 59 by the LSWR.

In 1961 the 'Cornish Riviera' managed the non-stop run from London to Plymouth in 4 hours (exactly the same time that it took in 1938), while the 'Atlantic Coast Express' took 5hr 25min with 11 intermediate stops. Fastest times from Exeter to Plymouth were 1hr 16min (Western) and 1 hr 44 min (Southern).

The 'withered arm'[108] (the Southern lines west of Exeter) were run down once the regional boundary had been moved to Wilton and the Western Region had taken over all points west in 1962. The Beeching Report proposed closure of the line between Okehampton and Plymouth, but that between Exeter and Okehampton was to be retained, together with the Barnstaple line. Intermediate stations, apart from Crediton, were also to be closed. Further south, the inadequate roads of the Bere peninsula, together with the natural barrier of the River Tavy, meant that alternative bus services could not be provided to replace the southern section of the line, so St Budeaux to Bere Alston was retained and singled, being linked to the Great Western line at St Budeaux. Trains then followed the former Callington branch to Gunnislake, where the line terminated. Callington had enjoyed a direct service by bus to Plymouth from the opening of the Tamar road bridge in 1961.

The link between Okehampton and Bere Alston closed in 1968, while the LSWR loop from St Budeaux to Plymouth via Devonport (Kings Road) had closed in 1964. The line to Okehampton (not listed in Beeching's 'Reshaping' report), deprived of its feeder services from Bude, the North Cornwall line and Plymouth, closed in 1972.

The southern part of the route survives and prospers as the Tamar Valley Line, a thriving community rail line, as does the northern end from Yeoford to Exeter as part of the Tarka Line, another busy community rail route, both being actively promoted through the Devon & Cornwall Rail Partnership. On the Tamar Valley Line, business has more than doubled over the last 15 years and the line is actively promoted, together with its attractions, such as walks and a visit to Cothele House or Morwellham Quay. The Partnership also supplies booklets of rail tickets for local shops to sell, and no less than a third of the population of the Bere peninsula has these carnet tickets, a remarkably high figure for rail penetration in any rural market.

Indeed, extension of this line north to Tavistock is proposed, and the scheme is supported by Devon County Council, with part of the funding coming from a major housing and community development at Tavistock. The new station site proposed is to the south of the original, but would serve the new development well and be linked to the old town by shuttle bus. The addition of Tavistock would effectively triple the population in the line's catchment area.

Okehampton, however, had a rather different history. Although closed to passengers in 1972, the line remained open to serve Meldon Quarry, which continued its traditional role of providing ballast for Southern Region lines. In 1993 the line from Coleford Junction (where it joined the Barnstaple branch) to Meldon, together with the quarry, was sold to English China Clays. Four years later the station at Okehampton was restored and an operating company, Dartmoor Railway, began running passenger trains on parts of the line, while Wessex Trains provided Sunday trains under contract to Devon County Council from Exeter to Okehampton. Bus links at Okehampton allowed car-free days out to points all over Dartmoor and a connection to Gunnislake, for trains to Plymouth. Sampford Courtenay station, between Okehampton and Crediton, reopened in 2004. In that year the quarry had been used to supply ballast for the restoration of double track between Probus and Burngullow, a

ALTERNATIVE ROUTE
The 8.25am Paddington to Penzance train (with a portion for Perranporth) rolls off Meldon Viaduct behind No 6973 *Bricklehampton Hall* of Old Oak Common, diverted from the normal route via Newton Abbot on Saturday 26 August 1961. *S. C. Nash*

MELDON STONE
The 15.00 Meldon Quarry to Bristol East Depot train approaches Yeoford behind Class 45 'Peak' No 45069 on 17 February 1983. The second track is the Barnstaple line, both continuing as parallel single lines from Coleford Junction to Crediton. *Peter Medley*

scheme funded by the Strategic Rail Authority. In 2008 the railway lease was taken over by Iowa Pacific Holdings, the operator of a number short lines in the USA.

The last stone trains ran in 2010, and sadly, from that point on, it has been all downhill. The quarry closed and the equipment has been removed. The freehold of the quarry and the railway has been offered for sale, but, at the time of writing, remains with Camas Aggregates, successor to English China Clays. The 'heritage' service is limited and currently without steam as an attraction, and plans to extend to Yeoford or even Exeter have not been implemented. Freight has ceased and, apart from the summer Sunday FGW 'Dartmoor explorer' service from Exeter, supported by Devon County Council, the weekend heritage diesel service between Bow and Meldon, and some special events, the line sees little business today. It does perform a useful role for driver training (the gradient up to Okehampton offers perfect conditions for lessons in how to counter rail-slip), and at Christmas it becomes the base for running the successful 'Polar Express', based on the popular children's film with Tom Hanks[109] providing the voice of the computer-generated old-time railroad conductor.

Conclusions

If the line had survived, or if it were restored, it would provide an additional route between Exeter and Plymouth, improve rail access for West Devon, and provide a closer railhead for North Cornwall. The success of the Exeter-Barnstaple line, supported by the Devon & Cornwall Rail Partnership and the very active Tarka Line Rail Users' Association, also suggests that a local service for Okehampton and Tavistock could be successful, particularly if supported by a community rail partnership.

However, decisions are never straightforward, and there are a few potential pitfalls as well as some very obvious benefits.

As a diversionary route, the Okehampton line would not serve Torbay or the South Hams at all. A breach of the wall at Dawlish or a blockade for engineering work would still mean a bus to Newton Abbot. It would not serve Cornwall so well, given the need for a reversal at Plymouth and backtracking over the 3 miles to St Budeaux.

The A30 is a fast road with quicker journey times to the railhead at Tiverton Parkway than would be possible by train with a change at Exeter. The station at Okehampton and the site of the former station at Tavistock were singularly badly sited, hundreds of feet above the towns they served and a long walk from the centres.

On the face of it, once trains have returned to Tavistock, only 15 miles will separate the new terminus from Meldon. But this does not mean that there is just a small gap in the track to close. Both lines are operated as stub ends with a train staff for 'one train working'. Restoring a single line of railway between the two would only be the first step; resignalling the entire route from Crediton to St Budeaux would be required and, with a minimum of two intermediate crossing loops and probably a third to provide for diverted services, this will not be a simple or cheap task. So too, if double track were specified, enhanced signalling would be needed and a lot more work involving the clearance of cuttings and the stabilising of embankments as previous track-doubling schemes have demonstrated, together with the need for a second platform at stations and fully accessible footbridges.

The first part of the Okehampton route, from Exeter to Yeoford, is in a flood plain and would require work if it were to become the resilient all-weather alternative route that is required.

In July 2014, Network Rail published its study[110] into providing a resilient rail link west of Exeter and considered a number of options including:

- Providing greater protection for the existing coastal route
- Rebuilding the Teign Valley line as a double-track railway
- Restoring the Okehampton route
- Five options for a new line bypassing Dawlish, a similar approach to that for which the Great Western secured powers and on which the company started work in 1939, stopping short on the outbreak of the Second World War

The estimated cost of providing a double-track main line from Cowley Bridge Junction to the junction at St Budeaux was £875 million, although this includes a 66% contingency, making the base cost £527 million. The cost of a single-track route with dynamic loops to allow trains to pass at speed was estimated to be £655–700 million (£395–422 million without the contingency).

The estimated non-stop running time for a Class 220 'Voyager' between Exeter and Plymouth via Okehampton would be only 53 minutes, just 4 minutes longer than the run via Dawlish. A time penalty would apply for reversing trains at Exeter, however, and at Plymouth for trains continuing to Cornwall.

Clearly, the first priority is to protect the existing Great Western route with its large population centres. However, the added value of the Okehampton route is clear and, had it not closed, it would today be both a valuable line of regional significance serving areas of Devon and Cornwall that are today remote from a railhead. With rising sea levels, and the need for higher levels of maintenance of the coastal route, it would also have had a clear added value as a diversionary route.

Apart from that, Plymouth with its population of a quarter of a million is the only city in Britain of that size with just a single rail link with the rest of the country. In 1968 that was not seen as an issue. In 2015 it is, and a second line is needed, not just because of the vulnerability of the single route at Dawlish, but because from time to time it will be closed as a result of failure or incident, and quite frequently for maintenance. Something better than the present arrangement is needed for the 21st century.

Salisbury-Exeter

The eastern end of the Southern main line to the West remained open and has prospered. East Devon and Dorset are thriving and the line from Exeter Central to Salisbury and Waterloo is busier than ever with passenger trains. It was not listed for development in the second Beeching Report, and was singled between Pinhoe and Wilton in 1968, after the local stations had been closed (in 1966). The Western Region wanted to provide a good semi-fast service to London to remain competitive with road (the A303 was to be upgraded and parallels the railway), and allocated 'Warship' diesels to achieve this. Local opposition to retrenchment left too many

stations and a rather slow and definitely second-class service. Gerry Fiennes[111], the General Manager at the time, recorded his frustration in his autobiography:

'We drew up timetables to introduce as soon as the small stations were closed, accelerating the expresses by up to 20 minutes and giving the remaining stations an express to and from London every two hours. Dorset started to manoeuvre. Keep Yeovil Junction open as well as Crewkerne and Sherborne within three or four miles on either side. Templecombe must stay… Tisbury, of course… I got fed up with them; and they have got what they deserved: an express service far slower than before: and to my belief uncompetitive with road.'[112]

Indeed, in 1968 the best time between Waterloo and Exeter was 3hr 23min with eight intermediate stops. In fact, road speeds deteriorated faster, while rail speeds have subsequently improved, and the railway now enjoys double the level of service – an hourly service to London. Interestingly, the present service takes 3hr 17min from Waterloo to Exeter Central, with 14 intermediate stops, a little quicker than the 'Warship' service of 1968 and just 12 minutes longer than the 'Atlantic Coast Express' in 1959, which made just two stops at Salisbury and Sidmouth Junction. The market is probably large enough now to contemplate two trains an hour, one fast and one semi-fast, to meet local and long-distance markets, not only to London but also for South Coast destinations via Salisbury.

The right decision was taken to retain the line in the 1960s, and only with the benefit of hindsight could one criticise the lack of capacity resulting from the singling. In 1968 nobody expected the business to grow, and everyone thought, together with Gerry Fiennes, that the A303 would make further inroads into rail passenger numbers.

The pattern of loops left was matched to the requirements of a locomotive-hauled 2-hourly service, a solution designed for the technology of the time, but setting the service pattern in aspic. More frequent services required the additional loop at Tisbury, while the newer generation of Class 159 units, with faster acceleration, meant that the loops were in the wrong place. This has been addressed with a new 3-mile loop at Axminster, but inevitably further increases in services or the next generation of trains will mean more investment in future capacity.

This was a feature common to all the singling schemes such as the Cotswold line, East Suffolk, Bolton-Blackburn and the Glasgow & South Western route via Dumfries. All have proved inadequate and significant investment in the first and last have been needed to meet the requirements of today's business (and in the case of the Cotswold line, more is needed to complete the redoubling between Evesham and Norton Junction, and Wolvercote to Charlbury).

Through the Vale of Evesham: Cheltenham-Honeybourne-Stratford

The lost opportunities of Cheltenham's stations are set out in Chapter 10, but the route to Honeybourne and Stratford is a story of incompetence and prevarication that would strain credulity, even as an episode of *Yes, Minister*.

Like the Great Central, the Great Western's route from Cheltenham to Birmingham via Stratford-upon-Avon was a late arrival on the scene, opening throughout in 1906, with through expresses starting in 1910. It was one of a series of cut-off lines in which the company invested to reduce journey times and provide for expanding business. Like the Great Central, it was a competitive route designed to give the company an edge over a rival, in this case the Midland Railway.

In terms of intermediate traffic, the new line only served a string of small villages in Gloucestershire and Worcestershire, although Broadway generated quite a bit of traffic for the local auto-train. However, it was as a through route from the West Midlands to South Wales and the South West that the line had real value. While not a fast route, it provided plenty of capacity and avoided the constraint of the Lickey incline on the Midland route. While linked to the North Warwickshire line, the through trains ran via the Hatton north curve, giving them a fast run into Birmingham over the four-track section from Lapworth. Its high point was in the 1930s when it carried a substantial service of expresses from Birmingham and Wolverhampton to the West Country and South Wales, some of the latter being operated by the streamlined Great Western diesel railcars. Between 1952 and 1962 'The Cornishman' used the route between Wolverhampton and Penzance.

Local stations on the route south of Honeybourne had closed in 1960, with the through express trains, including 'The Cornishman', being rerouted via the Midland route in 1962. The residual through passenger service on the line (two trains a day each way between Leamington Spa and Gloucester) was finally withdrawn in 1968, with

the useful Worcester-Honeybourne-Stratford service coming off in 1969. By 1971, though, the route was still being used by five freight trains daily each way and was a diversionary route for passenger trains between Cheltenham and Birmingham while engineering work was taking place on the route via the Lickey incline. With the freight contracts then in place, a future for the line was seen at least until 1974. Other developments on the Lickey route were the planned introduction of HSTs on the cross-country service, with a 125mph capability, and the expected subsequent introduction of the gas-turbine APT with a capability of 155mph. The West Midlands PTE had also started to plan the cross-city service, originally intended to run from Lichfield to Frankley, but later cut back to Longbridge, with some trains going through to Redditch. All these developments meant that capacity on the Midland route was going to be tight.

In September 1971 minds were concentrated by a proposal from the Department of the Environment to use part of the line at the southern end for a Cheltenham relief road. For BR, closure of the line would mean a grant of £136,000 from Government for eliminating the surplus capacity, £104,000 for the scrap value of the

CORNISHMAN AT CHELTENHAM
Coming off the Stratford line at Lansdown Junction in June 1960 behind No 5031 *Totnes Castle* of Stafford Road shed, this express has come from Wolverhampton Low Level and is going to Penzance. It is taking the line towards Gloucester, and the diverging route in the foreground is that for Andoversford and Kingham. *John C. Baker*

track, signalling and structures, an annual saving in operating costs of £45,000, and a rather optimistic assumption that it could secure compensation of perhaps as much as £2 million for giving up the route for the road.

Decisions on the future of the line changed frequently during 1972. On 23 March the Western Region General Manager had recommended closure (from 1974), but the Chief Executive at the Board, David Bowick, decided[113] on 16 May that the line should remain open. Within five weeks, however, he had changed his mind and a letter of 21 June indicated that the line should close from the end of 1973. On 15 September the Board's Chief Operations Manager wrote to confirm that the date for closure had been brought forward to January 1973. Within three weeks there had been another change of heart and the Executive Director, Systems & Operations at the Board had written to halt the closure, and this was followed by an exasperated letter from the General Manager on 11 October. He had already agreed the freight train diversions with the London Midland Region; he had consulted on the proposal with the trade unions at sectional council, and they had objected, referring it to head office level. He had authorised the signalling alterations required to convert the Honeybourne-Long Marston section to a siding, and the savings were already in the budget for the following year. Could the Board give him guidance on how to explain this to staff, colleagues and customers?

Worse was to come, for this decision also meant that the formation could not be used for the road in Cheltenham. In an

USEFUL DIVERSION

The disused station at Malvern Road, Cheltenham, is the meeting point for northbound and southbound freight trains on 6 July 1971. All trains were diverted via Stratford following a derailment on the Midland route at Eckington. The disused bay platform between the two trains had been used by the Honeybourne to Cheltenham Spa St James auto-trains until 1960. *Eric Ilett*

angry letter of 6 April 1973, the Cheltenham Town Clerk expressed incredulity at the decision, but perhaps this was because he had commissioned consultants to draw up proposals for the road using the line of the old railway, at a cost of £40,000. Local press reaction was hostile to BR, and also inflated the cost of the report to £60,000. DoE was unhappy, and a stiff letter from Bill Sharpe followed saying they should have been advised beforehand, and that it had caused problems with its regional office and local MPs. BRHQ, quite rightly, dismissed these narrowly based objections and on 9 October 1973 the Railway Investment Panel (which handled investment expenditure within the Chief Executive's delegated powers) approved the retention and restoration of the line for 75mph running, at a cost of £1,110,000.

The work was not put in hand, and in August 1976 the future of the line was overtaken by events. An up freight train was derailed approaching Winchcombe, and a lot of damage to track occurred. The derailment was caused by a serious slip in the embankment on the famous 'Chicken Curve', which was to be the site of a further

LIMIT OF SHUNT
No 37235 hauls a short train of vans from Long Marston MOD depot to Didcot on 17 February 1992. It is heading south towards Honeybourne and is just regaining the formation of the former line to Cheltenham. Behind the locomotive can be seen the overgrown formation of the route to Stratford.
Peter Tandy

devastating slip in 2012 that severed the heritage Gloucestershire Warwickshire Railway for 18 months. The inherent problem stemmed from the original poor construction of the embankment, where spoil had been tipped directly on to the field without preparation, and the heritage railway has now rebuilt it properly, so a recurrence is unlikely.

While the Winchcombe accident meant that traffic ceased on the railway, its future remained undetermined. On 30 September 1977 the General Manager (by then Jim O'Brien) wrote to David Bowick[114] to advise him that he would have to replace the junction at Lansdown with plain line, as the poor condition of the fittings on the connections had resulted in the imposition of a 20mph temporary speed restriction on the main line at that point. By this time the whole line had deteriorated quite badly as no maintenance or renewals had been undertaken for a few years, and O'Brien's letter indicates that, 'Indeed, no movement is allowed over this section without the express permission of the CCE[115].'

In June 1977 the London Midland Region issued a consultation document concluding that there was no justification in retaining the line as a diversionary route. The report quoted a cost of £1,273,000 to restore the line for 50mph running. The trade unions, however, which had been somewhat supine during the height of the closure controversy 15 years earlier, were a lot more active in opposing closures now. All three unions objected to the removal of track from the Honeybourne line, and were prepared to back this with non-cooperation. In 1979, therefore, Ian Campbell, the Board's Chief Executive, wrote to instruct the General Manager to let the contract

for track-lifting 'without recourse to the use of railway resources'. Lifting was complete at the end of that year.

Fortunately, that was not the end. In 1977 the Gloucestershire & Warwickshire Railway Trust was formed to reopen the line between the Stratford and Cheltenham racecourses. A base was established at Toddington in 1981 and opened to the public, with just a quarter of a mile of track laid in April 1984, the opening ceremony being performed by the Secretary of State for Transport and Cotswold MP Nicholas Ridley[116]. The line was extended south steadily and was formally opened to Cheltenham Racecourse by the Princess Royal on 7 April 2003. Subsequently the line has been extended north from Toddington, with the aim of linking to the picturesque village of Broadway in 2017, the limit of the company's ownership. Setbacks occurred with an embankment collapse at Gotherington in 2010 and another at Winchcombe ('Chicken Curve') in 2012, but have been overcome by this determined and successful railway.

Looking to the north, the possibility of the Gloucestershire Warwickshire Railway eventually reaching Honeybourne must be considered good. The case for reopening Honeybourne to Stratford-upon-Avon as part of the national network is even stronger, and was enhanced by the major landslide on the Chiltern main line between Banbury and Leamington on 31 January 2015. That closed this busy route for many weeks, and meant that journeys on Chiltern and CrossCountry trains had to be interrupted by an unwelcome bus journey around the closed line.

Had the trains continued to operate to Stratford from the south (and Oxford, with the reinstatement of a chord to the east of Honeybourne), there would have been an ideal ready-made diversionary route, as well as the basis of a new semi-circular route serving Worcester, Evesham, Stratford and Birmingham, used by commuters and tourists. It would also be attractive to Vintage Trains, the operators of the steam specials from Tyseley to Stratford and places further afield.

Conclusions

So, should the line have been kept as part of the national network and would it today have value as a link in the network?

BR's prevarication in 1972 suggests that there was genuine uncertainty as to whether the line was required or not. Under these conditions, the default position should surely have been to retain it, on the grounds that it is so much harder to replace a line that has been closed than to expand the use of one that has been retained, even if little used for a period. However, as we have seen, retaining the line would not have been without cost. Following the derailment, around £1.25 million (£14.3 million at today's prices) would have been required to restore the line to a useable condition. During the 1980s freight continued to decline and the case for an alternative freight route would have been correspondingly weaker. Operation as a diversionary route would have been useful, however, both for track renewals on the Barnt Green route and during the electrification of the cross-city line. It might also have found a useful role with the expansion of cross-country services where one of the constraints on Virgin's 'Operation Princess' in 2002 was limited route capacity. There is no doubt that a service from Bristol, Gloucester and Cheltenham to Stratford and Birmingham would be providing a useful alternative to the A46 today. If it were there, the line would be a significant link in the national network, similar to the route from nearby Worcester to Birmingham via Kidderminster, but if that were the case the Gloucestershire Warwickshire heritage railway would not have developed and a major tourist attraction for Gloucestershire (and a significant local employer) would have been lost.

So, a potentially useful link was lost, but a significant heritage line replaced it, initially from Toddington to Cheltenham Racecourse. Sadly, the encroachment of development in Cheltenham appears to have prevented the heritage line from connecting with the national network at that end, and perhaps performing a dual function in the future. It should be a different story at Honeybourne, though, with the heritage line getting its main-line connection there, and linking to a reopened Honeybourne to Stratford line.

Steaming through Strathmore: the Caledonian main line to Aberdeen

From Perth the double-track main line heads north for Inverness, but 7 miles on at Stanley Junction it becomes single. This is where the Highland Railway started and the formation of the first main line from the south to Aberdeen continues straight on. Opened in 1848, it became part of the Caledonian in 1866 while the arch-rival, the North British, did not arrive until the opening of the Tay Bridge in 1878 (and, more particularly, the replacement bridge opened in 1887), while its route was only completed with the opening of that Scottish icon, the Forth Bridge, in 1890. The NBR relied on running powers over its rival north of Kinnaber Junction, where the two lines joined. The double-track Caledonian main line ran for 44½ miles through Strathmore from Stanley Junction to Kinnaber, which was effectively the winning post in the 'races to the north' between the east and west coast companies that culminated in the summer of 1895. Mileposts from this point to Aberdeen are still measured from Carlisle by the Forfar route.

Journey times were some 15 minutes quicker via Forfar than the alternative line via Dundee used by Scotrail express trains today. The Strathmore line was a racecourse over which latterly the thoroughbred 'A4s' ran with the 3-hour expresses between Glasgow (Buchanan Street) and Aberdeen as their swansong. In September 1966 the song ended and a year later the line itself lost its passenger service. Today's best timing between Queen Street and Aberdeen is 2hr 33min via Dundee.

While 1967 saw the end of the line as a through route, Stanley Junction to Forfar remained open for freight until 1982, while at the eastern end Kinnaber Junction to Bridge of Dun and Brechin closed for freight in 1981. The 4 miles from Bridge of Dun to Brechin now forms the Caledonian Railway heritage line.

The line was both a competitive route and served a rural corridor to the north of Dundee. In any reduction of capacity, it was inevitable that it would lose out to an alternative that served the much greater population and industry on Tayside. So it is unsurprising that it was included in the Beeching Report for closure, together with the remaining intermediate stations at Coupar Angus, Alyth Junction, Forfar and Bridge of Dun. Some 214 written objections were received, together with 1,702 objections registered via a form circulated by objectors.

The TUCC for Scotland found evidence[117] of severe and extensive hardship for users from Forfar, a large market town, with a big rural hinterland and 14 miles from the nearest alternative station at Dundee. Consequently the minister, in approving the closure, required the provision of replacement buses between Forfar and Perth, two of which should have rail connections to the south, as well as buses from Coupar Angus to Perth.

Inevitably, the A90 has had huge investment since the closure of the railway and is dualled all the way from the M90 junction to Aberdeen, including bypasses around Forfar and Brechin. The A94, however, which follows the old line through Strathmore, remains a single-carriageway road, albeit with bypasses including a relief road using the formation of the railway through Coupar Angus, opened in 1997.

It would be hard to argue the need for the restoration of the line today, and ScotRail runs an excellent service between Glasgow and Aberdeen, planning to operate this with high-speed diesel trains to meet the capacity needed and expectations of journey times between the two cities. However, Forfar did lose out when its railway closed and the line did provide a useful alternative route to Aberdeen, in particular as it avoided the single-track pinch point between Usan and Montrose.

4

THE LOST LINK LINES

'The railways were England's gift to the world.'

G. M. TREVELYAN, *ILLUSTRATED ENGLISH SOCIAL HISTORY*, 1942

Leeds Northern

The southern part of this main line from Leeds to Northallerton was opened by the Leeds & Thirsk Railway in 1848, the section north of Melmerby following in 1852, by which time the company had become the Leeds Northern Railway, a constituent of the North Eastern Railway, which was formed two years later.

The line from Harrogate to Ripon and Northallerton lost its passenger service on 6 March 1967 and was closed completely north of Melmerby. The remaining freight service was withdrawn two years later.

Why was there not more fuss when this important through route was threatened? Just prior to closure the line carried 10 up trains and

11 down, with 15 each way on Saturdays. These included the 'Queen of Scots' Pullman train between Glasgow and King's Cross and two Newcastle to Liverpool expresses as well as local services, some starting from Middlesbrough. BR's view was that the through trains could be diverted via York, and that as there was already a four-track railway between York and Newcastle this would meet all normal requirements[118]. Nevertheless, a painful reminder of the value of the

RIPON BY RAIL
Class 'B16/2' No 61435 of Hull Dairycoates passes Ripon with an RCTS special, 'The North Yorkshireman', heading for Hawes on 25 April 1964. *M. York*

MELMERBY

The Masham branch goods train heads down the branch behind 350hp diesel shunter No D3313 in 1960. The modest but neat platforms have oil lamps and the down platform is reached by a barrow crossing. The straight and level line gives an idea of the speed potential of the Harrogate-Northallerton route. *R. E. James-Robertson*

line came just three months after closure when it was reopened to take services diverted following a serious derailment and collision at Thirsk on the East Coast Main Line on 31 July 1967.

The line employed 107 staff prior to closure, including station masters at Melmerby and Ripon and three booking clerks at Ripon. Savings of £82,800 would be achieved (twice the allocated earnings), while the residual goods service from the south to Melmerby would earn £20,300 against costs of £17,400.

The files are pretty anodyne and do not indicate a sense that this was a significant closure, but then, while it was being progressed, it was just one of so many closures on which the North Eastern Region was working. The Harrogate to York line was put up for closure at the same time (consent refused by Barbara Castle in 1966[119]). Indeed, the whole route from Leeds to Northallerton was included in the Beeching Report for closure. The enormity of the proposals must have been overwhelming for the staff trying to deal with their implications.

The case against closure was well made by staff representatives, and the notes of the consultation meeting with the trade unions reflect an eclectic mix of strategy (the route could be used for the proposed 'liner' – Freightliner – trains), and detail (concern at the proposed use of a goods porter at Ripon to work as a shunter). But the ramifications were huge and linked to a number of other closure and rationalisation proposals being pursued at the same time. They were baffling even to experienced local railwaymen, as revealed by the meeting notes: 'At this point, the Staff Side representatives expressed their difficulty in following the proceedings as there seemed to be so many schemes involved about which they had not been advised.'[120] This came at the

point where the implications of the closure of the Harrogate to York line and the line to Pateley Bridge were being explained.

There has been strong pressure to reopen the line for a number of years. In 2004 the Countryside Agency published a 'rail reopenings toolkit' using the Ripon line as an example. In 2005 Arup carried out a study into reopening Ripon-Harrogate, and estimated a benefit to cost ratio of 1:3. The local campaign group has struggled on, and indeed extended its ambitions to restoring the Wetherby line as well, but little further progress has been made, and North Yorkshire County Council has not been able to prioritise funding to take the work forward. The case for reopening rests on a number of key strategic issues:

1. The line would relieve capacity on a congested part of the East Coast Main Line. The earlier view that the ECML would cope without difficulty was immediately shown as erroneous by the Thirsk collision, and the argument that four tracks were already provided between York and Newcastle is no longer true following the closure of the Leamside line.

2. In the context of the seven-day railway, the route would provide a valuable alternative to a very busy section of the

East Coast Main Line, which, in addition to freight trains, carries six passenger trains an hour each way, with such large numbers of people that using road coaches as an alternative during engineering work is not an option. Reinstatement would complete a good alternative route to the East Coast Main Line from Doncaster all the way through to Ferryhill near Durham.

3. Harrogate is an important conference centre (the fourth largest in the UK) and the station already attracts a higher proportion of long-distance rail journeys than the national average.

4. A station just to the south of Bramhope Tunnel would provide an effective link to Leeds/Bradford Airport, which could offer new journey opportunities for longer-distance passengers using services diverted to run via Harrogate.

The use of the Ripon line by one Transpennine Express and one CrossCountry train each way each hour, serving both Ripon and Harrogate, would provide a high-value service and open up the potential referred to above as well as offering access to the rail network for many more people in North Yorkshire, using Ripon as a railhead. In our view, the strategic value of this link would make it one of the priority routes for reinstatement.

Lewes-Uckfield

Uckfield was first served from Lewes in 1858, ten years before the line from the north at Groombridge was opened, and it was a further 20 years before the direct line between Ashurst Junction and Eridge (used by today's London Bridge to Uckfield trains) opened in 1888. Indeed, the pattern of train service for many years was regular Tonbridge to Brighton trains and an infrequent service from Victoria to Brighton via Uckfield.

Consent to closure was given on 16 August 1968 and part of the deal was to facilitate the new Lewes relief road, which at that stage was so much more important to the town than its rail link with Tunbridge Wells and Oxted. To ensure that the deal was delivered, more bus services were required and an hourly service between Uckfield and Lewes was agreed between operator Southdown and BR with intermediate stops only at Isfield and Barcombe Lane end. The variation of consent letter from the ministry[121] (the Minister was Richard Marsh) approved the extra services to complete the process as soon as possible 'in order that the closure may be implemented and progress resumed with the construction of phase I of the Lewes Relief Road…'

Train services had been withdrawn from 24 February 1969 because of the deteriorating condition of the cast-iron viaduct approaching Lewes from the north. Replacement buses ran until formal closure of the line on 4 May.

For almost the whole of the last four decades campaigners have been working to reopen the Uckfield to Lewes line as part of a new electrified railway between London and Brighton, via Uckfield and Lewes. This is seen as providing access from the Weald to the employment centre of Brighton and an additional route between the South Coast and London, relieving the Brighton main line.

As Railfuture points out:

'Travelling across or around Sussex isn't quick or easy. Roads are congested, bus services are slow and finish early, and rail routes do not all link up.

Wealden residents can only get work or education in Lewes or Brighton by congested roads and bus services. Uckfield Line commuter services take 20 minutes longer than equivalent

journeys on the Brighton Main Line. Newhaven needs regeneration but has only two through trains to London. Trains from Eastbourne, Lewes, Worthing, Hove and Brighton to London are overcrowded.

The major employment and tourist centre of Brighton is dependent on a single overutilised rail line from London. Journey times between Hastings, Brighton and Worthing are too long.

The Department for Transport has published the Network Rail report on the Brighton Main Line, capacity challenges and options for improvements. The DfT agree with the recommendation that Lewes-Uckfield re-instatement could make a longer-term contribution to capacity on the Sussex Route, after the constraints of flat line junctions and fast line platforms between Stoats Nest Junction and London have been addressed in Control Period 6 (2019-24) – so reopening is a question of when, not if.'

To assess the evidence of economic and transport needs in Sussex, Railfuture engaged independent advisor Jonathan Roberts Consulting. The key points were that Brighton is the largest employment centre in

LEFT: LEWES
The 10.18am Brighton to Victoria train via Uckfield waits at Lewes on 16 August 1949. The platform on the right is the up main line to Victoria via Haywards Heath. The locomotive is 'L1' 4-4-0 No 31784 – note the route headcode. *S. C. Nash*

LOST LINK
The 13.55 Brighton to London Bridge semi-fast train runs through Barcombe Mills on 30 December 1968 with unit No 1115 leading. The following week a temporary Lewes–Uckfield shuttle service replaced through trains. *A. D. McBird*

the South East outside London, the Weald has a very high daily outflow of people for work, and Hastings has a high level of unemployment. The recommendations to promote economic growth in East Sussex were:

- Uckfield-Lewes reopening to achieve affordable and effective journey times between the Weald, the Sussex Coast and Brighton
- Faster travel and extra capacity between the Sussex Coast and Gatwick, Croydon and London
- Electrification and other infrastructure, which expands services and connections, reducing journey times – by through trains, not changes
- Electrification of Marshlink and provision of 'Javelin' services via Ashford to achieve acceptable London-Hastings journey times
- Investment in a direct Coastway connection between Polegate and Pevensey to reduce journey times to attractive levels along the main coastal corridor, between Brighton, the Sussex Coast and East Kent
- Coastway Metro service linking Eastbourne and Hastings, with more stations.[122]

One obstacle that the reopening of the Uckfield to Lewes line will need to overcome is the 2.75-mile heritage railway from Isfield station, the so-called 'Lavender Line' (named not after the plant, but a firm of coal merchants – A. E. Lavender & Sons – which had operated from the station yard there). An attempt by the preservation society to acquire the trackbed from its northern boundary to Uckfield and allow heritage trains to run over it was successfully opposed by the county council, which claimed that reopening as a heritage line would prevent or at least hinder the reopening of the entire route to Lewes.

Leicester-Burton

One of the earliest railways in the country, the Leicester & Swannington, formed part of this 29½-mile cross-country route to Burton-on-Trent. Built to bring coal from local pits to Leicester, it opened as early as 1832 from Leicester (West Bridge) to Bagworth and was extended to Swannington (16 miles) the following year. The engineer was Robert Stephenson. The line was taken over by the Midland Railway in 1845, which extended it to link with the Birmingham and Derby line at Burton-on-Trent in 1848. The link from Desford to the Midland main line at Knighton Junction, just south of Leicester (London Road), followed in 1849.

The passenger service was withdrawn on 7 September 1964, but the line remains open for freight and, indeed, is still double track on two sections totalling 13¼ miles. The line serves a number of large towns and the population along the route totals 94,000. Traffic currently handled includes coal, aggregates and movements of new London Underground rolling stock from Bombardier at Derby. The north-facing spur at Knighton Junction was, however, removed and the site is covered by an industrial estate; the existing junction faces south towards Wigston.

The passenger service along such a populous corridor in the 1950s was poor. Seven trains a day linked Leicester and Burton, with two on Sundays. A through train to Blackpool ran on summer Saturdays. There was no departure from Leicester to Burton between 9.08am and 3.15pm, and the timetable was built around the needs of miners, industrial workers and schoolchildren. The service had been increased to eight a day and nine on Wednesdays and Saturdays when the closure case was considered.

Nevertheless the TUCC received 289 written objections, which it considered at its hearing in Ashby de la Zouch on 26 February 1964.

Cases of hardship were identified, the most extreme being two schoolchildren from Desford to Ashby who, in the absence of the train, would have to change buses twice, one connection involving a walk of a mile. The other disadvantaged group whose needs would have been given greater weight today was 190 disabled miners from the area who travelled to the National Union of Mineworkers' convalescent home at Skegness by train.

Earnings on the line were put at £28,000 per annum, and £29,000 in contributory revenue was generated. Of this, £34,000 would be lost, but costs would be reduced by £71,500, giving a net saving from closure of £37,500.

The verdict came quickly and the Ministry's consent letter is dated 31 July, and was published on 7 August, just one month before closure. There was an angry reaction from the local authorities, which in 1963 had been seeking in vain to meet BR to discuss improvements to the service that would have increased earnings. They also sought the intervention of the new Prime Minister, Harold Wilson, who had taken office in October 1964, but with no success.

The line remained open for freight and at Coalville also for parcels. The passenger closure released three loco-hauled corridor coaches (which were withdrawn) and part of an engine diagram, together with two two-car diesel units, which were redeployed in the Chester District.

Reopening the line was planned by British Rail together with the Leicestershire and Derbyshire county councils in the early 1990s, at the same time as the successful 'Robin Hood Line' was being developed with Nottinghamshire. Branded the 'Ivanhoe Line'[123], a horseshoe-shaped service was proposed, from Loughborough south to Leicester, then north-west to Burton and north-east to Derby. Phase I of the scheme saw a new local train service between Loughborough and Leicester with three stations at Barrow on Soar, Sileby and Syston, all closed in 1968, and these were reopened on 27 May 1994. Originally served by a separate shuttle, they now form part of the hourly Leicester to Nottingham and Lincoln trains run by East Midlands Trains. Phase II would have extended the service to Moira and Phase III to Derby. Willingdon station, between Derby and Burton-on-Trent (closed as Repton & Willington in 1968), reopened on 26 May 1995 with Ivanhoe Line branding, but is now served by Arriva CrossCountry trains between Nottingham and Birmingham or Cardiff. East Midlands Trains is the station facility owner.

Privatisation and the consequent fragmentation of BR stopped the further development of Phase II of the Ivanhoe project. A study in 1996 demonstrated that the line would incur an annual operating loss of £0.8 million. Further studies were undertaken in 1999, 2000 and 2004, and in 2008 Scott Wilson undertook a reappraisal for Leicestershire CC, demonstrating that the annual loss had risen to £4 million per annum.

Journey times by road in the corridor are slow, with heavy congestion in and around Leicester. From the Coalville direction, access to Leicester station involves crossing the city. With a reduction in freight traffic passing over the line (there is no regular freight traffic north of Bardon Mill), it is time to look again at upgrading this important route for a regular passenger service. Apart from the beneficial effects it would have in transport terms, it would also support regeneration of this former mining area. It runs through the National Forest and would support car-free tourism with the

OVERSPILL TOWN
Trains cross at Haverhill: Brush Type 2 No D5551 heads the train for
Cambridge, while a train for Colchester runs into the loop. Earmarked in
1956 as a London 'overspill' town, the population was 5,445 and has since
grown to 24,534 at the 2011 census, and is still growing. *Chris Austin*

economic benefits that brings. It would also have the potential to be
a useful diversionary route between Leicester and Derby as part of
the seven-day railway.

Cambridge-Colchester

Opened in 1849 between Marks Tey and Sudbury, then extended to
Shelford, near Cambridge, in 1865, the line was the core of a network
serving Essex and Suffolk that extended to Bury St Edmunds (closed
1961), Halstead via an independent line through the Colne Valley
(closed 1962), and Saffron Walden (closed 1964).

The line from Shelford Junction to Sudbury was closed in 1967,
leaving the southern end of the route from Marks Tey on the Great
Eastern main line to Sudbury as a branch line.

The closure between Cambridge and Sudbury was perhaps
surprising in this prosperous and highly mobile part of the country,
not least because it coincided with the development of the principal
intermediate town of Haverhill, which became home for thousands
of Londoners under the 'overspill' (rehousing) programme at the
same time. Together with the loss of the lines from Cambridge to
Bedford and to St Ives, closure has left limited access to the successful
Cambridge cluster of technology companies, linked with the
University and the ever-growing population. Property prices and
limited accommodation in Cambridge mean that a high level of
inward commuting is now inevitable. Apart from local traffic and
journeys between the principal towns of Cambridgeshire and Essex,
the Stour Valley railway was also used as a holiday route, including a
Leicester to Clacton train on summer Saturdays.

At the time, however, the explosion of economic growth that is
the predominant feature of Cambridgeshire and Essex today could

not be foreseen. Even the Eastern Region General Manager at the
time, Gerry Fiennes, who had invested in both the East Suffolk and
Hunstanton lines, concluded that 'the Stour Valley was not in the
category of lines which we could make pay by conversion to a basic
railway.'[124]

The Sudbury to Marks Tey section, however, did well to survive
against the extreme scepticism within the BR Board at the time. As
early as November 1963 the Eastern Region sought to retain this
section as a variation from the closure of the complete line as
proposed in the Beeching Report eight months earlier. The reason
was that, while traffic was declining on the Cambridge to Sudbury
section, it was actually rising quite strongly at Sudbury, Bures and
Chappel & Wakes Colne. Passenger numbers had risen by 20% and
revenue by 40% between 1962 and 1963, 'and the full effect of
electrification to Colchester and beyond has not yet been
achieved.'[125] Apart from that, 6,000 people from the London
overspill programme were expected to move to Sudbury, and 200
new houses were already being built over the following 12 months.
The line was being retained for freight, which at that stage was still
substantial, and the incremental cost of the shuttle to Marks Tey
(to Colchester off-peak) was £6,600, compared with the risk of
£7,600 contributory revenue loss if it were not provided. The total
saving from withdrawing the Cambridge-Colchester service was

estimated to be £31,700. The finance side of the Board was not convinced: 'This position cannot be regarded as satisfactory particularly when it is remembered that a continuing service should be covering interest and replacement reserve charges in addition to annual expenses.'[126]

The Sudbury line was reprieved, however, and under the title of the 'Gainsborough Line' has prospered, with a thriving community rail partnership and an enthusiastic group of station friends who have kept the intermediate stations as welcoming and secure access points to the railway. Passenger numbers have doubled over ten years.

Had the line north of Sudbury survived, however, it would have been a successful local railway with similar characteristics to the Cambridge-Norwich line. It would also provide a useful alternative route for container trains between Felixstowe and the North of England when the direct route via Bury is closed for engineering work or as a result of mishaps, such as the extensive damage to the Ouse river bridge at Ely following the derailment of a stone train in 2007, which resulted in the closure of the line for six months.

ABOVE: CLARE
A Derby lightweight unit forms a Colchester train at Clare, between Haverhill and Sudbury. *Chris Austin*

BELOW: SUDBURY
Unit No 156402 leaves for Marks Tey on 21 May 2014. The line to Cambridge ran to the right of the picture behind the lines of cars. The 'new' station is on the site of the former goods yard. *Chris Austin*

The Somerset & Dorset line

Although it closed in March 1966, the line from Bath to Bournemouth remains popular and has probably had more books devoted to it than any other railway in the country apart from the GWR. It was an interesting line operationally with heavy trains, steep gradients, an amazing performance at Templecombe for through trains, and the locomotives even carried headlamp codes unique to the route. The staff were a dedicated, hardy and independent group, and the railway ran through some wonderful scenery to destinations with magical names like Midsomer Norton, Sturminster Newton and Blandford Forum.

It was a busy route, too, with coal trains from the Somerset coalfield, shoes from Clarks at Street and agricultural products throughout. Local passenger trains provided useful links, particularly into Bath and between Blandford and Bournemouth (which has no direct bus today, although an hourly service runs to Poole), but it is the long summer holiday trains that are best remembered, bringing visitors from the North West and the West Midlands to the seaside at Bournemouth. It even had, until 1962, its own named restaurant car train, the 'Pines Express', running once a day from Manchester and Liverpool to Bournemouth, taking 7hr 17min. (Today's 'Voyager' journey time from Manchester is 4hr 43min, and the service runs every hour.)

It was also an interloper into territory that the Great Western Railway clearly regarded as its own, particularly on the northern section of the line, and with the long branch from Evercreech Junction across the Somerset levels to Highbridge and Burnham-on-Sea.

This was a weakness, however, as it crossed the Great Western at Bath, Radstock, Shepton Mallet, Bruton, Bridgwater, Wells and Highbridge, but with no proper connection for running through trains at any point.[127] So the S&D provided few links in the network, and cut across the grain of the main communication routes in the corridor it served. Glastonbury, for example, looks to Wells, Bristol and Taunton to do business, but the railway ran across the empty levels to Highbridge. Operationally, it was hugely expensive with its own station in Bath, gradients that required double-heading on all but the lightest trains over the Mendips, and a double reversal at Templecombe that required two engines and a lot of 'mucking about', representing a big delay for through passengers. These major drawbacks would have been reduced with diesel units, but not eliminated, and it is hard to imagine how the line could have been developed to serve passengers' travel needs effectively.

MENDIP SUMMIT
The double-headed southbound 'Pines Express' breasts Masbury summit. *Chris Austin*

This characteristic reflected the line's history, having been developed by two local railways, the Somerset Central and the Dorset Central, which merged in 1862 to form the Somerset & Dorset Railway with the primary aim of linking the Bristol and English channels by rail, with ferry connections from Cardiff to Burnham and from Poole (Hamworthy) to Cherbourg. The Bath extension was an afterthought completed in 1874, and one that was financially disastrous for the company, which had already been in receivership between 1866 and 1870. Negotiations with the Great Western for taking over the line were well under way in 1875 when it was snatched from under their noises by a better offer involving some rather underhand dealings by the London & South Western and Midland companies. As with the Exeter & Crediton (see Chapter 3), the Great Western lost out and the line was leased to the LSWR and the Midland and worked by a Joint Committee from 1875 to 1923, when ownership of the S&D company was transferred to the two companies. In 1948 the Joint Committee came to an end on the formation of British Railways.

Yet, even in its latter days when through services had been withdrawn, the southern end of the line did play an important role in linking Wincanton to the main line, and linking Blandford and Bournemouth. A rail link from Radstock to Bath would certainly relieve traffic on the A367. The demographics have changed, but the route of the railway still does not align with principal travel corridors. Proximity to the Bath-Castle Cary-Weymouth line also weakens the case for any restoration.

As a railway, the Somerset & Dorset line was magnificent, but as a transport link its role ended with the decline of the great British summer holiday, the closure of the Somerset coalfield and the transfer of most shoe production to the Far East.

TRAFFIC CALMING
Traffic waits and drivers fume as a Bath to Templecombe stopping train crosses the main road in Radstock. The signal protecting the Great Western level crossing on the far side of the S&D line can be seen just beyond the locomotive. *Chris Austin*

5
GREAT WAY ROUND – LONGER JOURNEYS

'The public will always prefer that conveyance which is the most perfect, and speed within reasonable limits is a material ingredient in perfection in travelling.'

I. K. BRUNEL, LETTER TO DIRECTORS OF THE GREAT WESTERN RAILWAY, 15 AUGUST 1836

Much has been written about how the railway closures of the 1960s and 1970s cut off whole communities from access to Britain's railway network. But the gloomy mood of retrenchment and contraction that permeated the British Railways Board throughout those decades as the network was further 'rationalised' also had a further effect on a number of towns, which, while not losing their services entirely, finished up with significantly worse and slower services as a result.

This chapter looks at some of the worst examples.

Whitby

In *Holding the Line* we described in some detail the fate that befell the Yorkshire seaside town of Whitby, which prior to the Beeching Report was served by three lines – one to Middlesbrough, one to Scarborough, and one to Malton. There were through services between Scarborough and Middlesbrough, stopping at both the Whitby stations – West Cliff and Town – and the line through Pickering to Malton provided connections to the main York to Scarborough main line, and thence to the West Riding cities of Leeds and Bradford, and to London.

Beeching had proposed the withdrawal of all services. There was a major battle that the protestors thought they had won because of what they believed was a promise by the Labour leader Harold Wilson made prior to the 1964 election to keep the lines open, and a powerful report on hardship delivered by the Transport Users' Consultative Committee.

But the decision by the outgoing Conservative Minister, Ernest Marples, to close the Malton and Scarborough routes (though not the line to Middlesbrough) was upheld by the new Labour transport minister, Tom Fraser, on the grounds that he did not have the power to reverse a decision taken by his predecessor, despite the introduction of a private member's bill by Whitby's MP, Alexander Spearman, to give the minister exactly that power. We recounted how the Cabinet decided on 11 March 1965 to support Fraser in blocking Spearman's bill, preventing the reversal of the closure of Whitby's lines to Scarborough and Malton, which had already taken place by then.[128]

It was felt at the time – and this view is maintained today – that the wrong line had been reprieved. If only one route to Whitby was to be

ROUND IN CIRCLES
The 1.28pm Middlesbrough to Scarborough train climbs from Whitby Town to West Cliff station on 23 July 1958. Having reversed at the Town station, the railcar will reverse again at West Cliff and cross Larpool Viaduct in the background on its was south to Scarborough. *M. Mensing*

LONDON EXPRESS
The 8.52am Cleethorpes-King's Cross runs into Boston in February 1961
behind 'Britannia' 'Pacific' No 70040 *Clive of India* of Immingham shed,
nine years before the East Lincolnshire route was lost. *Ian Allan Library*

kept open, the case for the service up to Pickering and Malton was far stronger than that serving the thinly populated areas of North Yorkshire on the way to Middlesbrough, which survived because several of these villages were inaccessible by bus. The success of the North Yorkshire Moors Railway, which has reopened the line from Pickering (though not Malton) to Grosmont, with through running into Whitby, as a heritage steam-operated line, demonstrates the potential.

In 1938 the London & North Eastern Railway ran through trains with restaurant cars between King's Cross and Whitby, completing the journey in 4hr 55min, and as late as June 1961 Whitby appeared in the timetable for the East Coast Main Line from King's Cross to Newcastle and Edinburgh as a place reached by connecting at York, though by then the journey time had deteriorated to 6hr 13min (off the 11.00am from King's Cross).

In 2014 the shortest journey time from London to Whitby by train, travelling via Darlington and Middlesbrough, was 4hr 35min (one service only). The mileage travelled was 282½; that by the direct route to Whitby, via York and Malton, would have been just under 245. On the assumption that York to Whitby could have been covered in around an hour and a quarter by modern rolling stock, a

Whitby to London journey could have been accomplished in less than 3 hours, with corresponding improvements to cities such as Leeds, Bradford and Manchester.

Despite the circuitous route by rail, Northern offers a cheap ticket to York for shoppers that is actively marketed by the line's community rail partnership and is an attractive alternative to the very limited bus service.

Peterborough to Grimsby, Cleethorpes and Skegness

There were few areas of England that were hit harder by the Beeching closures than Lincolnshire, with numerous branch lines and longer-distance routes axed. A particularly short-sighted closure (on 5 October 1970) was the line across east Lincolnshire from Peterborough to Grimsby and Cleethorpes. This served a series of medium-sized towns such as Spalding, Boston and Louth, and branch lines also brought thousands of holidaymakers to seaside resorts such as Skegness, Sutton-on-Sea and Mablethorpe.

The East Lincolnshire line offered the most direct route from London to Grimsby and Cleethorpes – 158 miles as against 183 via Lincoln and Newark, and 208 through Doncaster – and up to the date of closure there were two through trains in each direction, each taking almost exactly 4 hours. Current journey times via Doncaster are around 2hr 50min, but there are no through trains, although local politicians are campaigning hard for them.

LINCOLNSHIRE LINKS

Spalding had been a busy Lincolnshire junction between the joint line and the main line to Boston and Grimsby until 1970, as well as being served by the Midland & Great Northern line until 1959. In July 1961 'B1' Class 4-6-0 No 61066 of March shed waits at the town with a local train to Peterborough. The diesel shunter in the background has just attached a van to the rear of the train. Such tail traffic was a common way of providing direct transits for parcels until the 1970s. *John C. Baker*

It is reasonable to suppose that with the track upgraded to modern standards and 90mph running, it would have been possible to cover the 78 miles from Peterborough to Grimsby in around 85 minutes, even with stops at Spalding, Boston and Louth, thus making possible a London to Grimsby journey in little more than two hours.

Peterborough-Spalding escaped and, within eight months of closure, had been reopened with a grant from Lincolnshire Country Council. The full story is told in Chapter 7. Today, the best journey from Spalding to London takes just over an hour and a quarter, with a change at Peterborough.

Despite a succession of attempts to close it in the 1970s and '80s, the rail service to Skegness – unlike those to many other seaside towns

FULL STOP

The Lincolnshire Wolds Light Railway has brought trains back to a short section of the East Lincolnshire line between Ludborough and North Thoresby. It has plans to extend southwards to Louth, but for the moment this is the closest the line gets to Grimsby. *Chris Austin*

in eastern England – survived, and there are now, remarkably, around 15 trains a day in each direction between Nottingham and Skegness, with the trains linking Grantham, Sleaford and Boston. Travellers to and from London now have to change at Grantham, and the distance at 162 miles is 17 miles longer than the original route via Peterborough.

Edinburgh to Perth

From 1848 a roundabout railway route between Edinburgh and Perth via Stirling was established by the opening of the Scottish Central Railway, which later merged with the Caledonian. The same year the Edinburgh, Perth & Dundee Railway (later part of the North British) completed the route from Burntisland to Perth via Ladybank, although Edinburgh passengers had to take the train to Granton, with a ferry connection to Burntisland. The direct route via Kinross was formed of a number of local railways, the last piece of the jigsaw being put into place with the opening of the line between Mawcarse and Bridge of Earn in 1890, providing a route of 47¾ miles between the two cities, 23 miles shorter than the route via Stirling and 9¼ miles shorter than the route taken by today's ScotRail expresses via Ladybank.

EDINBURGH EXPRESS

Bursting into the daylight from the northern tunnel at Glenfarg, the 14.55 Perth-Edinburgh is hauled by 'V2' 2-6-2 No 60824 of St Margarets shed in Edinburgh on 3 July 1965. *Maurice S. Burns*

In 1954 the best train took 1hr 29min for the journey, compared with 1hr 46min from Edinburgh (Princes Street) via Stirling, and 1hr 13min today via Ladybank.[129] The line carried three through trains from Edinburgh to Inverness, two with refreshment cars. Five local trains served the route and two trains from Glasgow to Perth were routed via Alloa and Kinross Junction.

The line was not included in the Beeching Report but, as with others during the late 1960s, the unwillingness of the Department to pay grant under the 1968 Act for more than a year drove the closure process that BR was obliged to initiate as there would be no money to support it. In the first grant allocations after the Act, the Minister of Transport, Richard Marsh, told Parliament that he considered that the service between Edinburgh and Perth, which he would grant aid, would give better value for money if it were rerouted via Stirling, and that BR had agreed that this would be feasible. 'I understand that they intend shortly to publish a closure proposal for the section of route between Cowdenbeath and Hilton Junction including Kinross Station.'[130]

With the introduction of diesel locomotives, services between Perth and Edinburgh had been considerably accelerated from 82 minutes for the fastest train in 1958 to 67 minutes in 1968. Via Stirling, BR was promising 71 minutes.

Kinross was pretty upset at the loss of its railway as, although it had a population of only 2,300, it was the county town for Kinross-shire and was the railhead for a wide area including the Devon Valley, whose railway had disappeared in 1964, while the service between Kinross and Ladybank had gone even earlier, in 1950.

The TUCC hearing was held in the Town Hall at Kinross on 19 March 1969, and objections flooded in, not just from local users but also from local authorities across the Highlands, as far north as Ross & Cromarty, Caithness and Sutherland, all concerned that the journey to Edinburgh would take longer. The Scottish Women's Rural Institutes objected, as did the Scottish Railway Development Society and individual campaigners such as the redoubtable Frank Spaven. The committee's report also referred to an objection from a young David Spaven, later to campaign himself so effectively, and to be the authoritative chronicler of the Waverley Route. David used the train from Inverness to visit friends and watch rugby in Edinburgh, and would be prevented from doing this with the closure of the Kinross route. An interesting objection was from the National Small-Bore Rifle Association, as ammunition and other requirements of their sport were distributed from a supplier in Kinross. A local mushroom-grower relied entirely on the train to distribute his produce and was threatened with going out of business with the loss of the railway.

Nevertheless, the committee found that the hardship would be alleviated by trains running via the alternative route, except for a small number of passengers at Kinross – and the unfortunate mushroom-grower.

The decision to close had been made by Richard Marsh, although he had been sacked by Harold Wilson just four days before the consent letter was signed on 10 October 1969. Ironically, the signature on the closure decision letter was that of Reg Dawson.

Looking today at the traffic streaming down the M90, it is hard to understand the logic that considered it worthwhile to invest £4.3 million in the road in 1970, but could not even find the money to maintain the parallel railway.

Kinross station has been replaced by a supermarket and a park & ride interchange for the express buses that run from Perth to Edinburgh, but the old road through Glenfarg is still straddled by a mighty viaduct, leaping from the tunnel portal and following the road for some way.

Gone beyond recall, the line would have been of value had it survived, as the quickest route from Edinburgh to the Highlands, and probably as an alternative to the Ladybank-Hilton Junction route.

Carlisle to Stranraer (the 'Port Road')

For a town of only 13,000 people, Stranraer has a railway history greater and more interesting than many others in the UK. Its principal claim to fame is that until 20 November 2011 it offered the shortest sea crossing from the mainland to the island of Ireland, with regular services from Stranraer Harbour to Larne in Northern Ireland and directly to Belfast.

The first boat trains from London Euston to Stranraer started in October 1862, using the newly opened line from Dumfries through Galloway, which became known as the 'Port Road'. Fifteen years later, in 1877, the first boat trains ran between Glasgow and Stranraer.

The Victorians' original intention was to develop the Irish traffic at Portpatrick, 7 miles to the south-west of Stranraer (and thus even closer to Northern Ireland), but Government support for the building of a commercial harbour there, particularly for the Royal Mail traffic, was not forthcoming, and Stranraer stepped in and developed its own facilities. A short branch line from Portpatrick town to the harbour was a commercial failure, and was open to passengers for only a matter of weeks in the autumn of 1868. The rail service from Stranraer to Portpatrick struggled on until 1950, when other rural railways in the region also closed.

The railway across Galloway was used by John Buchan's fictional spy character, Richard Hannay, in his *The Thirty-Nine Steps* novel, set in 1914 (though none of the film versions of the book has Hannay going anywhere near south-west Scotland).

By the early 1960s the Dumfries to Stranraer service consisted of one morning and one afternoon train in each direction, together with the prestigious 'Northern Irishman' sleeper car service. The down train left London at 7.10pm (7.15 on Mondays), conveyed a restaurant car as far as Crewe, and arrived in Stranraer Harbour at 5.36am ('Sleeping car passengers may remain in their berths until 6.25am'). The steamer for Larne left at 7.00am, arriving there at 9.15am, where it connected with the 'Stranraer Boat Train' to Belfast York Road at 9.30am, giving an arrival in Northern Ireland's capital at a civilised 10.05am. The journey in the reverse direction entailed leaving Belfast at 5.55pm, and picking up the sleeper at Stranraer Harbour at 10.00pm. Arrival time in London was 8.35 the following morning.

Unsurprisingly 'the Paddy', as the boat train was affectionately known, attracted a popular following, and when the Beeching Report proposed the closure of both lines to Stranraer (that from Ayr, as well as the 'Port Road' from Dumfries), there was sufficient opposition to allow the minister to reprieve the Ayr to Stranraer service, largely so that the overnight sleeper could continue to run. Communities across Northern Ireland rallied to the cause, and as far west as the City and County Borough of Londonderry joined the list of objectors, as did a merchant in Strabane who consigned 100 boxes of salmon a week via the route to customers in England. Of the 190 objectors, 87 were from Northern Ireland, and Northern Ireland MPs even came to the TUCC public hearing in Stranraer Town Hall on 28 February 1964. They stressed that this was not just a local issue, but that the line was part of an important through route to Ireland.

In his letter to the British Railways Board of 17 July 1964, Ernest Marples, then Minister of Transport, wrote: 'I consider that an overnight service between London and Stranraer on schedules similar to the present ones and connecting with the morning and evening boats must continue. I have been assured by the Railways Board that such a service can be provided by an alternative route.'

The 'alternative' was to take 'the Paddy' up the Glasgow & South Western main line as far as Mauchline, where it turned left for Ayr, then went south to Girvan and Stranraer. This rerouting was almost 50 miles longer than the direct Dumfries to Stranraer line, but that

CROSSING LOCH KEN
The afternoon Stranraer to Carlisle train approaches Parton behind 'Black Five' No 44996 of Dumfries shed on 11 June 1963. *Derek Cross*

was seen as relatively unimportant bearing in mind that total journey times for sleeping car trains were – and are today – of less significance than daytime inter-city services. For the benefit of local passengers, three express buses were to run each way, connecting at Dumfries with London trains. In particular, and somewhat surprisingly, the consent letter said that the minister wished 'to ensure that users of New Galloway station [one of the remotest on the line] should have access to a bus service.'[131] In 1975 the train was rerouted even further north, via Scotland's oldest railway, the Kilmarnock & Troon, as the Mauchline to Ayr line was to be closed.[132]

There were various scares that the Ayr to Stranraer line would close during the 1970s and '80s, and real concern that as the grant for the sleeper service was only renewed for six months at the end of 1969, it was not long for this world. The then Conservative MP for Galloway, John Brewis[133], spoke up eloquently for its retention during an adjournment debate in the Commons on 29 January 1970:

'In 1969, 550,000 passengers used the crossing and the roll-on roll-off facilities attracted 25,000 commercial vehicles. The profit, which must now be approaching £1 million a year … makes this the most profitable of all British Railways shipping services.

Local people on both sides of the North Channel who man the ships and contribute so much to the service are naturally extremely proud of its success, one element of which is the London train, which enables a businessman to leave his Belfast office at 5pm and be in London by breakfast time the next morning. The train is also essential to the Post Office parcels service to Belfast, which carries on average 1,000 mailbags every night.'[134]

Brewis's enthusiasm was not shared by the minister, Bob Brown[135], who said:

'The hon Member says that 550,000 passengers used the Stranraer-Larne ferry in 1969, but a minute proportion of these passengers used the Euston boat train. The average number arriving at or leaving Stranraer on the trains on winter weekdays is less than 30, and even in summer the average is only just over twice this figure. The number of passengers joining and alighting from this train at Stranraer has fallen by about half since 1963. This rail service now performs a very minor role in travel between Great Britain and Northern Ireland.'

Given such an extremely negative view of the value of the Stranraer sleeper, it is remarkable that it lasted for another 20 years. It finally disappeared during the final years of British Rail.

The *Glasgow Herald* reported on 14 May 1990 under the headline 'The Paddy' makes its last sleepy run':

'LAST-DITCH attempts to save 'The Paddy' overnight sleeper train from Stranraer to London have failed.

The 10.46pm to Euston made its final run last night.

The ferry ports of Stranraer and Cairnryan handle hundreds of thousands of passengers a year. British Rail said only a handful used the sleeper service, which was losing £200,000 a year.

Strong opposition was mounted by trade unionists, councils, and tourist boards in South-west Scotland and Northern Ireland to try to save the service, which was re-routed through Ayrshire after the Dumfries-Stranraer rail line was closed 24 years ago by the Beeching cuts.

Dumfries and Galloway roads and transportation chairman, Mr Jim Heron, said he was disappointed the service was being axed. He went to London on Thursday to see Transport Minister, Mr Cecil Parkinson[136], to no avail.'

The boat train from Glasgow continued to run to Stranraer until 2011, when Stena Line moved its Irish ferries from Stranraer to Cairnryan (which is not rail-connected, although it was the site of an earlier military railway). Although there are ambitious plans for the redevelopment of the former ferry terminal area in Stranraer, it is unlikely that boat trains will return there. 'Classic' foot passengers to Northern Ireland now have a variety of low-cost airlines to choose from, so the train and boat market on this route has substantially disappeared.

As far as the railway to Stranraer is concerned, all is not lost. The rail service to Glasgow survives and is specified in the franchise for railways in Scotland, with a reasonable though not frequent service.

It is still possible to travel from London to Stranraer in the day – the 11.30 from Euston, with changes in Glasgow and at Ayr, will deliver passengers in Stranraer at 18.54. The journey time of 7hr 24min is a great deal faster than anything that was possible on the direct line from Dumfries, and there is a similar service in the reverse direction taking exactly 8 hours.

The question asked by supporters of the 'Reopen the Dumfries-Stranraer' campaign on the Facebook social media website is if it's possible to reopen the Borders railway from Edinburgh, why not that to Galloway? They would like to see stations serving Dumfries West, Garroch, Dalbeattie, Castle Douglas, Tarff (Kirkcudbright), Creetown and Newton Stewart, but not, interestingly, New Galloway which was of such concern to Ernest Marples. Certainly if trains ran from Stranraer to Carlisle in 2 hours or less, that would give a journey time to London of less than 5½ hours – a very considerable improvement on what's currently possible through Glasgow.

Should the 'Port Road' not have closed? Almost certainly not: it would have been seen as an important element in the Trans European Network, which Britain, as a member of the EU, is committed to supporting. Linking Belfast (and other communities in Northern Ireland) to Larne, and from Stranraer to elsewhere in Scotland and to England by rail would be a desirable objective. In 1978, such a proposal surfaced[137] when the A75 became a Euroroute and the Scottish Development Department announced that it was proposing to spend £20 million on building no fewer than ten bypasses between Dumfries and Stranraer. Unsurprisingly, BR dismissed the idea of

MEETING OF THE WAYS
The fireman of the 09.25 from Kirkcudbright hands over the token at Castle Douglas on 18 April 1965, three weeks before closure of the branch. The loco, BR Standard Class 4 2-6-0 No 76073, was also based at Dumfries. The track on the right is the 'Port Road' to Stranraer. *Gerald T. Robinson*

reopening the railway, pointing out that between one third and one half of the roadbed had been sold.

Is reopening feasible? With Stranraer losing out to Cairnryan for the ferry traffic, and the substantial drop in the number of passengers using rail as part of their journey from Scotland, the economic case would be difficult to assemble. It is unlikely to be a priority for Scotland compared with the many other worthwhile rail schemes being pursued.

York to Hull (the 'Minsters Line')

Opened from York to Market Weighton as early as 1847, by George Hudson's York & North Midland Railway, the line did not reach Beverley until 1865 when through trains to Hull started. Running through a predominantly agricultural area, the line saw eight trains each way on weekdays prior to closure, and apart from local traffic it was a strategic link between the two cities. There was also holiday traffic with through trains on summer Saturdays between Leeds and York and Filey Holiday Camp. The line carried freight until withdrawal of the train, which latterly ran three times a week, on 1 November 1965. The principal goods depots were at Pocklington and Market Weighton, and the annual traffic figures quoted in the staff consultation document showed a total of 1,500 wagons received at the two depots and 340 forwarded. Principal traffics were coal, scrap metal, timber, agricultural products, beet pulp, seed corn and potatoes.

The distance from York to Hull via Market Weighton was 42¼ miles, and the best journey time for passenger trains just prior to closure on 29 November 1965 was an hour, coincidentally the same as today's best train on the 52-mile route via Selby.

Much of the formation of the line remains, although it has disappeared in the towns it passed through. The population of the places served is modest (the largest between York and Beverley is Pocklington at 8,500), but road congestion is bad, particularly approaching York. A previous study in 2005 showed that reopening was feasible and that a benefit to cost ratio between 1.26:1 and 2.04:1 could be expected.

The 'Minsters Rail' campaign has developed in outline route proposals that bypass the intermediate towns to avoid property demolition, but at the same time this would lose accessibility to stations, particularly on foot. An alternative approach would be to rebuild the line as a light railway with street running through the towns to improve access, and tram/train vehicles to allow them to continue on the conventional railway into York and between Beverley and Hull.

It is a classic illustration of the problems created by abandoning infrastructure, and makes the whole question of restoration so much more difficult. Like other closed lines, the nature of the market towns served has changed since 1965 from self-sufficiency to close dependency on the nearest major town or city (in this case York), generating large numbers of car trips in the process. While there is no easy solution, there is every reason to protect the remaining alignment for the future and to protect alternative routes through the towns as well.

Oxford to London

In Chapter 3 we described in detail the campaign to reopen the east-west line from Oxford to Cambridge, and covered Chiltern Railways' imaginative proposals for a London to Oxford service via Bicester.

This will give Oxford a choice of two routes to London – Chiltern's to Marylebone in 66 minutes and First Great Western's to Paddington in an hour (although this should come down to 45-50 minutes with the completion of electrification).

Neither service, however, will operate what would have been the most direct route between the two cities: had it not been for a pre-Beeching closure, the route from Oxford through Thame and Princes Risborough would have occupied that role. The three mileages were 55¾ via Princes Risborough, 63½ through Didcot, and 65 via Bicester.

The line from High Wycombe to Thame opened in 1862, being extended to Oxford two years later. Thame's station master when the extension was opened was Ernest J. Simmonds who, writing under the pseudonym 'Ernest Struggles', immortalised the station as 'Fame' and pointed out that railways were not always an unmixed blessing to the towns they served.

'The Fame people clamoured loudly for the new line to be opened to Snorum [Oxford], which expected event was to be an immense boon, but which has, in reality, worked against them by bringing the trade of the town into competition with that of a much larger one, and by affording means of escape for commercial travellers and others who were obliged in the old days to stay the night.
Railways drain small towns and feed large ones.'[138]

Almost a hundred years later the line closed to passengers in 1963, three months before the Beeching Report was published, but remained open for freight throughout until 1967, when the section between Thame and Cowley was closed completely. Princes Risborough to Thame was retained to serve an oil depot, finally closing in 1991, the trackbed forming the 'Phoenix Trail' cycle route. The remainder of the line survives to this day between Kennington Junction at Oxford and Cowley, a 3¼-mile branch to serve the BMW car plant.

Thame reappeared in railway timetables from 1987 with the opening of Haddenham & Thame Parkway on the Chiltern main line to Banbury and Birmingham.

The Western Route study published by Network Rail in 2014 lists the Cowley spur as a candidate for reopening to passengers, to serve both the car plant and the huge Blackbird Leys housing estate.

A more ambitious plan was developed by Adrian Shooter in 1997 with a proposal to attract traffic from the M40 by a possible link to Lewknor (Junction 6) on the former Watlington branch, served by some Oxford-London express buses, or to Oxford via Thame. One of your co-authors was advising him at the time and recalls looking at aerial photographs of the latter route in his office in Aylesbury. There had been a number of incursions on to the formation of the route, especially west of Thame, and it was apparent from the number of swimming pools attached to large houses that there would be a battle to restore the railway, with a wealthy and articulate opposition. The route via Bicester has the advantage of both avoiding such conflict and of serving the successful Bicester Village outlet stores and Water Eaton Parkway to the north of Oxford.

6

THE 'SPELLER' LINES – REVERSING THE DECLINE

'Acts of Parliament do not, as a rule, afford entertainment to the general reader, especially those relating to such prosaic and sternly business-like operations such as railways and other works of public utility.'

AMMON BEASLEY, 'HOW PARLIAMENT HARASSED EARLY RAILWAYS',
WITHIN *THE RAILWAY MAGAZINE*, VOL XXIII, 1908

The election of the Conservative Government in 1979 under the leadership of Margaret Thatcher was greeted with alarm by many in Britain's railway. She had shown little interest in the industry, rarely travelled by train, and was known to be antagonistic to state-owned monoliths heavily influenced by powerful trade unions. In addition she was receiving consistently ferocious anti-rail briefings from her personal guru, Sir Alfred Sherman[139], who lobbied for their conversion into roads.[140]

But it was not all gloom. On 7 November 1979 the Transport Secretary, Norman Fowler, faced with a newspaper story that 41 services were threatened with imminent closure, responded to a question in the House of Commons, saying that it was untrue and he saw 'no case for another round of massive cuts in the railways'[141] and other ministers gave similar commitments.

Not only were very few lines and stations closed by the Conservative Government between 1979 and 1997, but a remarkable programme of reopenings was undertaken, initially thanks almost entirely to Antony Speller[142], a little-known Tory MP who had been elected in 1979 for North Devon, defeating the former Liberal Party leader, Jeremy Thorpe[143].

Using the 'Ten Minute Rule bill' procedure, he introduced a private member's bill that had the effect of amending the 1962 Transport Act in a way that allowed British Rail to reopen a line or station experimentally, so that if the reopening failed it would be possible for BR to close it again, without going through the expense of a full closure procedure, which involved TUCC hearings and an eventual ministerial decision.

Remarkably – and unusually – Speller's bill received a second reading without a debate in the Commons on 27 March 1981. It was then sent to a committee of the whole house and considered in a single day, 15 May.

He opened his speech with these words:

'In bringing this measure to the attention of the House, let me first explain how it came into being. It is common belief that this is the age of the train[144] and that it is time that, wherever possible, we got people off the roads and back on to trains. Moving into a new house, I discovered without surprise that adjacent was a railway line that carried a fair amount of goods but no passengers. It goes from Barnstaple to Bideford and on to the constituency of my hon Friend the Member for Devon, West (Mr Mills[145]). With commuters crowding the road outside my back door, it seemed logical that they would be more comfortable on a train, particularly as the line was already there.

That small and fairly obvious thought brought me to the discovery, as a new Member of Parliament, that British Rail has every right to open or reopen a line, but, if the experiment fails, it is a lengthy and extremely expensive process to close the line. Principally for that reason many perfectly good lines carry only a little freight, when they could be used much more usefully.'[146]

Speller's bill was supported by the Government. The junior Transport Minister, Kenneth Clarke[147], said:

'…there should be no role for the Secretary of State in experimental rail passenger services of this kind … the railway board should begin and end an experiment and not involve the Secretary of State or the Government. That could lead, under some Governments, to political and other difficulties in the process. We tried to draft the Bill so that it would allow a simple procedure whereby proper notice is given to the public that a service is being opened on an experimental basis outside the 1962 Act safeguards and that proper notice is given to the public if the experiment fails and the service has to be withdrawn.'[148]

Consideration of the bill took just one day in the Commons, and it passed to the Lords, where it got a second reading, without opposition, on 18 June, after a debate of less than half an hour.

There were no amendments tabled for consideration in committee, so the Lords was able to pass the bill without further debate, and it received Royal Assent on 2 July.

More than 30 years on, what has the 'Speller Amendment' (or 'Speller Act') achieved? The answer is more than anyone thought possible.

On 16 January 1987 Speller himself had been told in response to a written question that '32 stations and two passenger services had been opened or reopened on an experimental basis under the 1981 Act, and that a further 11 stations and five passenger services were expected to be opened or reopened in the next 12 months.'[149]

Just over a year later, the Commons Hansard for 5 December 1989 records this question and answer:

'Freight Railway Lines
Mr Malcolm Bruce[150]

To ask the Secretary of State for Transport how many freight railway lines have been opened to passenger traffic under the Transport Act 1962 (Amendment) Act 1981; and if he will list these with mileages of track, dates of opening and whether they remain open to passenger traffic.

Mr Portillo[151]

Fifteen stretches of freight line have been opened or reopened by British Rail to passenger traffic under the Transport Act 1962 (Amendment) Act 1981. The details are as follows:

TRAILBLAZER

The 1980s saw a number of important lines reopened. Perhaps the most significant was the Edinburgh-Bathgate line in 1986. Four days after opening on 28 March, one of the newly branded Bathgate trains awaits departure at Waverley. *Murdoch Currie*

Line	Year	Approximate mileage
Penistone-Barnsley	1983	7.5
Newbridge Junction-Bathgate	1986	10.2
Kettering-Corby	1987	5.5
Dore Curve (Derbyshire)	1987	0.25
Morecambe-Heysham Harbour	1987	4.0
Oxford-Bicester	1987	10.0
Coventry-Nuneaton	1987	10.0
Coatbridge Central-Motherwell	1987	5.0
Cardiff City	1987	4.15
Abercynon-Aberdare	1988	5.75
Lichfield City-Lichfield Trent Valley	1988	1.25
Bishop Auckland-Stanhope	1988	9.6
Walsall-Hednesford	1989	9.75
Thornton West Junction-Thornton South Junction (Fife)	1989	0.25
Altrincham-Stockport	1989	8.0
Note: All these lines remain open to passenger traffic.'[152]		

There appear to have been few attempts to produce a more recent comprehensive list of Speller Act reopenings, but one creditable effort has been made by Phil Deaves, owner of the http://www.railwaycodes.org.uk/ website. This table is reproduced in Appendix B with his permission, and with the grateful thanks of the authors.

This long list demonstrates just how many stations and lines were opened and reopened following Tony Speller's private member's bill becoming law in 1981. Not all came about because of it, though a great many did. The most remarkable feature of the list is the tiny number of services that were subsequently withdrawn – the only one not operating today in one form or another is that from Bishop Auckland to Stanhope (and even there the Weardale Railway has restored part of it as a heritage line).

The sad irony for Speller is that the one service he wanted to see restored in his lifetime (and mentioned in his initial speech on his bill) – that from Barnstaple to Bideford – has not been, and indeed in 2010 Devon County Council indicated that it did not believe a case existed for reinstating the line. As a tribute to Speller, however, and because of its importance to tourism, we have included the line as far as Bideford in our list for reopening in Appendix A. Torrington station was the original terminus for most passenger services, but it is a long way from the town it served.

The 'experimental' status of those in the list is now of largely historical interest, since virtually all the services have been included in franchise specifications since the privatisation of the railways from 1995. Speller deserves immense credit for spotting a legislative opportunity to help satisfy the public's growing demand for rail travel, even though the national mood in the preceding years had been for contraction and decline.

7

FREIGHT LINES FORGONE

The decline in rail freight traffic was dramatic during the period under review. Partly this reflected the steady loss of heavy industry in Britain during the 1970s and 1980s, but it also reflected a much more hard-nosed commercial approach to rail freight than was applied to the carriage of passengers. It is widely, but perhaps incorrectly believed that there are no votes in freight, and no equivalent grant system to support the operation of rail freight services was applied until privatisation.

The freight facilities grants[153] did provide a contribution to the capital costs of terminals and rolling stock from 1974 onwards, but there was no equivalent of the PSO grant for passenger services, and freight was expected to pay its way. That included paying for the infrastructure, which, in the case of road haulage, was provided at the taxpayers' cost. More than this, the huge programme of motorway construction, the dualling of many A roads and the thousands of bypasses and other improvements of the last 50 years were all provided at public expense (sums raised through vehicle excise duty are regarded by HMT as general taxation, and not hypothecated to road construction). The haulier did not have to pay one penny towards the huge improvements from which he benefited. Rail improvements were paid for by BR and the cost recovered from the customer. Beyond that, the rate of return expected of rail freight was progressively increased, so that even profitable freight

had to be turned away if it failed to meet the required rate of return. No wonder the rail share of the market had sunk to a very low level indeed by the close of the 20th century.

Interestingly, on privatisation a large transitional grant was required to support Freightliner to make it saleable. The rest of the freight business was split into four companies, but this was not what the market wanted, and they were all bought by Wisconsin Central during 1995 and 1996. The SRA expanded the grants available but was forced to cut back and abolish grants in 2003 when Government support for the authority was cut dramatically by Alastair Darling.[154]

Rail freight since privatisation has bounced back and is growing strongly again, and we are at the remarkable point where containers are overtaking coal, the railway's traditional principal traffic since the beginning of the 19th century, and promising a much brighter future for rail freight.

The stories of three key freight lines, together with the Woodhead route, are told in this chapter, demonstrating how these policies worked out in practice and how they left the core network without sufficient capacity to handle the demands now being made on it.

LIVING LEGEND
No 3440 *City of Truro* comes off the Newbury line at Shawford Junction with Shawford Viaduct in the background on the right of the picture. The M3 now crosses the South Western main line at this point. *L. Elsey*

The 'Desert Line': over the downs from Didcot to Southampton

'That child of sorrow, the Didcot, Newbury and Southampton.'
C. Hamilton Ellis, *British Railway History*, Vol 2 (1959)

A failure of the market and of state planning

This is a remarkable story of Victorian enterprise driven by competition to complete a strategic north-south route linking Southampton Docks with their hinterland, and of a market failure to make best use of it. Two world wars underlined the potential of the route, and state intervention in the 1950s allowed British Railways to start to correct this market failure, but the lack of a transport strategy or of dialogue between the parties involved let one of the key rail routes wither and die, while billions of pounds were spent upgrading the parallel road and the second rail route to create the capacity needed. The route of the Didcot, Newbury & Southampton line could have been developed as a valuable part of the national network, but a decision to achieve short-term savings in the 1960s and the overwhelming desire to improve the A34 road reflected a failure in coordinated planning that ignored the potential of the railway, except as a route corridor through which to drive the dualled trunk road. This was compounded by the mindset of policy-makers in the 1960s who could not conceive the role that rail might play in meeting Britain's transport needs. This particular corridor also suffered from the disgraceful campaign by the Transport & General Workers Union in 1977 to prevent the development of the rail-served inland port and distribution centre at Didcot.[155] The result left us with consequences that are still being addressed at considerable cost today, both for the A34 road and the rail route via Reading.

Southampton Docks

Southampton had been a port from Roman times, and indeed was the embarkation point for Henry V and his army before Agincourt. But it was the arrival of the railway from London in 1840 that triggered the development of the modern port. Opened originally in 1842, it was bought by the London & South Western Railway in 1892 and remained as part of the railway until 1963, when it was vested in British Transport Ports, being privatised as Associated British Ports in 1983.

Southampton was looking to improve links to the port from the railway mania of 1845 onwards. From 1860 onwards, the need became greater, not just to improve access for exports, but also to provide a through route for coal (from South Wales and the Forest of Dean) as steamships replaced sail. A number of new railway proposals were developed to improve access and to overcome the major problem of break-of-gauge at Salisbury. Hampshire became a hotly contested county between the expansionist plans of the Great Western and London & South Western railways. In 1862 a truce was reached, but the agreement was repudiated by the LSWR in 1869 to allow it to expand its network in Devon and Cornwall[156]. When the Midland and the LSWR took over the joint lease of the Somerset & Dorset Railway in 1875 and the LSWR reached Plymouth in 1876, the GWR General Manager, James Grierson, felt encircled and invaded[157], and the DN&S became a pawn in this wargame. The feud even led the LSWR to promote and build the line from Hurstbourne

to Fullerton Junction as a competitor to the DNS, but it survived only until 1931 as a through route, thereafter losing its passenger service and being cut back from Hurstbourne to Longparish. There was also considerable local rivalry between the DN&S and the Swindon, Marlborough & Andover Railway (later the Midland & South Western Junction Railway), a north-south line some 16 miles to the west of the DN&S, for which Parliamentary powers were being sought at the same time.

Building the railway

The Didcot, Newbury & Southampton Junction Railway was authorised by Act of Parliament in 1873 as an independent company following a route from Didcot, passing to the south of Newbury and joining the LSWR main line at Micheldever. It proved impossible to raise the money required for construction, and in 1876 extension of powers was sought and a working agreement with the GWR was concluded. One of the stipulations of the GWR was that the ruling gradient should be no steeper than 1 in 106, and this meant that the line was particularly suitable for handling long goods trains and would have been ideal today for Freightliner services. Three years later, in 1879, when little further progress had been made and a bill to abandon the railway had cleared most of its parliamentary stages, a last-minute reprieve came with financial support from local landowners and a new board of eminent local directors. John Fowler[158] was appointed engineer and on his advice a new parliamentary bill was promoted in 1882 for a revised route that joined the GWR's Berks & Hants line through Newbury and, instead of connecting with the LSWR at Micheldever, provided an independent route via Winchester and Chandler's Ford to Southampton. This caused further tension between the GWR and the LSWR, but the former's General Manager, Sir James Grierson, supported the bill in committee. Following authorisation, this scheme was itself scaled back and the line finished at Bar End, Winchester, under a compromise imposed by James Staats Forbes[159], the new Chairman of the DN&S company. Further acts of 1888 and 1889 authorised the completion of the line to its junction with the LSWR at Shawford, part paid for, and subsequently worked by, the LSWR. As a result, the line was handicapped by the need to change locomotives at Winchester from its opening until 1953. The fact that for northbound trains this involved two locomotives being inside the tunnel on the same track was an added complication.

The line between Didcot and Newbury was opened in 1882. Some of the cuttings through the Berkshire Downs had been dug with a 'steam navvy', thought to be the first case of such a machine being used in Britain. From Newbury to Winchester, services started in 1885, and the remainder of the line to Shawford was finally opened in 1891.

Working arrangements

From its opening until it was absorbed by the GWR in 1923, the development of the line was held back by the fact that it was owned by an independent company, dependent on the GWR to work its trains. The terms of the agreement with the GWR were onerous. The latter kept around 60% of the receipts to cover the working expenses. The remaining 40% was generally kept to cover interest payments on the debenture stock, which the GWR had guaranteed. The DN&S

shareholders had every reason to complain about the 'hostile and disparaging' attitude of the GWR[160]. Worse than this, there was no incentive for either the GWR or the LSWR to route traffic over the line. Indeed, they benefited from traffic staying on their own lines via Basingstoke. The approach of the company was reflected by that of the train crews working over the line. To Didcot men 'it was known locally as the 'Desert" or the 'Suakin and Berber' line.'[161]

The DN&S struggled to build its own business and achieved limited success in securing traffic from France through Southampton Docks. It also secured through carriages from Leicester to Southampton under an agreement with the Great Central Railway. Two years later, this developed into a through train with a restaurant car from Newcastle to Southampton, timed to connect with the overnight ferry to Le Havre. The 1902 timetable shows this train as well as two through trains from Paddington, smartly timed at 2hr 1min to Winchester and 2hr 34min to Southampton Town. This compared with 1hr 27min from Waterloo to Winchester and 1hr 45min to Southampton West by the LSWR. All these trains disappeared at the start of the First World War.

An interesting development currently in the thinking of the Wessex Alliance, the combination of Network Rail and South West Trains, is the idea of a Southampton to Paddington service running via Reading and Heathrow. Perhaps the GWR was just ahead of its time.

While local passenger traffic on the line was relatively light, the railway played an essential role in supporting the local economy in terms of goods traffic. It is hard to recall today how essential to the local economy was the pick-up goods train from the 1880s to the 1930s. Apart from local coal wharves, movement of agricultural products and machinery, and parcels, the DN&S was particularly important for the movement of livestock, notably at Upton & Blewbury, Sutton Scotney and Winchester; racehorses at Upton, Compton, Hampstead Norris, Hermitage, Burghclere, Whitchurch, Sutton Scotney and Kings Worthy; iron for foundries at Compton and Kings Worthy; bitumen at Hermitage; timber at Woodhay and Highclere; coal and gunpowder for Forders lime works at Burghclere; milk from Highclere and Litchfield; and jam from a factory at Whitchurch. A siding was provided for the newly formed Flying Corps' depot at Worthy Down, and coal arrived and coke left the gasworks at Winnall Siding at Winchester, while Bar End yard at Winchester handled bales of wool, biscuits, oil, coal for a local laundry and bottled mineral water as well as general merchandise and substantial quantities of sheep and cattle.[162]

Even after it had absorbed the line in 1923, the GWR continued to work it as two branch lines north and south of Newbury, and again its biographer, T. B. Sands, illustrates the position graphically and lyrically:

'The picture of the DN&S that comes most vividly to mind is not of a heavy goods train rolling southwards behind some grimy giant of the locomotive world, but of two or three elderly coaches and a horsebox trailing through the Berkshire Downs behind a Great Western 2-4-0 tank engine, sprightly and immaculate in the summer sunshine.'

The position of the railway as an independent company and the tense relationship between the GWR and LSWR combined to produce this market failure, which meant that a well-engineered route with reasonable capacity was ignored while traffic was routed over lines that were 9 miles longer and where capacity was stretched as the demands of other traffics grew.

Supporting the war effort

All this changed in wartime, and the line took on a new and serious purpose. It proved invaluable in moving men, horses and equipment to Southampton during the South African War. In the First World War it became an essential part of the logistical chain that linked camps established north of Winchester with Southampton, as well as bringing horses from Newbury and the Berkshire Downs to the port for embarkation. The depot of the Royal Army Ordnance Corps was at Didcot and a major tented camp was established at Churn. A military stores depot was established at Bar End yard in Winchester, and a 3-mile branch line (now obliterated by the M3) was built to serve new camps at Avington Park. The line was used by ambulance trains moving wounded troops to the Winchester hospitals, to Burghclere and to Highclere for temporary hospitals established at Sydmonton Court and Highclere Castle[163]. Passenger services on the line were suspended for short periods at the start of the war to provide capacity for troop movements. Greater things were planned, without, it seems, much consultation with the company owning the line. In April 1918 Frank Potter, the Great Western's General Manager, wrote to Beresford Turner of the DN&S to advise him of additional capacity being required and of 'the possibility of the DN&S line being utilised for the passage of heavy traffic to and from the camps at Winchester.' However, by November that year the plans were shelved. Potter wrote again to say that in view of the elaborate nature of the works, the cost could not be justified. The War Office 'had contented themselves with arranging for the provision of rail access between the Avington, Winnall Down and Horn (sic) Hill[164] camps and the DN&SR near Cheesehill Tunnel, Winchester.'[165]

Similarly, during the Second World War the line was a key link during the preparations for D-Day. The need to move large numbers of troops, and huge quantities of stores, vehicles and ammunition to Southampton for embarkation gave the little railway a serious purpose in the defence of the nation. From 4 August 1942 to 8 March 1943 the passenger service was withdrawn and the line was effectively rebuilt, as part of the wider project 'Bolero' to ensure American troops could reach the South Coast ports in short order, and the papers refer to that name in relation to the DN&S works. The northern half, between Didcot and Newbury, was doubled, and double track was extended south from Enborne Junction west of Newbury to Woodhay. Further south, although the formation and bridges were built for double track, rock falls and the need to strengthen embankments meant that the solution chosen was to extend passing loops at Burghclere, Highclere, Whitchurch and Sutton Scotney, and to reinstate the loop at Litchfield as well as providing new loops at Lodge Bridge and Worthy Down. A new spur linking the Southern's up main line at Winchester Junction with the single line just south of Worthy Down was also constructed, effectively providing grade separation for the Southern main line (down trains could continue to join it at Shawford). An up goods loop was provided alongside the Berks & Hants line at Enborne Junction at the same time. Total cost of the works was £412,000[166], or £15.9 million at today's prices.

TWYFORD DOWN
The monstrous scar left in the fragile environment of Twyford Down is evident from this picture of the busy M3 with the moribund railway in the foreground, crossing the restored Shawford Viaduct. Optimistically, the restored signal is in the 'off' position as if expecting a train. *Chris Austin*

The long loops in remote rural areas called for a new technical solution, too, as the points were too far away from the controlling signal boxes to be worked by the signalman via conventional point rodding. Instead, point motors were installed, with power provided by a hand-operated generator worked by the signalman. Having pulled the point lever, he would operate the generator, and a point indicator would show when the points had moved and been detected 'normal' or 'reverse', and he could then clear the protecting signal.

Strategic significance of the line

The modest gradients, coupled with the double-track sections and long loops created an excellent heavy freight route, and it would have been ideal for long Freightliner trains hauled by Class 66 locomotives. The wartime spur at Winchester Junction provided grade separation with the South Western main line, and at the Didcot end a flyover could have been provided to take the line over the Great Western main line to the Didcot avoiding line, all easily accomplished in the years before housing had spread to the boundaries of the railway here.

Elsewhere along the South Coast there is little rail freight activity, but Southampton is a major rail freight centre, with the growth of the container port and the plans for its further expansion. Numbers of container trains have grown and the main line also handles cars and vans between the Eastern Docks and Morris Cowley, Castle Bromwich and Halewood.

So, we do not argue here for the retention of a local passenger service, as the larger communities served were all on other east-west rail routes. It is also recognised that the commercial pull of Reading would always have meant that cross-country services would have

been routed this way. But as a freight-only route, and a diversionary route for passenger services as part of the seven-day railway, the DN&S line would have been a valuable link in the network.

Ironically, closure came just as the Freightliner concept (one of the more positive proposals from the 1963 Beeching Report) was being developed and rolled out. The first Southampton Freightliner terminal (at Millbrook) was opened in 1967, just as the track on the DN&S was being lifted. Ten years later, the proposed inland port at Didcot was being blockaded by members of the Transport & General Workers Union in a most unfraternal battle with the railwaymen.[167] The line, and a major distribution depot at its northern end, might have brought a profound change to the development of logistics in southern England.

Last years and closure

The line lost its passenger service between Newbury, Winchester and Shawford in 1960, although main-line congestion meant that a DEMU service from Southampton to Winchester continued to use Chesil station until 1962. The passenger service between Didcot and Newbury was also withdrawn in 1962, leaving the line as a freight-only route. It was one of the lines on which the iconic GWR locomotive *City of Truro* had worked in regular passenger service during the late 1950s.

WELL ENGINEERED
The sylvan setting of Bullington bridge between Whitchurch and Sutton
Scotney shows a substantial viaduct to carry the DN&S across the River
Dever. *Chris Austin*

From 1957 onwards, more through freight was routed this way, including oil trains from Fawley to Bromford Bridge and traffic from Southampton Docks. The route north of Newbury also carried two freight trains daily from the West of England to the Midlands via Oxford. So, by the time the traffic surveys on which the Beeching Report was based were carried out in April 1962, the line was in the second category (5,000-10,000 tons a week) alongside routes such as Basingstoke to Reading and the Bournemouth main line between Brockenhurst and Hamworthy Junction. The Beeching Report also showed Compton goods depot as being in the most heavily used category (25,000 tons a year or over), while Bar End and Sutton Scotney were in the intermediate category (5,000 to 25,000 tons a year). By this time, though, the approach was not to identify what sort of railway would be needed to cater for the demands of the future, but how could the existing (and known future) traffic demands be accommodated on a smaller network of core routes.

The line closed as a through route in August 1964, and ironically one of the last through trains to use it was the 'Pines Express', diverted because of a derailment on the main line. The final goods trip to Winchester was in 1966. The Department of Transport gave approval to sell the land between Didcot and Newbury in January 1967. Berkshire County Council originally showed interest in purchasing the line, but decided not to proceed. Newbury Borough Council also had plans to purchase a mile at the Newbury end for a road scheme, but this too came to nothing. In the event it was sold piecemeal and its value as a transport corridor destroyed.

Development of the A34

Prior to the Trunk Roads Act 1936 there was little in the way of national strategic planning for main roads, which were managed by the local authorities through which they passed. The A34 was designated in 1922 as the route between Winchester and Oxford. In 1934 it was extended to run north to Manchester, and from the 1936 Act onwards was known as the 'Winchester to Preston trunk road'. As early as 1937, traffic growth impacted on the railway at Sutton Scotney where the road joined the A30[168] in the village, passing under the railway through a narrow bridge and dividing again to the east of the line, and a wider bridge was constructed that year.

Access to Southampton was continued over the A33, and as early as 1940 the Winchester bypass was opened. As an indication of future priorities, the railway south of Winchester Chesil had to be slewed some 50 yards to the west to make way for the road. An earlier suggestion had been that the line should be linked to the Southern main line at

Winchester Junction (as happened in 1942) to allow the route through Chesil to Shawford to be closed and used by the new road.

The 1946 Trunk Roads Act gave a new stimulus to planning and road construction. Over the next decade a master plan was produced based on making the A34 a dual carriageway road from Winchester for much of its length to Rowstock (near Harwell) where it ran parallel with the DN&S. Towns would be bypassed with single-carriageway three-lane roads.

The new sections of road, with the years in which ministerial approval for their construction was given, were:

1955 Winchester Northern bypass (Kings Worthy link road to A33)
1956 East Ilsley bypass
1957 Newbury north-south relief road
    Sutton Scotney bypass
1960 Bullington Cross and Manor Farm diversions (where the A303 crossed the road between Whitchurch and Litchfield)

An engineering appreciation of the road carried out by the Ministry of Transport in 1957 showed that widening the road and building the bypasses would cost a total of £5,604,000 (the equivalent of £114.5 million today).[169]

At that stage the work was not planned to use any of the alignment of the railway, and indeed the costs included replacing a narrow railway overbridge at Litchfield and strengthening the weak Tothill railway bridge at Burghclere.

By the time the plans were to be implemented, however, through trains had finished and the first scheme, the Kings Worthy link road, was planned to use a mile of the railway formation. The scheme was actually delayed until the track had been lifted in 1967. The Kings Worthy link road was opened in 1969.

The formation was also used for the expanded road at Whitchurch when the bypass was built in 1976.

This continuing expansion of the A34 and the huge investment entailed did not go unchallenged. In 1977 a well-argued paper[170] in favour of making more use of the railway via Basingstoke and Reading was sent to the Department for Transport's South Eastern Road Construction Unit (SERCU) by Peter Hayden, the Southern Region's Chief Passenger Manager. It argued that the railway (via Basingstoke) had spare capacity for passengers and freight and that more could be provided at marginal cost. It also indicated that rail had at that stage 26% of the passenger traffic over the route, and 50% of the longer-distance flows. Apart from passengers and containers, the route carried the Stirling to Brockenhurst Motorail train, coal and chemicals, aggregates, irradiated fuel flasks, parcels and mail traffic. Twenty-two Freightliner trains ran daily, keeping 218,000 HGV journeys a year off the road. Hayden was sympathetic to the need for bypasses, but said he could 'see no need for upgrading the country sections of the A34 between the bypasses'.

> 'It would be in line with Government policies if all efforts were made to use this line to the full, instead of investing more in a parallel facility. This would also save resources – energy, aggregates, capital, environment and human life.'

Coming just 12 years after Beeching's trunk routes report, the strong and effective arguments show just how far BR's thinking had come.

The response from the Director of SERCU came a few days later and was quite dismissive. Even a doubling of rail traffic would only reduce demand by 1,000 vehicles a day and 'any transfer of traffic from road to rail was considered not materially to affect the proposals for improving the road.' But this was challenged by the Southern with a detailed analysis of traffic showing that the actual reduction from doubling rail traffic would be 7,000 vehicles a day, and an internal memo from Hayden expressed concern that the Department's view of how much the railway carried was so far below the figures collected by BR.

Newbury Bypass

So the juggernaut rolled on and led to a hugely controversial scheme that became known as the 'Third Battle of Newbury'[171]. It illustrates two points very well. First, that traffic expands to fill the road space available, and second that it has become impossible to deliver major new road schemes at an acceptable price in economic, social and environmental terms.

Traffic through the centre of Newbury had grown to the extent that the first bypass was built in 1963, just a year before most freight was withdrawn from the parallel railway. The scheme was approved by the Transport Minister, Ernest Marples, at a cost of £625,026[172] (£11 million at today's prices), which was, however, less than the £800,000 estimated in the master plan six years earlier. Further growth, stimulated by the progressive upgrading of other sections of the A34, meant that by 1980 this first bypass had reached capacity and planning started on a second one further west. A report from Mott, Hay, McDonald of that year identified 39 route options from Tothill to Donnington (north and south of Newbury), 20 of them running to the west and using part of the formation of the DN&S.

This highly controversial scheme had been the subject of a public inquiry in 1988, and it was not until 5 July 1995 that it was approved by the Secretary of State, Dr Brian Mawhinney[173]. Thirty minutes later he resigned. Work started a month later. It was eventually completed in November 1998, at a cost of £100 million, 40% more than the original estimate (£149 million today).

Ultimately this 9-mile route through three sites of special scientific interest involved the clearance of 360 acres of land and the loss of 10,000 trees. Indeed 'tree-sitting' was one of the ways in which the protestors sought to prevent the onward march of the bulldozers. At the height of the protests in 1991, 7,000 protestors were on site and 800 arrests were made during this period. It hit the national headlines over an extended period and one of the principal activists, known as 'Swampy'[174], entered the lexicon as the archetypal environmental protestor. The total cost of the policing operation and the use of private security firms was £24 million.

The opening of the Newbury bypass produced two measurable results. The first was to move the congestion point from Newbury to Chieveley, where a roundabout remained as part of the interchange with the M4. Sorting that out was another major project requiring the construction of ten bridges and 3 kilometres of new carriageway, costing a further £34 million (£44.2m at today's prices).

The second consequence was initially to provide some relief to the huge traffic levels on the first bypass. However, this capacity was soon taken up by suppressed demand for local trips that could now be made by car, and the traffic levels in Newbury are back to where they were prior to the opening of the new bypass, in addition of course to the through traffic passing on the new road. The Newbury Movement Study, undertaken by West Berkshire District Council, showed that traffic on the road network around Newbury (including both bypasses) had increased by 50% since the new bypass had opened in 1998.

Twyford Down

The other highly controversial road scheme that was to be used by road traffic from the West Midlands to Southampton resulted in the battle of Twyford Down. Two decades earlier a six-lane motorway along the line of the railway was considered and approved in 1973. However, it was opposed by Winchester College, which owned the water meadows alongside the River Itchen, some of which were required for the road, and was dropped in 1981 when Kenneth Clarke was Transport Minister, and he instigated a new study.

The geographical pressures of the Itchen Valley in which the city of Winchester lies meant that the motorway route chosen was over the downs to the east, and at Twyford Down it was to drop down to the river valley through a deep and wide cutting south of St Catherine's Hill. This was one of the most protected landscapes in southern England, with two sites of special scientific interest and two scheduled ancient monuments affected, all within a designated area of outstanding natural beauty. None of this, however, prevailed against the big yellow machines that started to tear into this fragile landscape in February 1992.

There were significant protests against this, ruthlessly controlled by Group 4 Security, the Department's contractors, culminating in a violent eviction of the protestors on 'yellow Wednesday' (named from the colour of the contractors' high-visibility jackets) on 9 December 1992. In July 1993 the Department secured an injunction against protestors entering the work site, and several protestors who ignored this and joined in a mass trespass were imprisoned for 28 days. The following year an even larger mass trespass of 1,500 people took place on 2 July 1994. Subsequently the Department for Transport sued 76 named protestors for costs of £1.9 million, and the issue was subsequently debated in the House of Lords. It was not until 31 July 1995 that the case against the protestors was dropped, the motorway having opened the previous month.

The Department may have forced the issue in the case of the Newbury and Winchester bypasses, but it was a Pyrrhic victory. The public pressure for new motorways had dropped and increasing environmental concerns had changed the context of new road building permanently. After 35 years, people realised that you could not go on like this, even if it took the civil servants a little longer to come to terms with the new reality.

The A34 continues to consume significant sums of public money, whether for maintenance and resurfacing or for relieving continuing congestion under the Highways Agency's 'pinch point' programme. Recent work undertaken in 2013 was a further £0.5 million spent at the junction with Easton Lane just north of Winchester to provide additional lanes for vehicles queuing at the traffic lights.

Three sections of the 47-mile DN&S line now underneath the A34 are:

South of Enborne Junction to north of Burghclere (3 miles)
South of Litchfield to north of Whitchurch (3 miles 10 chains)
Near Kings Worthy (1 mile)

Some sections of the line have been used as farm tracks at Churn (50 chains), north of Compton (1m 15ch) and south of Burghclere (1m 30ch), and in total some 8m 25ch have been converted to road. There has been encroachment on the formation at many other points along the route. Shawford Viaduct has been restored by Winchester City Council and forms part of a very pleasant walkway into the city from the south following both the railway and the River Itchen navigation; a number of the station buildings are now in private hands. While rebuilding railways is always possible at a price, reinstating the Didcot, Newbury & Southampton line, sadly, is certainly in the 'too difficult' category.

Rail investment in the corridor

With the DN&S closed, substantial investment has also been required on the alternative rail route formed by the London & South Western main line from Southampton to Basingstoke, the former Great Western branch thence to Reading, and the Great Western main line to Didcot. Resignalling and electrification of the South Western route would have happened anyway, but specific to the north-south 'A34' flows have been the gauge clearance works for container traffic from Southampton Docks and the investment in creating additional capacity at Reading. Providing clearances on the DN&S route for 8ft 6in containers would have been a relatively straightforward task as there were no tunnels between Winchester Junction and Didcot.

The big investment has been at Reading, to address the problem of conflicting train movements at Scours Lane Junction to the west of the station, where Freightliner trains from Southampton crossed the down and up main lines to reach the down relief line for the run to Didcot, Oxford and beyond. Here, the main lines have been raised onto a flyover and the Freightliner trains pass underneath them, releasing capacity for further growth and improving reliability.

For the future, this route to Southampton will form part of the 'electric spine', and the alternative route via Laverstock Junction and Romsey will also be electrified at 25kV overhead. The main line via Winchester is at capacity now and future plans in Network Rail's long-term planning process include extending the up goods loop from Eastleigh northwards, and some four-tracking between Wallers Ash loops and Micheldever. The possibility of four-tracking through Winchester is even being considered, so a heavy price is now being paid for the loss of this useful but unappreciated railway. Many millions will be spent, rightly, to create the capacity now needed, but the wasted asset running between Didcot and Shawford could have provided much of what is now needed so much more cheaply and effectively.

Conclusions

Across the Berkshire Downs the clear line of the former railway is still there, built on in places, partly obliterated by roads and with bridges missing. But an embankment or a fence line or a station, now an attractive home, all remind us of the wasted opportunity offered by the DN&S over a period of almost 80 years. These are monuments to the lives of men lost during the construction of the line, to the lives of those who served the railway throughout its existence and of its key role in two world wars, the latter suitably recorded in memorials embedded in Shawford Viaduct. It is also very visible evidence of the disinvestment resulting from a failed policy, or of any effective coordination between the agencies planning transport in Britain from the Trunk Roads Act of 1936 to the privatisation of the railways in 1997.

Some £700 million has been spent so far on upgrading the A34 and the alternative rail route, and more is planned, and the question is how much of this would have been needed had the DN&S been used effectively.

Another independent cross-country railway, further west, the Somerset & Dorset line, has a strong band of enthusiastic supporters even today, but the sad remains of the DN&S lie forgotten and half hidden in the undergrowth, unseen and unremarked by those driving on its inadequate replacement, the A34, or travelling on a 'Voyager' via the 9-mile-longer rail route, with its reversal at Reading. It is too late to turn the clock back on this route, but the lessons it holds in keeping options open and protecting routes for future transport use are there to see and learn.

The Joint Line: across the Fens from March to Spalding

The Great Northern & Great Eastern Joint Line (Cambridge to Lincoln and Doncaster) had its origins in the deposit of two competing bills by the Great Northern and the Great Eastern in 1878. Parliament approved the Great Northern bill for a railway between Spalding and Lincoln, with the proviso that there should be joint working with the Great Eastern. The line was opened in 1882, and a Joint Committee was formed to operate not only this line, but also the Lincoln-

SUMMER SATURDAY
The Joint Line was particularly useful for freight and summer Saturday services to the East Coast and East Anglian holiday resorts. The 09.12 train from Manchester Piccadilly to Yarmouth crosses the River Welland just south of Spalding on 28 August 1982. Spalding-March closed three months later and the following year holiday trains ran the additional 11½ miles via Peterborough. Welland Bridge signal box is now preserved at Peterborough on the Nene Valley Railway. *John Honnor*

Doncaster and the Spalding to March and Cambridge (via St Ives) lines[175], together with a number of branches. Crossing the wide open (and lonely) spaces of north-west Cambridgeshire and Lincolnshire, its role as a strategic route was more important than the service it offered to local communities. From 1891 it carried the 'York Continental', the first all-class dining car train to run in Great Britain.

In 1909 a parliamentary bill sought approval for a perpetual joint working arrangement between the Great Northern, Great Eastern and Great Central railways, which promised both working economies and a better integrated service for passengers and freight forwarders. The bill was eventually withdrawn, but from that date the Joint Line working arrangements changed, with the Great Northern operating the whole line north of March and the Great Eastern from March to Cambridge, although ownership remained vested in the Joint Committee.

It has always been an important freight route, providing relief to the East Coast Main Line between Doncaster and London. Gerry Fiennes had been assistant yard master at Whitemoor, the vast marshalling yard established near March, and describes the infinite variety of work and the wide range of traffics on the line:

'…the fruit and vegetables and potatoes and cider and mustard of East Anglia would stream down the joint line direct to Newcastle and York and the West Riding and Sheffield and Manchester and Liverpool and Nottingham… We had a basic heavy trunk haul of coal and goods from Whitemoor direct in train loads to the principal towns of East Anglia.'[176]

The local train service was sparse (two trains each way daily, with a third on Saturdays) and the two southernmost stations at Murrow (West) and Guyhirne had closed as early as 1953. The remaining three stations with the evocative names of Cowbit, Postland and French Drove & Gedney Hill closed in 1961.

BRAIN TRAIN
March was also linked to Wisbech and formed part of a through route to King's Lynn. It lost its passenger service in 1968 and freight finished in 2001. Now there are plans to reopen the line between March and Wisbech to link the skilled population in the town to the economic powerhouse of Cambridge. In 1966 a train for March leaves Wisbech and heads across the Fens. *Chris Austin*

March-Spalding closure
The very significant closure of the East Lincolnshire line in 1970 had removed the passenger service between Peterborough and Grimsby, and seen the complete closure of the line between Spalding and Boston as well as Firsby to Grimsby (see Chapter 5). This had been a step too far, and with local authority support a local passenger service between Peterborough and Spalding had been restored the following year. The main objective at the southern end of the line was always going to be the city of Peterborough and its fast London connections, rather than the small fenland market town of March, so the reopening brought opportunities not only for Spalding, but for the whole of the Joint Line passenger service.

In 1980 the Eastern Region's General Manager at York, Frank Paterson[177], advised the Board's Chief Executive (Railways), Bob Reid, following a study he had concluded that the route between March and Spalding could be closed. This would yield £313,000 a year in savings (staff costs) and would avoid the need for £1.5 million of track renewals between 1982 and 1985.[178] It was decided to add to the March-Spalding proposal the closure of the Sleaford and Lincoln avoiding lines.

Traffic was light and only three weekday services each way were involved, and these would all be diverted to Peterborough. An additional five summer Saturday trains ran to Great Yarmouth, and these too would be diverted, but continue to run. So it was not surprising that only 17 objections were received. A number of objectors were from the Railway Development Society[179], some still active campaigners today, and correctly forecast the congestion at Peterborough that would result, not from the three daily passenger trains, but from the significant number of freight trains involved. The TUCC took a hard line in its report and found evidence of hardship, both from longer journey times and from the need to change trains at Peterborough. Underlying the report was a view that the line served an area where public transport was poor, and that closure would make things worse. The report, and the rather ungracious rejection of a late offer by the Divisional Manager, Doncaster, to extend four of the six trains to and from March and Cambridge, was evidence of a change in approach to closures evident in the 1980s. The political climate was different and the public mood had swung against further retrenchment. There was also deep suspicion of the figures deployed by BR and the Department, and of their ultimate plans for the railways, rightly so, as became apparent from the publication of the Serpell Report the following year.

The Minister, David Howell, approved the closure in August 1982, against the background of weeks of strikes, initially by the NUR, and latterly by ASLEF. Nevertheless, here too the political stance had changed in response to public pressure. The approval letter included the sentence: 'The Secretary of State is anxious that, if possible, some alternative transport use should be found for these lines after they are closed by the Board.' There followed a requirement to notify the Secretary of State before any bridges were demolished, or other action taken that might prevent the route's further use for transport purposes.[180] This was a change of direction, even though, in this case, it did not prevent Whitemoor prison being built on the formation of the line at a later date.

The line closed on 29 November 1982.

PEAK SWANSONG
A Manchester-St Pancras express races through Millers Dale in 1966 behind
'Peak' No D45 with the restaurant car leading the train. The station and
goods yard are intact and the track is in fine fettle. A Buxton train waits in
the bay. The following year the line and station had closed. *Brian Stephenson*

Conclusions

There was clearly no case to retain the southern section of the route as a passenger line, and diverting the service to Peterborough was the right thing to do. The loss of the link for freight, however, has resulted in real capacity problems, with some very expensive solutions now proposed for the construction of a flyover at Werrington Junction to carry the diverted freight trains across the East Coast Main Line and direct them towards Spalding. The cost will be many times the modest savings made at the time of closure. The need arises, despite the massive decline in coal traffic and other commodities that Gerry Fiennes described as using the route, because there has been significant growth in container traffic from Felixstowe to Yorkshire and Humberside and the North East, and that line retains an important role as a diversionary route for the southern half of the East Coast Main Line in support of the seven-day railway.

This was perhaps a classic case where what appeared to BR as a piece of sensible 'good housekeeping' at a time of huge cost pressures has turned out to be a real impediment to growth and a significant strategic constraint in today's network. We are today paying the price for the miserly economies of a quarter of a century ago resulting from the tight financial straitjacket imposed by successive governments and the limited strategic vision evident from contemporaneous documents such as Serpell.

The rest of the Joint Line has been upgraded, with signalling control concentrated at Lincoln under a £280 million scheme, completed in 2014. It is now an important relief line to the East Coast Main Line, although it has its own pinch-point at the High Street level crossing at Lincoln Central, something that would not have been such a problem had the avoiding line been retained.

Through the Peak and across the Pennines to Manchester

The Midland main line from St Pancras ran from Derby via Matlock and Chinley to Manchester Central. Its role was crucial during the electrification of the West Coast Main Line when this 'Peak Forest' route was served by a frequent service of express trains, including the 'Midland Pullman', so brilliantly interpreted by the 1960 British Transport Films production, *Blue Pullman*.

The Beeching Report proposed closure of the alternative Hope Valley route between Sheffield and Manchester and removal of stopping services from the Peak Forest route, but retaining the line for through trains together with the intermediate stations of Bakewell and Matlock. In October 1963 Bakewell was added to the list of stations for closure through a notice in *The Times*.

BACK TO NATURE
A decade later the line to Matlock had been singled and nature was trying to reclaim the rest. The 11.00 Matlock to Derby service brushes past the encroaching trees on 5 August 1976 as it runs into Whatstandwell station.
Brian Sellars

But the plan changed and, once the West Coast electrification had been completed, the decision was taken to divert remaining through services via the Hope Valley line and to close the whole route between Ambergate and Chinley. Further north, the Woodhead route was also proposed for closure, with services also diverted via the Hope Valley.

The London Midland Region considered early on in 1966 that it might be necessary to retain the line between Matlock and Ambergate, both for longer-distance travellers from Matlock and also for the considerable commuter traffic to Derby. Indeed, in giving her consent to closure of the route north of Matlock, Barbara Castle refused consent for the section of line between Matlock and Ambergate and required BR to retain the peak service to Derby. Through services were withdrawn in 1967 and the line was singled the following year. Track recovery was halted briefly when the BR Research Division at Derby considered using the line between Matlock and Rowsley as a test track, but it resumed in June 1970.

Members of Matlock Urban District Council, concerned about the loss of both through services and local stations, wrote to ask to meet the London Midland General Manager, Henry Johnson[181]. Surprisingly, he declined to meet them on the grounds that the matter was with the minister and the meeting would serve no useful purpose, although he was at least able to reassure them about the retention of the service between Matlock and Derby. Stakeholders frequently got short shrift in the headlong rush to complete the closure process as quickly as possible, and this approach set up tensions and mistrust between local authorities and BR for many years to come.

The planned diversion of through services included not only those from Derby but also from Nottingham to Manchester, and work proceeded on this, progressed by a team under the Line Manager at Derby. In April 1967, however, Peter Keen, the Passenger Manager at Euston, flagged up that the Nottingham to Manchester services were 'a heavy loss-maker' and might have to be withdrawn. This disconnect between HQ and local teams is both surprising and illustrative of the fairly chaotic state of planning at this turbulent time. The spreadsheets show an analysis train by train of income and expenditure, which must have made some heroic assumptions about allocation of revenues and costs, but were unlikely to be sufficiently accurate as a basis for assumptions about profitability.

The line north of Matlock to Chinley North Junction closed in 1968, although the remaining local stations and the branch from Millers Dale to Buxton had closed the year before.

North of Millers Dale the railway is still busy with freight from Tunstead, Great Rocks and Dove Holes. To the south, the Matlock branch now has an hourly train to Derby and Nottingham and is supported by the successful Derwent Valley community rail partnership, which actively promotes the tourist potential of a line that serves Matlock Bath and the National Tramway Museum at Crich as well as the Peak Rail heritage railway. Services have improved, as have stations, with national railway heritage awards in 2009 for the restoration of Cromford's station buildings as office accommodation and a holiday let. Ridership on the line has increased by a staggering 120% over the last six years, which gives an indication of the potential north of Matlock as well.

From Matlock a heritage steam railway, opened in 1991, runs north to Rowsley South and there are plans to extend the line to Bakewell, the closest station to Chatsworth House.

From Bakewell the railway has become the popular Monsal Trail as far as Millers Dale.

ABOVE: CROMFORD COTTAGE
Today's revival is reflected in the superb restoration of the former up-side waiting room at Cromford. It is now a holiday cottage that can be hired. Access by rail is excellent! *Tim Collis*

BELOW: RETURNED EMPTIES
The northern end of the Midland route to Manchester is still busy with freight. Prior to closure of the main line, two Class 37s arrive at Peak Forest with an empty stone train from Portwood Drops (near Stockport Tiviot Dale). *C. J. Tuffs*

CLIMBING TO WOODHEAD
The 15.10 Manchester Piccadilly-Sheffield Victoria train is seen at Torside near Crowden on 16 July 1964 behind EM2 locomotive No 27002. *John Clarke*

A report by Scott Wilson in 2004, part funded by the Strategic Rail Authority and Derbyshire County Council, found the formation in good shape and capable of restoration as a railway. In net present value terms all options produced a negative value, so the benefit-to-cost ratio was less than 1. However, the report indicated that in the longer term the prospects were better. An increase of 140% in road traffic in the corridor was predicted and a railway would take almost a million of those journeys each year. At the same time, the evaluation did not take account of any rail freight benefits but concentrated instead on the value of a local passenger service.

It is perhaps the Peak route's importance for freight that would be particularly useful, and this is why it is listed in Appendix A for reopening, although it would certainly not be universally welcomed as it runs through a national park, and can be expected to attract strident criticism, just as it did from Ruskin when the line was built.[182]

Today, the case for reopening the route rests upon three principal premises:

1. It would provide a faster and more reliable service between the East Midlands and the North West than the current services via Sheffield and the Hope Valley.
2. It would open up a new rail market between Matlock and Manchester and between Buxton and Derby, together with Nottingham, East Midlands Airport and Leicester.
3. It would be a new outlet for freight from Peak Forest to the East Midlands and points south and east, as well as an alternative route for containers from the London ports and Felixstowe to the North West, taking pressure off the West Coast Main Line.

Woodhead

Further north, the Woodhead route lost its passenger service in 1970, to clear the way for freight, but just over a decade later that traffic had been diverted too. The troubled story of Woodhead has been expertly chronicled elsewhere, particularly by Alan Whitehouse in his poignant book of the last days before closure.[183] Even if it had not been closed in 1981, the traffic it had been retained to carry was declining fast as imported steel replaced home production and the privatisation of the electricity supply industry changed the supply routes and triggered the closure of many British collieries. The core coal supplies from South Yorkshire to Fiddlers Ferry power station would have gone, even if the line had remained.

The real problem, however, was not commercial, but operational. The line was electrified, but at 1500 volts DC with overhead catenary, and this required at least one change of traction, and in some cases two, for any train that was routed that way. Locomotive utilisation was poor and changing engines meant time lost. From the passenger point of view, the line served Victoria station at Sheffield, whereas other services were being concentrated on the Midland station, and this made interchange difficult and access from Manchester via Penistone complicated, involving a reversal at Woodburn Junction or the detour via Barnsley, used by the successful Penistone line.

The question is whether the line would have value today. Pressure on the principal trans-Pennine route via Standedge Tunnel and also on the Hope Valley route suggests that additional capacity is needed, and indeed is planned through a mixture of additional signal sections and loops. The 2010 Coalition Government accepted the need for more capacity and

much shorter journey times across the Pennines in its Chancellor's articulation of the need for an 'HS3' to create a 'northern powerhouse' by creating new links between Liverpool, Manchester, Sheffield and Leeds.

A campaign has been running for some years to reopen Woodhead Tunnel and prevent its use by high-voltage cables (currently routed through the old tunnel), to keep open the opportunity for connecting the Lancashire and Yorkshire networks again by this route, and in terms of forward planning this is right. There are many ideas on how the link might be made, and what trains would use it, but it is important to protect the options for the future when the use of rail will have far outgrown even the expanded capacity of the existing routes. It is, to some extent, a choice between the Peak Forest and the Woodhead routes as to which would provide the best value, and the quarries around Peak Forest perhaps point to the former as a priority, but this does not negate the need to protect the latter where possible. Who would have foreseen the current levels of demand 34 years ago in 1981, and what will demand look like in 34 years' time, in 2049?

8

THE SEVERED SEASIDE TOWNS

*'The concentration on obvious loss-makers, cutting away the dead wood,
was meant to leave a healthier, well-pruned, more fruitful tree. In fact, that is not what
happened. The analogy would be more accurate if one saw the process as cutting off the
tributaries and drying up the main flow of the river – or perhaps it is Ibsen's onion in
Peer Gynt, where layer after layer is stripped and the heart never found.'*[184]

PETER PARKER, HALDANE MEMORIAL LECTURE, 23 FEBRUARY 1978

PROMENADE PRUNED
A major Lancashire resort, Morecambe is still rail-connected but, like others, the railway has been cut
back to release land for car parking. A train for Lancaster waits in the bay platform. Behind the buffer stop,
the line used to continue to the Promenade station on the seafront and opposite the beautifully restored
Midland Hotel, which can be seen in the distance. *Chris Austin*

Clevedon

On the Somerset coast of the Bristol Channel is the small town of Clevedon, traditionally a more genteel resort than its brash rival Weston-super-Mare, 10 miles away. Initially a smaller settlement than Clevedon, Weston prospered and grew from the opening of the Bristol & Exeter Railway between Bristol and Bridgwater in 1841, as a short branch line served the little town. Six years later, in 1847, Clevedon was linked by a branch line, 3m 45ch long, from a junction on the B&ER main line, which changed its name the same day from Clevedon Road to Yatton.

In the early days the railway encouraged trips to the seaside with a fare of one shilling between Bristol and Clevedon, although to separate the rough excursionists from the more refined townsfolk, a separate excursion platform was provided. This was swept away with the alterations of 1879 when the branch was converted from broad gauge and a 600-foot platform to accommodate longer trains was provided at Clevedon.

From 1897 to 1940 the line connected with the Weston, Clevedon & Portishead Light Railway, one of the remarkable Colonel Stephens[185] lines, with the two stations at Clevedon adjacent to each other.

Clevedon subsequently grew and prospered, both as a modest seaside resort and as a pleasant place to live for those working in Bristol, and through residential trains ran morning and evening to serve them in the days before they became known as commuters. For many years Clevedon passengers could take the rear coach of the 5.15pm from Temple Meads, which was slipped at Yatton for their convenience, being worked forward to Clevedon by the auto-train. Slip coaches had been introduced in 1858 and were widely used, particularly on the Great Western, as a way of serving stations without the need to stop the train. Instead, the rear coach (or portion) with a special coupling would be detached while approaching the station by the 'slip guard' who would then bring the coaches to a stand in the platform. (The last coach was slipped at Bicester North on 10 September 1960 from the 5.10pm Paddington to Wolverhampton.)

The branch was economical to operate, at one stage with a railmotor, then with a two-coach auto-train pulled or propelled by a '517' Class tank engine, and subsequently by the classic Collett '1400' Class 0-4-2T, with No 1463 as the regular engine towards the end of steam. Clevedon signal box had long ago become a ground frame and, with no intermediate stations, the train could be worked by the loco crew without a guard. From 1960 onwards, No 1463 was replaced by a single-car diesel unit with or without a trailer. Goods traffic was withdrawn from the branch in 1964 and Clevedon became an unstaffed halt the same year, with the guard issuing tickets on the train.

The line was included in the Beeching Report and the closure case was heard by the TUCC in the Council House at Clevedon on 5 October 1965. A 2,000-signature petition against closure had been sent to the Ministry from Clevedon UDC in February 1964. Prior to the hearing, the county, urban district and parish councils objected, as did a number of individual passengers, including a group of 19 mothers concerned that they would not be able to take prams on the replacement bus. The figures were modest – around 500 passenger journeys a day (half during peak periods) and a maximum of 44 on any one train – but against the depressing and run-down condition of BR local services at the time, this

CLEVEDON

No 1426 arrives with the auto-train from Yatton, with the goods shed on the right and the signal box (reduced to a ground frame) just visible on the left.
Jane Lilly

was perhaps not surprising. More surprising was the reaction of the Economic Planning Council for the South West Region, which saw it as a 'minor closure' that 'would have no economic planning significance'[186], a surprisingly short-sighted view, even for 1965. The Ministry of Housing and Local Government warned that 'Clevedon is a possible expansion area into which overspill from Bristol may be received.'[187] The Board of Trade reflected that the British Travel and Holiday Association recommended retention as 'closure would have an adverse effect on the holiday trade of the area.'[188]

While these latter arguments were subsequently overridden, when the papers were prepared by the Bristol Division for the Ministry it became clear that the figures favoured retention. Income was £4,600 per annum while movement costs were £9,000 and terminal costs £2,000, and £2,720 in renewals were due in three to five years' time.[189] But bus replacement costs were estimated to be £6,000, and some £10,000 of contributory revenue was at stake, as so many commuters travelled beyond Yatton to Bath, Bristol and Weston-super-Mare.[190] When this was put to the Board, however, Margetts rejected it out of hand as the service would have to bear full track and signalling costs following withdrawal of the freight service. In his view, the full annual loss would be £7,325 to receive contributory revenue of £10,100. He told the Region to proceed with the closure case, with the ironic comment that this was no more than a bus service on rails.[191]

But the Ministry picked this up at its working party that reviewed progress on closures on 27 January 1966, and remitted it to the Board for an explanation as 'the line appears therefore to be running at a profit'[192], noting that the bus subsidy would be greater than the gain that would result from rail closure. The reply from John Dewdney, who worked for Margetts at the Board, exposed the truth that the benefits actually came from asset-stripping. Noting that costs had risen as a result of a pay award, the value of the track recovered would be £3,150 and the Clevedon station site might realise £22,000. Meanwhile, from another quarter the Ministry was also aware that closure would save £125,000 in bridging costs as the line crossed the route of the proposed M5.

The Ministry accepted that 'This service is one of the smaller branch lines which the Board do not want to retain and although on

CLEVEDON HALT
With the track cut back and the station destaffed, the end is near as a railcar waits to return to Yatton. *Chris Austin*

the basis of operational costs they would not gain much (if anything) from closure, the main financial benefits would accrue from the recovery of materials and the sale of assets.'[193]

Barbara Castle gave her consent seven days after this memo, on 21 April 1966, and the line closed on 3 October, a replacement service of 18 buses a day each way being provided, running non-stop with through rail tickets issued by the conductor.

There were thoughts of revival as a private railway, and one of your authors worked with the redoubtable campaigner Owen Prosser[194] in forming the Clevedon & Yatton Railway Preservation Society. The correspondence remains on the Ministry file and shows an unwillingness to engage, which borders on obstruction. The Ministry advised the society to approach BR to seek to buy the line, while the approach to BR met the response that the first approach should be to the Ministry. In the polite but insistent way that made Prosser such an effective campaigner, he asks, 'Perhaps you would be good enough to let me know to which authority the next approach should be made.'[195] Local support for retention of the line was encouraged by a press report in the *Bristol Evening Post* in May 1966 that a mystery peer was prepared to promote a railway transfer bill in Parliament to allow the line to be taken over by a new company. The Ministry made clear that it would not meet the cost of bridging the M5, and Clevedon Urban District Council, while an objector to closure, wanted the station site for development, car parking and an

inner relief road. Against such formidable obstacles, the project foundered and died.

Subsequently, housing has encroached on the formation at the Clevedon end and the route was severed by a number of roads as well as being affected by drainage work on the Blind Yeo River. The Clevedon station site disappeared under a new shopping centre, car park and road.

The case shows three things in particular:

1. Buses are not a cheap replacement for trains. The bus costs for this short line were actually £8,500 for 18 buses and a service that ended an hour before the train service, which was costed at £10,250 for 30 trains and a longer operating day.
2. The Board had lost sight of the objective of the Beeching Report and was set on delivering outcomes rather than objectives. Clevedon had to go because it was on the list, even though closure produced a worse financial result.
3. At this early stage, 'selling the family silver' was seen as justification for destroying a perfectly good local railway.

It was perhaps cases like this that made many people determined to overturn this juggernaut of a policy, which threatened to do so much damage to local economies and to the environment, but also to the British way of life. To many, it looked like wanton destruction, particularly when the bulldozers moved in.

Today, Yatton is a busy Bristol commuter station with car parking at a premium and a thriving community café, the Strawberry Line, employing young people with learning difficulties and providing excellent local food. The buses no longer connect with the trains, and only an hourly service is offered during the day as part of the longer X5 route from Weston-super-Mare to the Cribbs Causeway shopping centre. There is no service in the evenings and buses run every 2 hours on Sundays. Clevedon is served every half-hour by express bus from Bristol bus station (more than a mile from Temple Meads).

Had it survived, the railway would have continued to play its valuable role as a feeder line, taken the pressure off the car parks at Yatton and Bristol Parkway (easily reached by the M5), and provided an integrated service for Clevedonians in a way that has never, in practice, been achieved by a bus/rail connection. The town would certainly have fared better as a tourist destination with its rail link.

Four years after the railway closed a second disaster struck Clevedon when its elegant Victorian pier failed during routine structural tests and two spans collapsed, leaving the landing stage isolated. It was to be almost 20 years before the pier reopened, and almost 30 years before restoration was completed as a result of local initiative. It is now a unique Grade I listed structure, of particular interest as it was originally built (in 1869) using redundant Barlow rails from Brunel's broad gauge.

This was a short rural branch line, with all the disadvantages of the need to change at Yatton for other destinations. Many of these have failed to attract enough passengers to ensure their survival, so what is different about Clevedon?

With a population of 21,000, the town is reasonably large and attractive enough to generate tourism and work and retail trips to itself as well as travel to work, shopping and educational trips to Bristol and Weston, so it would not be relying solely on seasonal tourist traffic. Cheap to operate and capable of supporting a high-frequency service with a single unit, it would also have offered reasonable value for money. How much better the dreary shopping centre might have been if it had had a busy railway station at its core.

One nice touch: the site of the station is marked by a simple stone and a plaque noting that this was the departure point for so many men from the town who left home to fight in the two world wars.

The local community showed determination and resilience in insisting on the restoration of their pier, and they now have a community cinema that survived because of local initiative. However, the community remains cut off from the rail network and, like Hunstanton (below), is, sadly, likely to remain isolated.

Hunstanton

The Norfolk coast was traditionally the summer destination of Londoners and of families from the East Midlands, particularly from the 1920s onwards when holidays with pay allowed large numbers of people to spend two weeks by the seaside. Cheap package holidays overseas have changed all that, but the area is still popular, particularly with north Londoners who migrate to the coast every weekend. Most of the resorts owed their development and economic success to the railway. Some, like Great Yarmouth and Cromer, were very successful and continue to attract large numbers of visitors today, many by rail. Other smaller resorts such as Mundesley, Caister and Gorleston, relied on the railway, but perhaps the largest one cut adrift by the loss of its railway, and still recovering from the consequences, is Hunstanton.

SUMMER SATURDAY AT HUNSTANTON
Brush Type 2 No D5504 backs on to a train while crowds alight from the latest arrival. The sidings are full of stock and the station hotel, built by the Great Eastern, can be seen behind the station. The area is now a car park.
King's Lynn Forum

Opened in 1862, the King's Lynn to Hunstanton line saw the early development of holiday traffic, which encouraged the building of the Sandringham Hotel next to Hunstanton station by the Great Eastern Railway in 1876. Indeed, early BR maps showed the main line from Liverpool Street and Cambridge continuing right through to Hunstanton, only later being shown as a branch from King's Lynn. This reflected its importance and the running of through trains from London as well as the local service. From 1949 'The Fenman' started from Hunstanton each morning, complete with restaurant car, and other through trains ran beyond King's Lynn, including three trains daily via the M&GN line, two of which provided a useful link to Peterborough, and one to Birmingham. Like many holiday routes, the disparity between summer and winter services was enormous. In 1954 the basic pattern of winter service saw 10 departures from Hunstanton. On summer Saturdays, the figure rose to 23.

The first part of the line from King's Lynn to Wolferton was double track, beyond which it was single with crossing loops at Snettisham, Dersingham, Heacham and Hunstanton. At Heacham, a branch line ran east to Burnham Market and Wells-next-the-Sea, an early closure to passengers in 1952. The following year part of the line at Holkham was lost to the 1953 floods, which also engulfed a train from Hunstanton near Heacham. The Hunstanton line reopened, but Burnham Market to Wells closed, the remainder of the branch from Heacham to Burnham remaining open for goods traffic until 1964.

The Hunstanton line was not included in the Beeching Report for closure, and indeed every effort was made by Gerry Fiennes when General Manager of the Eastern Region to cut costs and invest in signalling to enable the line to survive. Working with Claude Hankin, the Norwich Divisional Manager, stations were destaffed, level crossings automated, some crossing loops removed, and pay trains were introduced with simpler and cheaper fares to encourage local use. In fact, they did everything that campaigners had urged railway management to do. But this was not enough for the Board with its inflexible view at the time on the need for further retrenchment. Royal trains ceased to run to Wolferton (for Sandringham) in 1966, and the pay train experiment followed the next year. Two years later

RYDE PIER HEAD
A Ventnor train leaves behind No 35 *Freshwater* on 18 May 1964. On the right is the paddle steamer *Ryde* and in the foreground are the tracks of the pier tramway. *Leslie Sandler*

the line closed, amazingly from the May timetable change, right at the start of the summer season.

For anyone who wants to see this attractive line and the rich heritage of the county it served, an excellent British Transport Film survives in the British Film Institute archive. Made in 1962, John Betjeman goes by train along the whole line and proves to be an excellent guide to the architecture of both the railway and the local churches as well as idiosyncratic details such as the box hedge at Snettisham clipped to spell out the station name.

Millions of pounds have been invested in the parallel road, the A149, since the railway closed in 1969, including an eastern bypass at King's Lynn to link it to the A10 and the A47, but summer congestion remains acute and has constrained the development of the resort, particularly for day visitors. Peak congestion limits access to King's Lynn all the year round. Hunstanton itself has been impoverished by the loss of its railway, which has also made access to the spectacular North Norfolk Coast more difficult by public transport, although the County Council and the operator, Norfolk Green, deserve credit for the support and promotion of the 'Coasthopper' bus service from King's Lynn to Hunstanton and Cromer, which provides access today.

Much of the formation of the railway, and most of the stations (except Hunstanton itself) survive in private ownership. Over time, though, more encroachment has taken place, as Norfolk has not sought to safeguard the route. Local support for reopening has been patchy and lacks the drive and focus seen in other parts of the country where lines have been restored. Hunstanton appears condemned to remain remote from the rail network, forever held back by road congestion and peripherality.

Ventnor

The Isle of Wight Railway was opened from Ryde St Johns Road to Shanklin in 1864 and extended to Ventnor in 1866. Originally connected to Ryde Pier by horse tramway, a direct rail connection from Ryde Pier Head to St Johns Road was built jointly by the London, Brighton & South Coast and London & South Western railways and opened in 1880.

Its arrival was not greeted with universal acclaim. The author Henry James wrote in *English Hours* (1905):

'The Isle of Wight is at first disappointing. I wondered why it should be, and then I found the reason in the influence of the detestable little railway. There can be no doubt that a railway in the Isle of Wight is a gross impertinence, is in evident contravention to the natural style of the place.'

However, the railway brought mass tourism to the eastern coast of the island, and Ventnor, south-facing and protected by St Boniface Down (through which the railway ran in a 1,312-yard tunnel), developed as a popular and somewhat genteel resort.

So attractive was the Ventnor business that a second railway was built and worked by the Isle of Wight Central Railway as a branch from its Sandown-Newport line at Merstone, and this was opened in 1900 to Ventnor Town (renamed Ventnor West in 1923). This line never attracted significant numbers of passengers and with the onset of bus competition was reduced to a push-pull shuttle to and from Merstone. The branch closed at the end of the summer season on 15 September 1952, although the station buildings survive as houses within Castle Close, which now occupies the station site.

The Ryde to Ventnor line was always the principal route to the town and was marketed as an extension of the line between Waterloo and Portsmouth Harbour. Indeed, the carriage roof boards on the main-line trains read 'Waterloo-Portsmouth-Isle of Wight'. The train service was hourly in the 1950s and 1960s and there was a seamless connection between train, boat and train. In the more leisurely days before the City's 'big bang' a few stockbrokers lived in Ventnor and travelled to the City on the 6.35am train, arriving at Waterloo at 9.51, and returning on the 4.50pm from Waterloo (arriving at Ventnor at 8.10pm).

Run with locomotives that by their withdrawal in 1966 were 75 years old, and carriages some of which were by then were more than 60 years old, the intensive service worked to Ventnor on summer

ST BONIFACE DOWN
A train from Ventnor arrives at Wroxall and crosses No 24 *Calbourne* with a train from Ryde on 28 August 1964. No 24 will then head off to the tunnel under the down to reach Ventnor station, perched above the town. *Calbourne* was preserved and is now run by the Isle of Wight Steam Railway. *M. Dunnett*

Saturdays was an amazing achievement given the tight turnrounds, limited capacity and stiff gradients. Each hour five trains left Ryde Pier Head, two for Ventnor, one for Shanklin, one for Sandown, and one for Cowes. Six-coach sets were used with a capacity of 420 seats. The numbers carried in the 1950s were enormous and the average load on peak days was 454 passengers, with around 800 carried by the most crowded. The figures for passengers via Ryde Pier Head on a peak summer Saturday, 9 August 1952, collected by the Railway Executive and reproduced in the County Council's 1953 report, were:

Arrived by ferry	28,506	Left by ferry	30,894
Ventnor train	17,377		16,995
Newport train	1,365		2,023
% by train	66		62

This was not some idyllic rural network but a serious working railway with characteristics more akin to the busy suburban services into Waterloo.

By the time of the Beeching Report the bubble had burst and more people were taking foreign holidays, increasingly by air, but on the island numbers remained too high for the buses to cope with. The whole network was included in the Beeching Report for closure, but this was vehemently opposed by the County Council and the

island businesses. When it came, the consent letter from the Minister, Tom Fraser, had approved the closure of the Cowes line and that from Shanklin to Ventnor, leaving the core route from Ryde Pier Head to Shanklin to 'alleviate most of the hardship the closure proposal would cause'. The location of its station, high above the town, proved to be fatal for Ventnor, with closure being approved, the letter pointing out that 'bearing in mind the limited value of traffic between Shanklin and Ventnor and the siting of the station at Ventnor, the operation of bus services between Shanklin station and Ventnor would provide an adequate alternative service.'[196]

The retention of the service was costly as the railway required complete renewal, including electrification using refurbished Underground rolling stock and major works on Ryde Pier. However, the Ministry foresaw that the line would still not be 'profitable' and would in due course require subsidy, which proved indeed to be the case. Consequently, the letter suggested that 'it would be reasonable for the Board to consider increasing fares (in particular at peak holiday times) so as to reduce, if not to eliminate, the loss which is expected to be incurred on the new service.'

The connecting bus service from Shanklin required road improvements (although these were not a condition of consent), and these were to be carried out by the County Council with costs shared with the Ministry, which was to contribute £100,000. The Council, however, was unwilling to progress these while there was still a possibility of reopening the line.

The closure had a dramatic effect on Ventnor. There was an average loss of trade of 25% during the season following closure, and three businesses went into receivership.[197] The owner of the Hotel Pelham on the Esplanade wrote to the Minister in despair:

'In spite of the fact that I have increased our advertising by 100% our bookings are well down on last year. We still have rooms available for the peak time in July/August. This has never happened before.'

On 12 December 1967 a heavy fall of snow cut off the town by road and telegrams were sent to the Minister (by then Barbara Castle) by both the town's Hotel Association and the Professional and Business Association highlighting the inadequacy of the buses.

There were thoughts of reinstatement, and the Sadler railcar company planned at one stage to use it as a demonstration project, but nothing came of it. Even the Ministry was open to the suggestion, and Dr Stewart Joy (see Chapter 2), normally seen as something of a 'hawk' in these matters, pointed out that 'even if the total grant rose, the grant per passenger mile would almost certainly fall'. As an economics adviser to the Ministry, he was sceptical of BR's figure of £200,000 for reopening, and pointed out that the Board had procured enough rolling stock from London Transport to run to Ventnor.[198] This stock was used to provide the augmented service run to replace the pier tram. He pressed for BR to undertake a full evaluation.

A letter of 'no objection' to lifting the track had been sent to BR on 28 February 1967, and as nothing came of the reopening proposals the track was lifted in 1971. Interestingly, only the rails could be removed from the section through St Boniface Down Tunnel, which was shared with the town's water main. Surprisingly, this used to run in an open conduit when the trains were running,

and when the track was lifted after closure special precautions were required and the sleepers remained in situ, to avoid contamination. Steam services on the island were withdrawn on 21 February 1966, while electrification was completed and the superstructure supporting the rail tracks on Ryde Pier was renewed, then in 1967 the line to Shanklin reopened using 1927 rolling stock from London Underground. So unpopular was BR and the Ministry over the island closures that the junior minister declined an invitation from the Southern Region to be present at the launch of the new electric service on 20 March.[199]

Your co-author Chris Austin was appointed summer assistant to the Island Manager in 1969, the year the pier tramway closed and during which stations were destaffed in the winter and a pay train system introduced. It was still then a substantial operation employing more than 100 people. Apart from the railway operation, staff were employed at Pier Head to tie up and load the boats, train maintenance was carried out at Ryde, a parcels depot remained at Newport, and BR owned a toll road at Bembridge and employed staff to collect the tolls. Five trains an hour were run on peak summer Saturdays, one to Sandown and the rest to Shanklin, and a frequent service ran between Pier Head and St John's Road to replace the tram. The trains were run in seven-car formations.

Today, newer rolling stock (from 1937!) operates in two-car formations and two trains an hour are run. The whole operation is slimline compared with 1969, and the passenger numbers have dropped from their high peak to more modest levels in line with the reduction of visitors to the island since its heyday.

The decision to truncate the Ventnor line at Shanklin was, with the benefit of hindsight, a poor one. For some years a connecting bus met every train at Shanklin to provide a replacement service to Ventnor, but that disappeared, as replacement buses do, and no guaranteed connections operate today. For most, the direct bus from Ryde or Newport is more convenient than one requiring change of mode. Ventnor station site remains as a collection of industrial units and the tunnel is still there, carrying Ventnor's water supply.

With a running time of around 10 minutes, two trains an hour could have been provided by extending the service from Shanklin to Ventnor at the cost of an additional unit, and the capital costs would have required the addition of an extra sub-station, but the town would have remained on the network. While it reflected the desire by both civil servants and BR to minimise the cost of continuing an essential service, it has produced a sub-optimal result. The island's economy has gone through a tough time as holiday destinations and requirements have changed over the years, and Ventnor's ability to compete was certainly hamstrung by the loss of its railway.

The loss of the bridge at Shanklin, encroachment of building at Wroxall and the more demanding standards of the water industry today probably preclude reopening, and Ventnor will continue to lose out from being 'off the network'.

VENTNOR

No 29 *Alverstone* pauses while running round her train to receive attention and take on a tankful of water. The picture shows the narrow station site carved out of the cliff and the entrance to the tunnel beside the signal box.
Chris Austin

9

THE CLOSED COMMUTER LINES

'I said, 'Buses aren't the answer.' Mr Winch was looking at the oncoming train.
He said, 'Buses aren't even a good question.'

PAUL THEROUX, *THE KINGDOM BY THE SEA*, 1983

The demographic characteristics of all Britain's cities have changed dramatically over the last 50 years in ways that could not have been foreseen. Consequently, there are many suburban lines that were seen as hopeless loss-makers in 1963, that would today be useful suburban or light rail links, taking the pressure off inadequate and dangerous suburban roads. In general these are outside the PTE areas, where coordinated planning enabled more rational decisions to be made, and some illustrative examples are given below.

CROSSED LINES
The 3.55pm Leith North to Princes Street DMU crosses the main line at Haymarket Central Junction on 27 April 1962. Underneath 'A1' 'Pacific' No 60143 *Sir Walter Scott* heads the 4.03pm Waverley to Perth train via Kinross Junction. *W. S. Sellar*

Edinburgh: the Corstorphine branch
Edinburgh, in common with cities such as Nottingham, Bristol and Plymouth, once had an extensive suburban network that dwindled almost to nothing before the revival started in the 1980s. The story is told in detail below (Chapter 10), but is illustrated at this point by the last of the closures, the short Corstorphine branch, at the end of 1967.[200] Built by the North British in 1902, it was only 1½ miles long with one intermediate station (a second halt was added by the LNER in 1934). The service was affected by tram competition and by the drawback of climbing Waverley steps in the city centre (now supplemented by three banks of double escalators funded by Transport Scotland in 2012), while the trams ran along Princes Street.

Nevertheless the line proved to be a useful part of Edinburgh's public transport network for 65 years, diesel trains replaced steam in 1956, and in 1958 a clockface timetable was introduced, with most trains running

EDINBURGH, GRANTON, HAYMARKET & LEITH

through to North Berwick, some going to Musselburgh, and to Rosewell & Hawthornden for a short period after the Peebles loop had been cut back to that station in 1962. The line was not included in the Beeching Report, but nevertheless was proposed for closure by the Scottish Region and the Heads of Information it provided indicated that the line carried 1,415 passenger journeys on 18 trains each way daily, mainly in the peak periods. The busiest train was the 8.17am from Corstorphine, with 172 passengers, while the following 8.34 train carried 165. The train was significantly cheaper than the bus (a monthly season between Corstorphine and Waverley was 39s 6d compared with a four-weekly bus ticket costing 55 shillings). In its report of 26 April 1967, the TUCC for Scotland found evidence of hardship, but was divided on whether the additional peak buses proposed by the Corporation bus company would mitigate this. On a vote, 12 members thought they would, while seven did not, and there were two abstentions.

Also unusual was the rider the TUCC added to its conclusions that 'it appeared unfortunate that there should not be a place in the public transport system for a train service between a suburb and the town centre.'

There was a last-minute attempt by the local MP to save the service following bus reliability problems resulting from staff shortages and traffic congestion. Barbara Castle's minister, John Morris[201], made clear that her decision was a final one.[202] Earlier in the month, in answer to a parliamentary question, the junior minister, Neil Carmichael[203], had turned down a request to maintain the service pending completion of the East-Central Scotland Land Use Study, saying that Castle 'considers that the retention of the formation of the line is a sufficient safeguard.'[204] In the event, safeguarding was not included in the letter consenting to closure, nor was a requirement for additional buses, although these were provided. Retention of the track

was raised later by the TSSA in correspondence with the TUCC, but it was pointed out that no such requirement had been made.

The branch performed a valuable function in moving large numbers of passengers at low unit cost to and from work in Scotland's capital city and, as was the custom of the time, took them home for lunch as well.

Looking back, there is a surprising contrast between the euphoria of 1958, when faster and more frequent diesel trains on an interval service pattern were introduced on a number of Edinburgh suburban routes, and 1962, when many were closed and the writing was clearly on the wall for the others. This was a dramatic change over four years and all before the 'Reshaping' report of 1963. Only the North Berwick branch survived as a result of effective campaigning to prevent closure in 1969 led by Norman Hall, a former Conservative councillor who served on North Berwick Community Council, Lothian Regional Council, and North Berwick Burgh Council and who remains a resident of the town.

There is no doubt that, short though it was, the line would today be a useful, traffic-free link with the city centre, probably as part of the tram route, which crosses the route and has a tramstop close to the former Balgreen Halt. It remains as a pleasant walkway, although the Corstorphine terminus is no longer there.

Bristol: the Portishead branch

In 1867 when this line opened, the population of the little fishing village of Portishead was only 1,200 and the investment included a pier to allow steamers plying across the Bristol Channel to call and provide some more passengers to justify the investment in the railway. The branch, 9¾ miles long, leaves the Bristol & Exeter main line at the suburban station of Parson Street, and runs in a tunnel

BRIDGING THE GAP
With Brunel's suspension bridge in the background, ex-GWR railcar
No W23W heads for Portishead watched by some keen trainspotters
on the wrong side of the fence. *George F. Heiron*

In 1954 the construction of Portishead 'B' power station (now demolished) required the relocation of the station, and a long (12-coach) island platform was provided, together with an attractive modern station building in local limestone. Unfortunately the platforms were built on a base of fly ash and on a marsh, which caused subsidence, and for some time services were concentrated on a shorter length of one platform.

Then in 1962 the Sunday service was withdrawn and, as part of a major reduction in services in the Bristol area, weekday services were cut to six trains each way per day during the morning and evening peaks only. The line appeared in the list of closures in the Beeching Report, and the Urban District Council at Portishead was quick off the mark with a letter of objection to the Minister dated 5 April 1963, just nine days after the report had been published. This highlighted the inadequate road link to Bristol, the poor bus service and the likely effect on tourism if the line were lost. It noted that the station was still relatively new and, with a rare flash of gallows humour, said that 'it would seem ironic to close this station before the stonework of the station buildings has had time to mellow.'

The closure case had not been particularly well prepared by BR, and even the Ministry did not believe the figures provided. The original submission to the Minister referred to originating revenue of £6,100 and direct costs of £16,100. Further details were then provided and the contributory revenue also turned out to be £6,100. The Ministry officials dealing with the case recorded that, 'The Working Party noted with mild scepticism the identical figures for 'earnings' and for 'contributory gross revenue'.'[205]

The working party also gave short shrift to the needs of Portishead as a seaside resort, saying that 'the holiday trade aspect was not vital in this case'. The Divisional Roads Engineer advised that closure of the line would not present any problem, despite the views of the Ministry of Housing and Local Government. Indeed, a prophetic word of warning was sounded by that Ministry in a memo dated 30 December 1963. Referring to Portishead, it was noted that, 'Its population is expected to increase from its 1961 figure of 6,500 to 10,000 in 1981. The roads are tortuous and inadequate to cope with the increase in traffic which is likely; there is already considerable commuting between the two towns in both directions.' Growth was likely to continue because of the shortage of land in Bristol resulting from green belt restrictions.[206]

These warnings were duly noted and ignored by the Ministry, and consent to closure was given by Ernest Marples and notified on 16 July 1964.

This was a classic case where earlier economies in pruning the train service had resulted in a very low passenger base (the census for

underneath the Clifton suspension bridge and along the Avon gorge to Portishead, where the river meets the Bristol Channel. Initially single line and broad gauge, expanding traffic resulted in the line being doubled as far as Clifton Bridge in 1883, and subsequently additional loops were added to that at Pill: at Portbury Shipyard, when this was built during the First World War, and at Oakwood in 1929, built to support a half-hourly train service between Portishead and Ashton Gate. From 1906, a goods line branched off at Ashton Gate Junction on the up side to serve the city centre goods depots of Canons Marsh and Wapping Wharf, the latter line continuing back underneath St Mary Redcliffe churchyard to Temple Meads. At Portishead, between 1907 and 1940, the line connected with the Weston, Clevedon & Portishead Light Railway.

The line enjoyed a more frequent service of local passenger trains (roughly hourly) from the introduction of diesel units in the Bristol area, and from 1958, and on Saturdays, a mixed steam and diesel service ran at half-hourly intervals for part of the day. Ashton Gate Platform served the nearby Bristol City football ground and was particularly busy on match days. Goods traffic was carried to Portishead Dock, and a principal flow from the 1950s was coal from Radstock to Portishead power station (see later).

ASHTON GATE PLATFORM
A DMU picks up passengers for Portishead while Standard 2-6-2T No 82037 of Bristol (Bath Road) depot heads for Temple Meads on 7 June 1960. On the right are the goods lines to Canons Marsh and Wapping Wharf. The station served the Bristol City football ground. *R. E. Toop*

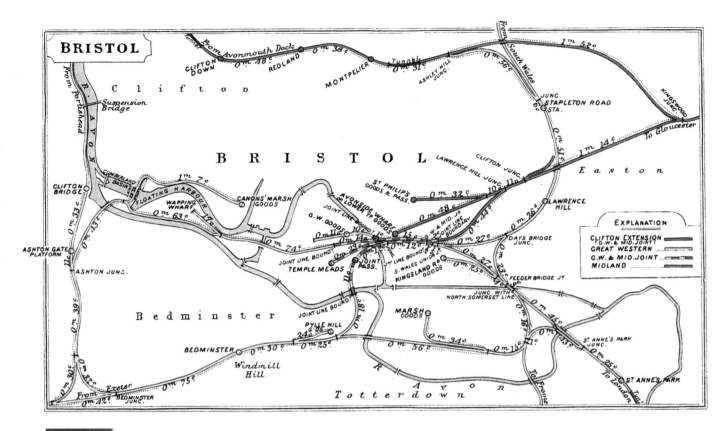

SOMERSET COAL
A Radstock to Portishead coal train approaches Clutton in 1960, just after the line had lost its passenger service. The locomotive is ex-GWR 'Prairie' tank No 5104 of St Philips Marsh. *Chris Austin*

the Heads of Information showed no train carrying more than 50 passengers). The alternative bus service was frequent – every 20 minutes – but at peak times took an incredible 102 minutes for the journey, compared with 30 minutes by train. Even so, the closure consent required three additional morning peak buses and five in the evening peak. The limitations of the A369 and the forecast growth in the area were ignored.

Passenger services on the line were withdrawn from 7 September 1964, although football specials continued to run from the Bristol end as far as Ashton Gate until 1977. Freight continued to be carried until 1981, after which the line had no regular traffic, but was used for steam excursions as part of the GW150 celebrations in 1985.

As early as 1966 the dynamic Urban District Council at Portishead was again writing to the Minister, asking her to give serious consideration to reopening the line for passengers because 'The result of all these pressures on the one road link between this part of North Somerset and Bristol is that it becomes heavily over-burdened during peak traffic hours…' The Ministry's classic response was that '…the Minister has no power under the Transport Act 1962 to withdraw a consent which has already been given to the closure of a railway line or station or to require the restoration of a service or the reopening of a station' (see Chapter 1). However, the writer went on to say on behalf of Barbara Castle that 'if national and regional plans show a real need for reopening a closed line, she will take whatever steps are necessary to meet the situation.'[207]

In April 1969 Portbury Parish Council wrote in similar vein, and pleaded for a return of rail services 'so that an adequate, reliable passenger service can be provided for the general public in the area between Portishead and Bristol.' The problem was the unreliability of the bus service, and an hourly railcar service 'would be fully justified on financial and ethical (*sic*) grounds.'[208] It received a similar reply.

In both cases the arguments for restoring passenger trains were that the line was still there for freight. That continued to be the case until the last traffic ceased to pass in 1981.

The opening of the Royal Portbury Dock led to the restoration of the line at a cost of £21 million, part funded by the SRA, in 2002, and

today this carries trainloads of imported cars as well as imported coal. It is operated as a long single line with no intermediate signalling or crossing loops. About 2½ miles of line from Portbury Dock Junction into Portishead remains unrestored.

Portishead has expanded hugely since the loss of its railway as a result of its attractive location, with thousands of houses spreading over the hills behind the town from which there are spectacular views over the Bristol Channel. The opening of the M5 and the Avon Bridge provided easy access from the town to Avonmouth and the industrial complex of Severnside. It also brought Bristol Parkway within easy reach in the early years before traffic congestion extended journey times. Its population rose from 6,500 in 1961, before the railway closed, to 22,000 today, and has grown by 50% over the last 20 years. Further growth of 8,000 is planned over the next three years, and the rate of growth has outstripped other towns in the area.

The town is close to Junction 19 on the M5, which is so busy that there are frequent tailbacks, blocking the slip roads and even the M5 itself, a classic example of poorly planned local developments resulting in unconstrained local traffic demand adversely affecting the strategic road network. The A369 road to Bristol has been improved at great cost since rail passenger services were withdrawn in 1964, but remains a single-carriageway road and is hopelessly inadequate at peak times. A high-quality local bus service, with Wi-Fi, operates every 15 minutes between Portishead and Bristol, but still takes a scheduled 52 minutes, or more if the traffic is bad, compared with a reliable 17-minute potential journey time on the train.

There is a clear case to restore passenger trains to Portishead in terms of reducing congestion, improving safety, in environmental terms and in support of economic development. What has prevented this from happening before? As we have seen, lobbying began as early 21 months after closure, but it was really in the late 1990s that the prospects of restoring the line for freight reawakened strong interest in bringing back passenger trains. The SRA was initially expected to support the project, but was not funded to do so. At that stage it was paying the huge bills resulting from the Railtrack collapse and was focussed on rescuing the major projects that had run out of control, such as the West Coast Main Line upgrade and the power supply strengthening required for new electric trains in South East England. Funding was also cut back by Government at this stage, eliminating all discretionary expenditure for the organisation. Avon County Council had long since disappeared, while North Somerset was a small and poorly resourced organisation in terms of sponsoring a major new railway project. Worst of all, the opportunity was lost to secure financial support from the huge housing and retail developments taking place in the town through Section 106 agreements to support the return of the trains.

The position today, however, is far more promising. The local authorities around Bristol are working together to promote Metro West, a revived suburban network for Bristol, and Portishead is its first priority for a reopened line. Funding has been agreed by DfT and local authorities, and work on vegetation clearance has been undertaken to allow detailed estimates on the cost of reinstatement to be made. North Somerset has defined the station location, and the target date for reopening is 2019. The result should put Portishead on track to a successful future and at last offer its residents a civilised alternative to the daily ordeal of driving to work in Bristol.

Bristol-Frome, and the Henbury loop

The Great Western Railway had a deservedly high reputation for running its express trains, its responsiveness to the demands of its freight customers and the picturesque nature of its rural branch lines, but not for running suburban services. Together with the LMS, it operated a comprehensive network of lines around Bristol but without the frequency or clockface departures of railways like the Southern. Specific flows were well catered for, such as workers at the Fry's chocolate factory at Keynsham & Somerdale, which enjoyed through trains from Henbury and north Bristol as well as from Temple Meads, known as the 'Fry's Angels' trains. A significant flow of aircraft workers used North Filton Platform to get to work at the Bristol Aeroplane Company (later BAE Systems), as did workers at Avonmouth Dock and, of course, the office workers around Temple Meads. Post-war development took the focus away from Temple Meads towards the centre and Broadmead areas of the city, and Bristol's main station was out on a limb during the 1960s and 1970s.

The Portishead line is covered in detail above, but another Bristol local line, now long forgotten, which would have formed a valuable commuter route today, was the North Somerset line from Frome and Radstock to Bristol. The country stations it served at Pensford, Clutton, Paulton (served by Hallatrow station) and Midsomer Norton are now commuter towns generating many thousands of car commuting trips to Bristol each day along the A37. When the line closed to passengers in 1959, development was just starting on a huge housing scheme at Stockwood, near Whitchurch, through which the trains ran without stopping. The line was used extensively during the Second World War for diverted trains when the main line was closed near Bath following bombing raids, and it would today have also formed a useful diversionary route for Bristol to Portsmouth or Weymouth services (or for diverted cross-country services) during engineering works or emergencies, as an alternative to the congested route via Bath.

At closure there was some criticism by the TUCC that BR had not even tried to run a more effective service with diesel units, and it is true that the line slipped through the Bristol suburbs unnoticed and few of the local residents knew where the trains went or how quick and cheap they were. The line survived until 1968 carrying coal from Writhlington Colliery at Radstock to Portishead power station, but after that date trains were diverted via Westbury until the closure of the colliery in 1973 and conversion of the power station to oil-firing. The southern end of the line survives to serve Whatley Quarry and the track remains in place as far north as Radstock, with a number of failed attempts over the years to revive it for passenger services. Sadly, however, the valuable part of the route, linking Radstock with Bristol, has long gone, leaving the magnificent 16-arch viaduct at Pensford as its memorial. Today the line is hard to find and has faded from local memory, seeming as remote in time as the Wansdyke, the ancient British earthwork it follows for part of its length.

The other Bristol route with potential for use again is the Henbury loop (Filton Abbey Wood to Avonmouth). The Severn Beach line and local services on the main line around Bristol have seen phenomenal growth over the last decade as people flock back to the railway to avoid the congested roads and expensive city centre parking. Also important are the comparative journey times. Yate to Temple Meads, for example, takes 20 minutes by train, 64 minutes by bus, and 45 minutes by car during the morning peak, with a great deal of uncertainty over the actual arrival time by car. The Metro West proposals cover the Henbury loop, are timely and deserve to be successful.

Leeds-Wetherby

The Yorkshire market town of Wetherby was served by three lines, but ended up with little more than a token service following years of retrenchment, and inclusion in the Beeching list was inevitable.

Today's traveller from Leeds to Harrogate might wonder why the railway climbs the east side of the Wharfe valley beyond Pannal, then turns sharp left to cross Crimple Viaduct. On the right, houses now obscure the track of the old railway and the entrance to Prospect Tunnel and the former line to Wetherby. This was the first line to reach Harrogate, and the line through Pannal used to head up the valley to Starbeck, while the spur linking the two is today's main line.

THIRTY MINUTES FROM LEEDS
Passengers alight from the 5.35pm train from Leeds City to Harrogate via Wetherby at the rural station of Bardsey. This is now Grange Road, a housing development. *J. M. Rayner*

The town was connected to the railway network as early as 1848 on a branch of the York & North Midland Railway engineered by George Stephenson, running from Church Fenton to Harrogate. Almost 30 years later, in 1876, a new line built by the North Eastern Railway was opened from Cross Gates on the Leeds-Selby line to Wetherby, where it joined the Church Fenton to Harrogate line, and in 1902 a new station was built on this line that could be served by direct Harrogate-Leeds trains. The original Wetherby station on the Church Fenton line remained as a goods depot.

Train services ran from Leeds to Wetherby and Harrogate, with some trains running fast to Wetherby and continuing beyond Harrogate to Northallerton or Newcastle. The Church Fenton route offered a service out and back from Leeds via Wetherby and Tadcaster. Wetherby racecourse had its own station and many racegoers arrived by train.

Like the Didcot, Newbury & Southampton route, the Church Fenton line performed an essential role during the Second World War, when a large ordnance factory was built on an extended site near Thorp Arch in 1941/42. Building materials were brought in by rail and a circular railway ran round the site with four platforms to allow workers to leave the train as close as possible to their part of the factory. Carriage sidings were also laid out within the site. At its peak, 18,000 people were employed there, most arriving and departing by train each day. After the war, the site was retained to provide ammunition for the forces until the last of the unadvertised workmen's trains ran in 1958. Today the site is occupied by a retail park, the northern reading room of the British Library and a prison, and many of the original buildings (but not the railway) remain.

Around 1951 the services were reduced to run only at peak periods between Leeds, Wetherby and Harrogate, and on the Church Fenton route only a token service survived to the end. The 07.44 from Church Fenton to Leeds City via Tadcaster and Wetherby was the only passenger train on the line, and there was no return working. With just half a dozen daily passengers, the train served little purpose, but the line did survive for goods trains to Wetherby until 1966.

The three lines to Wetherby were the first listed in the Beeching Report to be taken through the process and closed following its publication. On other lines closed in the latter part of 1963 (such as the Severn Valley), the process had been started prior to the Report's publication. Staff consultation took place as early as 24 May 1963, just six weeks after the publication of the 'Reshaping' report. Earnings of £13,700 were set against expenses of £57,500. The lines had six signal boxes and three staffed level crossings, and all the stations were staffed. A total of 50 people were employed on the lines as well as four drivers, a fireman and a guard, whose jobs would go with closure. There were also four station masters, one of whom, together with other traffic staff and footplate crew, would stay on to work the goods service from Church Fenton to Wetherby. The route from Crimple Junction to Cross Gates would lose its goods service and with it £1,815 of revenue for carrying a wide range of agricultural products and coal.

The figures make depressing reading. Only 27 passengers are shown as travelling between Wetherby and Leeds on the busiest train in the census, with a total of 964 daily journeys on the three lines.

Staff side pointed out the recent work between Cross Gates and Crimple Junction, which had replaced ash ballast with stone. Tadcaster Rural District Council and Leeds City Council objected to the closure, as did Barwick in Elmet parish council, but, surprisingly, Wetherby RDC could find no reason to do so.

The TUCC hearing found that hardship would arise only in isolated cases. There was, after all, a half-hourly bus service and the West Yorkshire Road Car Company was willing to run duplicate services as required at peak periods. Ministerial approval was given in a letter of 18 October 1963 and the public announcement was made on 24 October.[209] All passenger services were withdrawn on 6 January 1964, and the line from Crimple Junction to Cross Gates was closed completely on 27 April.

In 1961 Wetherby was a small market town on the Great North Road, with a population of 4,179, which had declined over the previous decade. Since then, however, it has grown steadily with many of its residents commuting to Leeds. Numbers almost doubled over the following decade and today stand at 11,155 for the town and 19,979 for the wider area covered by the ward. The town is now bypassed by the A1(M) and is served by four buses an hour to Leeds and two to Harrogate. Four buses an hour is often an indication that demand is strong enough for a rail service.

The comparison today is with the lines to Ilkley (population 14,800) and Skipton (population 14,300), both now electrified and very busy suburban routes feeding into the thriving powerhouse of Leeds. Had its railway survived, Wetherby too would be playing its part in meeting Leeds's transport needs, as well as providing an alternative route to Harrogate. How useful that would have been during the months of closure while major repairs were carried out to Bramhope Tunnel.

East Lancashire and North Yorkshire

A number of the suburban lines built by the Lancashire & Yorkshire Railway west of the Pennines and centred on Manchester have survived and prospered under the Greater Manchester PTE, now Transport for Greater Manchester.[210] However, many Lancashire lines were lost between the 1950s and 1970s, and while some closures (the former Cheshire Lines Committee route to Southport, for example) were inevitable, others removed valuable connections and the lines would today form a useful link in the rail network of North West England.

Southport to Preston

This was an important link between two significant Lancashire towns (Preston became a city in 2002) as well as serving the small towns and villages in between. The journey now has to be either by bus or a circuitous rail journey via Liverpool, so most people drive. The line appeared in the Beeching Report and, after the formalities had been concluded, closed to all traffic on 7 September 1964. Arrangements were put in hand to start track recovery three weeks later, on the 26th. The rolling stock savings from closure give an indication of the relative inefficiency with which the lines were run, and in this case were three gangwayed coaches, 21 non-gangwayed coaches, and two three-car electric multiple units – a total of 30 vehicles, together with the steam locomotives to haul the coaches (not quantified).

The train service was approximately hourly, with additional services on the electrified section between Southport and Crossens operated by EMUs. A reasonable low-cost alternative between Southport and Preston could have been provided by three two-car DMUs and would have maintained most of the revenue, saving 80% of the rolling stock costs, but nothing like this was considered.

Illustrating the depressing context of the time, the future of the EMUs was uncertain on closure, as even the busy principal route between Liverpool Exchange and Southport was being appraised for closure. Southport-Preston was to have been but a dress rehearsal for the main performance.

Conditions of closure required local operator Ribble to provide additional bus services as well as a bus shelter at Tarleton. Throughout October 1964 the Transport Users' Consultative Committee for the North West received a high level of complaints about the buses, both on reliability (Ribble was hit by industrial action at the time) and overcrowding, with examples of passengers (including schoolchildren) being left behind as full buses swept past. Lack of information on delayed buses was a further cause of complaint.

As on other lines, the principal players were quick to pass on this hot potato. The TUCC responded that its role finished when its report was made to the Minister. 'The ministry were not in a position to assist in matters of this kind as, once the Consent had been issued, the matter passed out of their hands.'[211] However, both the TUCC and the Ministry agreed that 'this question was one for the Railways Board to deal with'. Schoolchildren left behind by full buses or stranded when buses were cancelled were for the local education authority to sort out.

Despite the complaints immediately following closure, the replacement buses were not well used as time went on, and on 5 December 1966 the Ministry approved their withdrawal. People appear to have voted with their feet and to have got into their or other peoples' cars.

The track from Hesketh Bank to Southport was recovered, and some of it was sold to CIE[212]. The estimated values of this section of line illustrate the volatility involved in planning because of uncertainties on the cost of removal and the market fluctuations in the price of scrap metal. Originally estimated to be worth a net £21,732 on 4 November 1964, the value had increased to £55,840 just 15 days later when a revised estimate was provided by the Chief Civil Engineer.[213] In fact, the recovery of track and signalling netted £67,956.

Meanwhile, the eastern part of the line had a brief reprieve as the Central Electricity Generating Board planned to build a number of new coal-fired power stations at this time, and two possible sites at Much Hoole and New Longton on the Lancashire coast were reasonably close to the line. So, east of Hesketh Bank, the track was left in situ. As CEGB decisions on new power stations were taking time to be made, BR decided to lift the rest of the track, arguing reasonably that it was in poor condition and would require relaying anyway if it were to be used for heavy coal traffic. A letter of 'no objection' to this course of action was sent by the Ministry on 21 May 1965. In a letter of 21 October 1966, CEGB indicated that, whatever site was chosen, the new power station was likely to be fuelled by a nuclear power rather than coal. A nuclear plant could be served from a nearby railhead and would not require the line to be retained. Nevertheless, it was agreed that the formation would be retained in BR ownership both for potential CEGB traffic and because the Ministry wanted it for access to a proposed Leyland/ Chorley new town development. This latter embargo was not lifted until August 1972. In the event the nuclear power station was built at Heysham rather than Much Hoole or New Longton.

Today there is still a gap in West Lancashire's rail network between two of its principal towns, and there is no doubt that the line would provide a valuable and congestion-free link if it had remained. It would have become part of the West Lancashire community rail partnership and would be as valuable as the Southport-Wigan-Manchester line. While the restoration of the line itself may no longer be affordable, a possible alternative has been put forward with the restoration of the Burscough curves. These would link the Southport-Manchester line at Burscough Bridge (an excellent modern interchange sponsored by Lancashire) with the Ormskirk-Preston line. While it would not serve the smaller intermediate communities such as Longton, it would link the two towns effectively and attract many more journeys from the busy A565 road.

Manchester to Skipton

The first railway to reach Accrington was opened by the East Lancashire Railway in 1848, with a line from Stubbins Junction on the Bury to Rawtenstall line to Accrington, whence branches ran west to Blackburn and east to Burnley and Colne. The line was served by trains from Manchester Victoria to Colne from 1849, with two running through to Skipton via the Midland Railway route beyond Colne, which was also opened in 1848 (see below). From 1876 the Lancashire & Yorkshire Railway worked the through trains between Manchester and Skipton with its own locomotives, and from 1881 until 1964 a relatively frequent service of through trains was run. Then, from 7 September 1964, restructuring of the north Manchester suburban services to save money and eliminate steam suburban trains involved rerouting the Skipton and Colne trains via Bolton and Blackburn. A DMU shuttle service was introduced between Bury and Accrington with a limited number of peak trains from Manchester. Notice of the intention to close the Stubbins Junction to Accrington section of line was published the following month.

Earnings of £58,000 (including contributory revenue) were matched by total expenses of £79,700, suggesting a loss of £21,700. However, financial details provided to the Minister indicated that much of the revenue would be retained by the rerouted services, so the estimated revenue loss was reduced to £25,000, producing a net saving of £54,700.[214]

The short section of line between Stubbins Junction and Accrington was 7½ miles long and very steeply graded, with a ruling gradient of 1 in 38 on the climb from the Accrington direction towards the summit at Baxenden. Two intermediate stations had been closed in 1951 and 1960, leaving Helmshore as the only intermediate station to be closed on the route. Of the 1,266 passengers using the line, it was estimated that 579 would use the rerouted services. The line was closed in 1966 and much of it has disappeared under development, although the stretch climbing towards Baxenden summit from the site of Stubbins Junction, just north of Ramsbottom, can be seen from today's East Lancashire heritage railway.

Further north, the line from Skipton to Colne was built by the Midland Railway, even though the Lancashire & Yorkshire operated

through trains from Manchester to Skipton from 1876 onwards. This section of double-track railway was not listed for closure in the Beeching Report, and indeed the maps showed it as in the busier category with more than 10,000 passengers and 10,000 tons of freight passing per week. Despite this the line was put up for closure as a result of the unwillingness of the Ministry of Transport to pay grant aid for it under the provisions of the Transport Act 1968. Without support and with an estimated revenue of £6,000 against the claimed costs of £106,000 and no remaining freight traffic, it was unsurprising that BR advertised the proposed closure of the line at the end of 1968. Only 37 objections were received and the passenger census figures make depressing reading, with a maximum of 288 passengers using the line on the busiest day (Saturday), and only 39 'regular' passengers. While the TUCC found evidence of severe hardship, it thought this could be partly alleviated by diverting the X94 bus to serve Colne railway station. The Minister (Fred Mulley) gave consent to close, but did not make any direction as to buses.

Nevertheless, the case is interesting in that the TUCC heard important evidence from both the local MP for Nelson and Colne, David Waddington[215], and from Lancashire County Council in relation to the potential effect of closure on the local economy and on prospects for regeneration.[216] Inevitably, this went well beyond the scope of the TUCC's remit, which was focussed on hardship to individual existing passengers, so was not material to its consideration and recommendations. The Minister, as we have seen, chose to ignore this in reaching his decision, but it is reflected in the prospectus of SELRAP (Skipton East Lancashire Rail Action Partnership), the lobby group seeking the reopening of this line today.

Waddington asked the committee to consider the 'wider implications of closure on trade including, for example, the effect on trade and prospects for industrial expansion.' Better communication was a prerequisite for growth, he said, and referred to the importance of a link road from the Calder Valley towns to the M6. Closing the railway 'would mean even further isolation of the area and the disappearance of one more amenity which could influence the thinking of those – industries and individuals – who are wondering whether to come to the area…'

The Assistant Solicitor of Lancashire, Mr R. W. Bradley, urged that there should be no closure until 'all transport facilities and requirements in the county have been properly surveyed and coordinated.' With funding coming to encourage development of sites around the proposed link road, he nevertheless urged the retention of the railway even if it was at present uneconomic 'if the slow strangulation of road traffic on inadequate roads is to be avoided.'

The line was closed on 2 February 1970.

In its latest publication (*At a Glance, 2014*) SELRAP makes much of a study it commissioned in 2013 from the consulting engineers, designers, planners and project managers Arup. By February 2014 two parts of the study had been completed. Findings included

- A reduction in base costs for reopening the line – single track £38 million, double track £72 million.
- 414,000 new passenger journeys would be made by reopening Skipton-Colne and new stations at Earby and at West Craven Parkway (for Barnoldswick), rising to £620,000 within 10 years.

• The Benefit Cost Ratio (BCR) for a single-track scheme (which would allow for a half-hourly service between Leeds and Rose Grove) would be 1.52:1 with median passenger demand – it reaches 6.56 if demand for travel is 30% greater than that anticipated. The BCR would be higher if there were long-distance and inter-regional journeys or new freight traffic attracted to the line.

SELRAP is now appealing for funds to finance the third stage of the Arup research, which it hopes will lead to the reopening being included in a GRIP (Governance for Railway Investment Projects) stage 3 evaluation. It claims support from 198 MPs, 49 MEPs, 'more than 500 councils within the wider corridor of the Skipton-Colne rail line', and 150 businesses and trade associations.[217]

Like so many of the closures we cover in this book, Skipton to Colne is one that should not have taken place, and should now be reversed, at least on the basis of SELRAP's proposal for a single-track railway.

SELRAP rightly draws attention to the benefits flowing from the reopening of the Todmorden curve, to the south of Colne, which is making a 45-minute journey from Manchester to Burnley possible, and improving links to the Colne branch as a result of new interchange facilities at Rose Grove. Journey times from Colne to Leeds, however, will remain at 2hr 50min without the reopening to Skipton (which would bring them down to under an hour).

A further telling comparison is provided by looking at relative property prices. SELRAP says that the average in Colne is just £110,000, whereas the figure for Skipton, at the end of the electrified Airedale route used by seven million people a year, is £210,000.

It is a universal truth that investment in better rail services enhances economic activity across the board, and this is particularly marked in the case of house values.

Skipton to Embsay and Bolton Abbey

The transformation in the quality and extent of passenger services to Skipton has been remarkable, with the electrification of what is now a busy commuter route to Leeds and Bradford, and the reprieve of the Midland main line from Settle to Carlisle. As we have seen, the campaign for the reinstatement of the service between Skipton and Colne has a considerable head of steam behind it, and the reopening may come about within the next decade.

While on a different scale, and serving a different market, the reconnection of Skipton with the Embsay & Bolton Abbey Steam Railway heritage line also has an articulate and dedicated following. This line was originally part of the through route from Skipton to Ilkley, and closed in accordance with the Beeching Report recommendations in 1965. Beeching had also proposed the closure of both routes to Ilkley (from Leeds and Bradford), but the former was finally refused in 1972, and Ilkley too has now become part of the West Yorkshire electrified commuter network.

Protagonists for the Skipton to Embsay reopening have a modest, and relatively inexpensive, proposal. They wish to reinstate Embsay

Junction, which is on the freight-only Grassington branch, which serves Swinden quarry. They claim it would cost no more than £3 million and – according to consultants JMP Ltd – would 'over a ten-year period create nearly £3 million of employment during the construction and operation of the railway and nearly £9 million in additional spend in the area. Additionally it suggests there could be £57,000 of additional volunteer spend and up to half a million pounds of additional railway spend in the area.'[218]

The plan would be to run into the disused Platform 5 at Skipton station, and a further interesting – and unusual – feature of the campaign is that it is not seen as an opportunity to extend the operation of steam trains on the Bolton Abbey to Embsay line into Skipton. Instead the campaigners are proposing to run a diesel service operated by Class 142 'Pacers' to take passengers arriving at Skipton off the main line (from the north and the south) into the Yorkshire Dales National Park, and provide an alternative for the thousands of day-trippers who come in by car.

This would be an excellent example of the way a heritage railway could provide a useful new public transport service, of the sort recommended by the report of the heritage rail all-party parliamentary group, 'The Value of Heritage Railways', published in July 2013.[219]

Derby-Sinfin

Ironically, it was in Derby, that celebrated centre of railway excellence, where the reopening of a line proved to be a failure. The proposition was simple enough, and a brave experiment at a time when closures were still taking place and the climate for reopening lines was not favourable. In the early 1970s traffic congestion in Derby was acute during peak periods, and some of this was caused by a strong north-south flow from Duffield and Belper (north of the city) to a number of employers around Peartree and Sinfin to the south. The former stations were on the residual Matlock to Derby local service, and the latter were served by a freight line, which had formerly gone through to Chellaston Junction, but by then had been cut back to Sinfin. Funded by the County Council, the closed platforms at Peartree & Normanton were reopened, modest new platforms were built at Sinfin North and Sinfin Central, and the track and signalling was upgraded to carry passenger services. The new service of two trains a day was introduced in 1976, but never really took off. The city's declining industrial base meant that the factories and workshops served by the new stations were closing or reducing the number of staff they employed. The principal site at Sinfin Central was within the Rolls Royce complex and not accessible for the general public.

The service was cut back to one a day in 1992, and withdrawn the following year when 'Sprinters' were introduced on the Matlock service, being replaced by a taxi service, because the new trains were incompatible with the track circuits in use on the branch. Formal closure took place in 1998. The line remains open for freight.

Peartree station remains open, with a limited service provided by Crewe-Derby trains.

10

CUTTING CITY CENTRE STATIONS

'My own belief is that it is possibly too good for its purpose...'

SIR GEORGE GILBERT SCOTT ON THE ST PANCRAS STATION HOTEL,
OF WHICH HE WAS THE ARCHITECT[220]

The great railway stations are the gateway to the cities they serve, and part of the rich fabric of the 19th-century built environment, together with the town hall, the municipal art gallery and the great public institutions of 19th-century Britain. One such, the Newcastle Philosophical & Literary Society, was also the library that provided much of the material for the education of Robert Stephenson, who subsequently built the impressive station next door, designed by John Dobson.

Rolt wrote that the railways 'represent a colossal outpouring of creative energy unmatched by any other age; the embodiment of the pride, the hope and the aspiration of a pioneer generation expressed in the cyclopean masonry of arch and pier, and in the smoke blackened architectural splendour of the great stations. Such stations with their iron arcades and high vaulting of glass and slender roof rib are temples consecrated to an unquestioning faith in material progress.'[221]

The number of cities prior to 1923 with a single station was relatively small, and was normally found where one railway had a geographical monopoly. On the North Eastern Railway, Newcastle, Durham, Ripon and York[222] are the examples. On the London & North Western, it was Bangor, Salford, Lichfield and Coventry, while the Great Eastern alone served Ely, the North Staffordshire Stoke on Trent, the London & South Western Southampton, the LB&SCR Chichester[223], and the Great Western Truro. Single joint stations existed in cities including Aberdeen, Bristol, Carlisle, Hereford and Perth.

Indeed, it is surprising, perhaps, that more joint stations were not established in the early 20th century, when capital was available and growth was substantial. In America, despite strong competition between companies, many cities were served by Union stations shared by a number of railroads. Washington, Chicago and Los Angeles are but three dispersed examples of a common phenomenon. In Britain, some cities did indeed have joint stations, as shown above, but in most two or more were a feature of the railway until the 1960s and even beyond. Some remain for reasons of capacity or railway geography, including some quite small towns like Dorchester, Gainsborough and Dorking. Others are sorely missed as the residual capacity remains inadequate, like Nottingham, Oxford and Gloucester, the latter described in more detail below.

So, most cities and towns had more than one station, as well as some other very small settlements indeed, like Crianlarich, Kirkby Stephen, Builth Road and Savernake. Up until its last edition appeared in May 1961, *Bradshaw's Guide* contained a helpful list of distances between 'Stations in the same Town or between Stations serving the same Places'. Outside London the furthest apart were in Lincolnshire – Little Bytham and Castle Bytham ('2¼ miles'), where the number of interchange passengers must have been very small indeed.

This duplication was almost entirely due to competition between the companies, and on this basis, with the grouping of the railways into the Big Four in 1923 and particularly with the formation of British Railways in 1948, it would have been reasonable to expect rationalisation to take place and the number of main-line stations to be reduced by diverting trains from one into the alternative. However, it was not as simple as that. In some cases the connecting lines required did not exist, while in others the numbers of trains and passengers to be dealt with exceeded the capacity of any one station on its own.

From the 1950s onwards, however, an inevitable corollary of the retrenchment of local rail services and duplicate routes was the loss of major stations in cities outside London. Strenuous efforts were made to concentrate all remaining services on a single station to serve each city or major town both to save costs and release valuable city centre sites for redevelopment, as well as to improve connections between remaining services. This was done at a time when the financial pressures from Government to cut costs and release under-used public-sector land were intense, and it was quite impossible to conceive of the sort of rail growth that was experienced from 1995 onwards. Indeed, further decline seemed inevitable when the key decisions were made in the 1950s, '60s and '70s.

However, subsequent growth has indeed exceeded the capacity of the remaining stations, which can no longer handle either the numbers of trains being run or the numbers of passengers passing through them. In some cities, such as Birmingham, abandoned stations have been reinstated. In others, like Leeds, major investment has been required to provide additional capacity at the remaining station.

Apart from cost-saving, the resulting simplification certainly made travelling easier for passengers initially. Changing trains is an unwelcome complication in any journey, but having to change stations is even worse. Where services to the same destination left from different stations, the complexity could be baffling, as we illustrate below at Leeds.

A feature of this era of retrenchment involved moving stations to release sites for development. This was generally to the disbenefit of the passenger who had further to walk from the train, but it also removed the station from a prominent location on the high street or sea front. The picture of Morecambe illustrates this well, but it also affected a number of other terminal stations such as Blackpool North, Exmouth, Falmouth (later reinstated), Felixstowe, Fort William, Looe and Wrexham Central.

London stations

It is significant that attempts to reduce the number of terminal stations in London have met with relatively little success. At various times proposals have been made to close Marylebone, with trains being diverted to Paddington and Baker Street. Similarly, a plan was formulated to close St Pancras, with suburban services diverted to Moorgate and main-line services to King's Cross. Neither came to fruition, and London retains its 14 main-line terminal stations as well as Thameslink, linking routes north and south. Only Broad Street was closed completely, with trains being diverted to Stratford and, for a brief period, Liverpool Street.

Remarkably, the North London Railway's Broad Street terminus had once been the third busiest in London behind Liverpool Street and Victoria, carrying three million passengers a year from its nine platforms. For a period, it was even the starting point for an LNWR express service to Birmingham. But tram competition started to erode the suburban traffic after 1904, and each new underground line – Metropolitan, District, then the Northern, Bakerloo and Victoria – took more of the radial traffic on which this level of demand was built. The North London line has since found a strong role as an orbital route with a thriving and growing business base as part of London Overground, and remains an important freight route.

Moorgate has lost its platforms on the City Widened Lines to allow the expansion of Thameslink, while the Brighton side of London Bridge lost six platforms as part of the resignalling of 1976. Under the current redevelopment plans it will lose an additional platform but, crucially, gain three more through platforms for Thameslink trains. Holborn Viaduct (three platforms) was closed, although replaced by City Thameslink as a two-platform through station. The Brighton side of Victoria lost some platform capacity when the concourse was extended, and the old practice of 'northing and southing' (splitting platforms in two with a central crossover) was discontinued in the 1970s.

Contraction

Outside London, Manchester held the record at seven stations: London Road (now Piccadilly); Victoria; Central; Exchange; Mayfield; Oxford Road; and Deansgate.

Glasgow had four great stations until 1966: Central; Queen Street; St Enoch; and Buchanan Street. Central and Queen Street had both high- and low-level platforms.

Leicester too had no fewer than four stations until 1928: London Road; Central; Belgrave Road; and West Bridge.

There are many other cities and larger towns where the number of stations was reduced in the period of retrenchment in the 1960s and '70s, and these include Bath, Birkenhead, Birmingham, Blackpool, Bournemouth, Bury, Cardiff, Cheltenham, Chester, Derby, Dundee, Edinburgh, Glasgow, Gloucester, Lancaster, Leeds, Leicester, Lincoln, Manchester, Northampton, Norwich, Nottingham, Nuneaton, Peterborough, Plymouth, Reading, Sheffield, Southampton, Swansea, Swindon, Wells, Whitby, Wolverhampton and Yarmouth.

Dr Beeching addressed the issue head-on in his 'Reshaping' report in 1963:

'Competitive railway building in the past led not only to duplication of main arteries between some of the principal cities, but also to duplication of passenger stations and all the ancillary facilities such as carriage and cleaning sidings, motive power depots, buildings and equipment which go with large terminals. Very little has been done, so far, to rationalise the main line passenger services which use alternative routes and terminals, but it is clear, in many cases, that concentration on selected routes and stations would provide equal or better services and permit substantial economies.

For example, studies of the possibilities at Leeds and Bradford, each of which has two large stations, are at an advanced stage.'[224] (See below)

Expanding capacity

The principal towns and cities where the loss of a station or a reduction in its capacity in the 1960s and '70s has required investment to deal with subsequent capacity problems include

Bristol, Birmingham, Cardiff, Edinburgh, Gloucester, Leeds, Newport, Nottingham, Peterborough, Reading, Swindon and Wolverhampton as well as those in London, where additional platform capacity has already been provided at King's Cross, Marylebone, St Pancras and Waterloo.

The current Network Rail route studies consider increasing the number of platforms at many stations around the country, such as Oxford, Bedford, Bristol Parkway, Chesterfield, Derby, Nottingham, Ipswich, Norwich, Southampton, Winchester, Redhill and Gatwick Airport.

The next section looks at a number of examples in greater depth.

Birmingham

England's second city was the scene of retrenchment that, even at the time, looked like a step too far, and has since been followed by the recreation of most of the capacity wantonly destroyed in the 1970s. Even with the benefit of hindsight, it is hard to understand how such a situation could produce planning blight, inadequate transport and such a waste of public money with the complete closure and subsequent reopening of the former Great Western lines through the city's Snow Hill station.

New Street

The first railway to reach Birmingham was the Grand Junction from Warrington (where it joined the Liverpool & Manchester Railway) in

1837, initially using a terminus at Vauxhall, extending to a station adjacent to Curzon Street in 1839. This was closely followed by the London & Birmingham in 1838, built to the terminus at Curzon Street, which can still be seen from the train today.[225] The Birmingham & Gloucester[226] arrived in 1841, also using Curzon Street from the outset. The Birmingham & Derby Junction Railway opened in 1842 from its own terminus at Lawley Street, moving to Curzon Street in 1851.[227]

Three years later, in 1854, with the opening of the Birmingham, Wolverhampton & Stour Valley Railway, the LNWR opened its city centre station at New Street, to which the services at Curzon Street were transferred.

The great porticoed station building at Curzon Street remains on the site today as a memorial to this first great trunk route and as a reflection of the architecture of the original Euston station at the other end of the line. From 2026 the site will revert to its original purpose as it becomes the Birmingham terminus for HS2.[228]

New Street station was rebuilt at the time of the electrification of the West Coast Main Line between 1964 and 1966, and the Pallasades shopping centre, on a raft over the station, was completed in 1972. It was not a success and the stygian gloom of the platforms contrasted poorly with the light from the glazed station roof it replaced. The concourse was better, but the public areas became very crowded as passenger numbers grew in the 1990s and the following decade. It is now being rebuilt again with much more space and providing higher standards.

The elegant restored concourse at Birmingham Moor Street, where the Centenary Lounge uses GWR crockery, and express trains again depart for London. *Simon Clarke*

Snow Hill

The Birmingham & Oxford Railway[229] reached Birmingham in 1852, to a separate station at Snow Hill, extended to Wolverhampton by the opening of the Birmingham, Wolverhampton & Dudley Railway in 1854. Subsequent growth of suburban traffic, particularly associated with the opening of the North Warwickshire line, led to the building of a small suburban terminus at Moor Street in 1909.

While the electrification of the West Coast Main Line was under way, the principal route to London was from Snow Hill to Paddington, served by express trains including the 'Blue Pullmans', introduced in 1960 and offering a journey time of just 1hr 53min.[230] Indeed, the first use of 'Inter City' as a description of a fast and comfortable express service was in 1950 and applied to the 9.00am train from Paddington to Wolverhampton Low Level and the 4.25pm return. This reached Birmingham in 2hr 15min. The fastest service on the route in 1965 was only 1hr 52min by the 14.10 Paddington to Birkenhead train, hauled by a Class 52 'Western' diesel-hydraulic locomotive.

The GWR route north of Banbury was transferred from the Western Region to the London Midland Region from 1 January 1963. Snow Hill and its approach lines were not listed for closure in the Beeching Report, published on 27 March of the same year, but the following month the LMR announced that, following completion of the West Coast Main Line electrification from New Street to Euston, main-line services would be withdrawn from Snow Hill. Given the sensitivities at the time of the publication of the Report, and the undertaking by Beeching to hold over closure proposals to allow public debate following its publication, this is perhaps surprising.

The routes through Snow Hill were not listed for development in the second Beeching Report of February 1965.

With the loss of through trains or their diversion to New Street in March 1967, the short section of line in tunnel between Moor Street and Snow Hill was closed on 4 March 1968. Within the space of a year, the number of daily departures from Snow Hill had fallen from 181 to 10. For the following four years the only remaining services using the station were those 10 arrivals and 10 departures a day (operated by single-coach 'bubble cars' of Class 122), running to Wolverhampton Low Level (six) or Langley Green (four). Approval for their withdrawal was given by John Peyton as Conservative Transport Minister, and the service ended on 6 March 1972, after which Snow Hill station was disused.

The station buildings were demolished as unsafe in 1976-77.

Moor Street

This suburban terminus was on a spur and did not originally have platforms on the adjacent main line. Opened in 1909, it was designed to take pressure off Snow Hill following the opening of the North Warwickshire line the previous year and in anticipation of the traffic increase that would follow the completion of the 'cut-off' line from Ashendon Junction to Aynho, which would reduce the distance between Paddington and Birmingham by 17 miles, allowing journey times of 2 hours between the capital and the second city.

While not in the Beeching Report, plans to close the North Warwickshire line were developed and this would allow the remaining Leamington local trains to be diverted and Moor Street closed. Ministerial approval to close was secured, subject to the provision of alternative bus services and the date was set – Monday 5 March 1969.

However, this date was never met. Midland Red, the bus operator, was having trouble recruiting staff at the time and a number of local

cancellations cast doubts over its ability to provide the alternative services. The traffic commissioners granted the licences but a right of objection remained and was taken up. This meant that the issue had to be considered by the Secretary of State (who had also approved the closure), but this had not been dealt with as the closure date approached. The strength of local opposition resulted in the local authorities joining together and, through a local solicitor, Douglas King, applying for an injunction to prevent the line closing, and this was considered by a judge on 26 April and thrown out. The objectors appealed and on 1 May the case was considered by Lord Denning[231], Master of the Rolls, and two colleagues, and an injunction was granted on Friday 2 May. So, passengers going to work on the Friday were being told that the line would close, but on the Monday a full service was operated to and from Moor Street.

The bus licensing issue was expected to be dealt with by July and closure would follow, but the window of opportunity had been missed. The Ministry did not come to a conclusion, time went by and, despite pressure from BR, the strength of opposition was too great. The fledgling West Midlands PTE agreed to support the section of line within its boundaries and the group of local authorities under Douglas King continued to question BR on costs and how an affordable service might be provided. A freight train review with the Western Region had resulted in the North Warwickshire line carrying 11 freight trains each way, and these could not be rerouted via Lapworth because the Hatton to Bearley Junction route had just been singled. A major review of Birmingham area services was carried out by the London Midland Region in 1971 and the movements manager became concerned at the limited capacity of the route through Lapworth because of the pressure to run more Freightliner trains to and from Southampton.

Unfortunately this route had just been reduced from four tracks to two, an indication of the lack of forward planning that characterised so much of this period.

With the North Warwickshire line open, Moor Street was required, at least during the peak, so at the 11th hour the tide turned. Following the oil crisis of 1973 and the development of PTE plans, off-peak frequencies on the Leamington and Stratford lines were doubled in 1975, and a pattern of steady growth established that has led to the busy station that Moor Street is today. But it could all have been so very different.

In 1967 the capacity at the three central Birmingham stations was 12 platforms at New Street, 12 at Snow Hill and three at Moor Street, a total of 27 platforms. By the end of 1972 this had been almost halved to 14 platforms (12 at New Street and two at Moor Street).

Revival and growth

The West Midlands Passenger Transport Executive (now Centro) was established on 1 October 1969. As early as 1973 it proposed reopening Snow Hill, as part of a second cross-city line to complement the north-south Four Oaks to Longbridge service, and a scheme to do so received Government approval ten years later. Construction started in 1985 and services on the new route commenced on 5 October 1987. At the same time the three platforms at Moor Street were closed and replaced by two through platforms on the reinstated line to Snow Hill; this was the first time that trains had been able to serve both Moor Street and Snow Hill. To the north of Snow Hill, the 'Jewellery Line' to Smethwick West reopened on 25 September 1995 at a cost of £26 million. The timeline illustrates graphically the speed at which closure can be implemented compared with the years of planning, fundraising and implementation to reopen something destroyed in haste. Snow Hill took five years to die, and 12 to recreate as a through station. Like other great city stations such as Leeds Central (see later), it took decades for the abandoned site to be redeveloped.

The route to Wolverhampton was rebuilt as Line 1 of the Midland Metro, which opened on 31 May 1999. With 23 stations and a 6-minute frequency (compared with ten stations and six trains a day in the final BR service of 1972), this route is now pulling its weight in terms of meeting the transport needs of the Black Country.

Two of the three Moor Street terminal platforms were reinstated in 2010. The third remains to be reconnected. The extension of the Midland Metro to New Street, and later to Curzon Street, involves street running and the release of the fourth platform at Snow Hill, which will be restored to (heavy) rail use. The HS2 terminal at Curzon Street will have six platforms. So, by 2026 Birmingham's central stations will offer a total of 26 platforms, together with the capacity at the Midland Metro stops in the central area, appropriate for the needs of the 21st century and one short of the number existing prior to 1968.

Edinburgh

The first railway in the city was the Edinburgh & Dalkeith Railway of 1834, designed to bring coal from the pits of Monktonhall to burn in the homes of Auld Reekie.[232] Horse-drawn, with an incline worked by a stationary steam engine, its terminus was on the south side of the city at St Leonards, an early closure that became a coal depot until 1968.

The arrival of the Edinburgh & Glasgow Railway at Haymarket in 1842 was followed by extension of the line to Waverley in 1846 to meet the North British Railway from Berwick, opened in the same year. The extension was controversial, as it ran through Princes Street Gardens, then, as now, the pleasure gardens dividing the old medieval city from the Georgian new town to the north. Waverley station was built on the site of a loch. Between 1892 and 1902, with the increase in traffic following the opening of the Forth Bridge in 1890, the line from Haymarket was quadrupled and the station enlarged.

The Edinburgh, Leith & Granton Railway opened in 1843, with its Canal Street terminus at right angles to the North British line at Waverley, and is marked today by a notice behind Platform 20. The station was closed, leaving an abandoned tunnel under Princes Street when the route via Abbeyhill was opened in 1868.

The other route from Edinburgh to the south was the branch to Hawick, extended via the Border Union Railway to Carlisle in 1862.

The rivalry between the North British and Caledonian railways was intense and was partly responsible for driving not just the creation of two stations to serve Edinburgh, but two high-quality stations with excellent hotels attached, in keeping with the character of Princes Street, on which both were situated.

This rivalry partly stemmed from natural competitive pressures, which resulted in a network of competing lines throughout Scotland and culminated in the 'races to the north' in 1895, when both East and West Coast routes vied with each other to reach Kinnaber Junction first, on the headlong race from London to Aberdeen. There was strong competition too for traffic between Edinburgh and Perth, Edinburgh and Carlisle, and around Edinburgh, particularly to Leith (which had four stations) and Granton.

The other factor was that the Caledonian was a purely Scottish railway, running no further south than Carlisle and built with Scottish capital. The North British on the other hand was built with some English capital, one of the investors being George Hudson's York & North Midland Railway, and it also extended to operating railways in Northumberland, with running powers to Newcastle via Hexham, and its own line to Silloth in Cumberland. This added an edge to the competition and lasted well beyond 1923.[233]

The Caledonian Railway arrived from Carstairs at a terminus at Lothian Road in 1848, moving to its own Princes Street station, close to Haymarket, in 1870.

Both the North British and the Caledonian had an extensive suburban network from their respective stations, but many lines fell victim early on to tram and bus competition and the car. With closure dates given in brackets, trains ran from Waverley to Leith Central (1952), North Leith (1947), Granton (1925 – the year the Leith and Edinburgh tramways were combined, and through trams introduced), Gullane (1932), Haddington (1949), North Berwick (open and thriving today), Gifford (1933), the south suburban loop via Morningside Road (1962), Glencorse (1933), and Penicuik (1951), as well as the longer-distance services to Peebles (1962), Dolphinton (1933) and Galashiels on the Waverley Route (1969), to Bathgate (1956, reopened 1986), on the E&GR route to Falkirk and Stirling, and over the Forth Bridge to Fife as well as the short branch to Corstorphine (1968). No wonder Waverley became crowded at the end of the 19th century.

From Princes Street, Caledonian suburban trains ran to Leith

PRINCES STREET
The 1.25pm train from Stirling enters the smoke-blackened train shed of
Princes Street station on 20 July 1955. The locomotive is former Caledonian
Railway 4-4-0 No 54504 of Stirling shed. *G. M. Staddon/N. E. Stead collection*

(1962), Barnton (1951), Balerno (1943) and stations on the Shotts line (open today).

Both companies built excellent hotels adjacent to their stations, which survive and prosper as five-star establishments today. Most famous, perhaps, is the North British, now renamed the Balmoral, with its famous clock tower, thoughtfully showing the time 5 minutes fast for those hurrying to catch trains. The Caledonian Hotel still shows an elegant face to Princes Street and now incorporates part of the concourse and booking office as a bar and restaurant, even though it no longer fronts the busy station it was built to serve.

Although Edinburgh suburban services were severely cut back in the 1950s and 1960s, there has been strong growth again from the mid-1980s onwards. One of the most successful reopenings anywhere in Britain was to Bathgate, and took place while Chris Green[234] was Director of ScotRail in 1986. Subsequently the line has not only been doubled and electrified, but also extended to Airdrie, so that it now has four trains an hour linking Edinburgh and Glasgow, with some trains running beyond to Helensburgh.

Creation of the Fife Circle service and the opening of Glenrothes with Thornton in 1992 and Dalgety Bay in 1998 have also been hugely successful, attracting many Fifers to rail and providing significant relief to Edinburgh traffic congestion. North Berwick survived as a suburban service and has prospered with electrification,

also sponsored by Chris Green, as well as new stations at Musselburgh and Wallyford.

Local trains to Dunblane, and a restoration of the first part of the Waverley Route to Newcraighall, have all added trains at Waverley. At the same time, frequencies of long-distance trains have increased, with four trains an hour to Glasgow Queen Street, four via the Bathgate line, and more frequent services to Aberdeen and Inverness as well as the East Coast Main Line and the Carstairs route.

All this meant that Waverley was again short of capacity, as it was before the 1892 expansion. Signalling constraints limited parallel moves in and out of the bay platforms at the west end of the station, and there were only four through platforms. Resignalling has improved flexibility and two additional long through platforms have been provided, one next to the hotel and the other next to the trainshed wall on the south side of the station. Central crossovers allow them to be used by two short trains.

Roof renewal and the installation of escalators alongside Waverley steps have transformed the station and given Scotland's capital a station of which it can again be proud.

Edinburgh's tram network was also planned to attract back to rail some of the passengers travelling to areas served by the old suburban railways, including Leith, Ratho and the Caledonian's Granton line. While the plans have now been cut back – at the moment – to the core Airport to York Place route, the full network would effectively replicate some of the lost rail capacity.

The result has been to provide four additional platforms, just short of the five lost with the closure of Princes Street. Waverley now has a total of 18 platforms, more than any other station in Britain outside London, and the capacity to see it through the next stage of growth.

In terms of convenience, there have been advantages in diverting Princes Street services to Waverley. It has made connections easier for the Shotts line and has usefully grouped all the main-line services, including those West Coast and cross-country services via Carstairs, under one station roof, with onward connections to Fife, Dundee and Aberdeen.

Despite being so busy, the trains manage to slip unobtrusively through Prices Street Gardens, while the glazed footbridges remain a source of fascination for children of all ages who like to watch the trains go by.

The empty stock for the 11.30 to King's Cross is brought into Leeds Central behind ex-LMS 2-6-0 No 43130 of nearby Holbeck depot on 3 January 1967, just four months before closure of the station. The wagon hoist (now a listed building) is behind the locomotive. *M. Dunnett*

Leeds

Leeds was served by the first railway opened under the authority of an Act of Parliament, the Middleton Railway of 1758, part of which is now a successful heritage railway. It was also the start of a very early line, the Leeds & Selby Railway of 1834, linking a station east of the city centre at Marsh Lane with the port at Selby on the River Ouse and its river boat connections to Hull.

The North Midland Railway arrived from Derby in 1840 with a terminus at Hunslet Lane to the south of the city. The first city-centre terminal was opened in 1848 as the Wellington terminus of the London & North Western Railway's line from Dewsbury. The inadequacies of this rather cramped station led to the opening of Leeds Central in 1854, a joint station serving the LNWR as well as the Lancashire & Yorkshire, Great Northern and North Eastern railways.

The lines on either side of the city centre were not linked until 1869, when the New station was opened by the LNWR and the NER with a mile-long connection from Marsh Lane to the lines heading west. The adjacent Wellington station had been enlarged and was used by the Midland. In 1938 New and Wellington stations were combined to form Leeds City, and part of Wellington became a parcels depot. The splendid art deco north concourse and the Queen's Hotel were built at the same time.

By the late 1950s, both stations were showing their age and inadequacy, and were the subject of complaints from passengers,

local businesses and the city fathers. As early as 1959 the North Eastern Region had put together a scheme to combine the two stations with track alterations and concentration of signalling in a scheme that would have provided a single, convenient, modern station, with opportunities for development of the Central station site as well as building above the City station concourse. The cost, however, was a figure of £4,526,000 (£89,179,000 at 2012 prices)[235], huge in relation to the available investment levels of the time, although not unreasonable by today's standards.

Dr Beeching was drawn into the debate just five months after becoming BR Chairman. The Conservative MP for Leeds North West, Sir Donald Kaberry[236], had written to complain about the condition of the Leeds stations. Money was tight, however, and the Leeds scheme would take a large share of the funds available for investment. Very reasonably, Dr Beeching had replied that 'perhaps the city might consider following the example of some Continental cities and offer to contribute to rebuilding costs particularly in respect of such facilities as car parks and the concourse which will provide for the benefit of the public generally and not merely for railway passengers.' This response went down like a lead balloon, being widely condemned by the local press and businesses. The Chamber of Commerce thought it 'a bit of a leg pull', while the Conservative MP for Shipley, Geoffrey Hirst[237], expostulated that it was nonsense to say that it was an amenity and that the cost should be farmed out to ratepayers.[238] Yet Beeching has been proved right, and today stations are seen as the gateways to the communities they serve, while ratepayers do contribute to their improvement, either through the city council or through the integrated transport authority.

The Ministry of Transport crawled all over the Leeds submission, with a string of searching questions asked by David Serpell. Was it really necessary to combine the stations? Did they really need rebuilding to the extent proposed? Could not the question of interchange and parcels be dealt with 'in some other way?' Was the growth in traffic (following dieselisation of the West Yorkshire local services) continuing? In particular, he asked probing questions about the extent of resignalling and how far provision had been made for electrification. At this stage, the Ministry was still trying to scale back the West Coast electrification project, and the 'e' word was still a sore point with them. The winter of 1962/63 was particularly severe, and during a storm the roof at City station was badly damaged. In February 1963 the Ministry grudgingly gave approval for expenditure of £273,000 for the replacement roof, making clear that this included no commitment to subsequent stages in the project to combine the two stations.

This piecemeal approach to development is not a good way to manage major projects, and the authors are critical of the way in which the Ministry constantly double-guessed BR and left it little room to manage its own affairs. Yet in the case of Leeds it was right to challenge the scheme put up by the North Eastern Region on 1 February 1961. The following year (4 December 1962) a revised scheme was put to the Ministry by John Ratter from the newly formed BRB at a cost that was more than £2 million lower, at £2,358,822. The Ministry liked this scheme better, as 'rationalisation of stations is consistent with the aims of the reshaping proposals.'[239]

The other factor relating to the original 1959 submission was the huge growth in the use of West Riding local rail services as a result of a more frequent diesel train services replacing steam. The number of passengers using City station had grown by 50% since 1953 to 4.5 million. At Central the growth had been astronomic, from just over a million passengers in 1953 to 3.5 million in 1959.

SURPRISING SURVIVOR
The wagon hoist today is the only part of the old Central station remaining
and has been restored, surrounded by the glittering glass walls of the
offices that have replaced the railway. The change in the colour of the
stonework marks the original level of the tracks that approached on a
viaduct. *Chris Austin*

While not included in the Beeching Report, Leeds Central closed on 29 April 1967, and trains were diverted to Leeds City. Together with Central went eight signal boxes, Farnley & Wortley motive power depot, Farnley carriage servicing shed and a section of line between Copley Hill Junction and Central, a reminder of the cumulative cost savings linked with such closures.

There were only five objections from members of the public out of a total of 4,500 daily users, and the Transport Users' Consultative Committee did not even hold a public meeting to hear the objectors. They found no evidence of hardship and, indeed, thought that 'concentration of services at one station in Leeds would be of significant benefit to the vast majority of passengers.'[240]

Leeds City was rebuilt and was finally opened by the Lord Mayor, Alderman J. S. Walsh, on 17 May 1967. The station improvements were widely welcomed and the *Yorkshire Post* had a gushing four-page supplement giving a potted history of railways around Leeds and a very upbeat view of the new station, behind which one can see the professional guiding hand of the North Eastern Region's York press office. The new station had five through platforms compared with the former three and, as at Central, there were consequential changes to depots. Both locomotive-hauled stock and DMU maintenance was concentrated at Neville Hill's DMU depot, and the carriage depots at Neville Hill (Waterloo) and Copley Hill were closed.

The loss of Central's eight platforms put additional pressure on City's 12, although the number of services running in 1967 was low compared with the number today. The number of trans-Pennine services grew under BR, as did Metro services, with the Leeds North West electrification authorised in 1994. BR sought powers for two additional approach tracks to the west of City station in its 1991 General Powers Bill. These were brought into use as part of the 'Leeds First' project to increase capacity between 1999 and 2002.

This also met the demand for increased cross-country service frequencies and the half-hourly London service introduced by GNER. Five new platforms were provided, bringing the total to 17. One was built on the south side of the station, while the remainder used the former parcels platforms to the north, on what had been the Wellington station site. As well as the platforms and approach tracks, a new interchange deck with escalators was constructed over the station, refurbishment of the main and the 1938 northern concourses was undertaken, and a new entrance provided, as well as a multi-storey car park and cycle hub. Total project costs were £165 million at 2001 prices.

And there is more to come. To the south of Leeds City is the location of the HS2 station at New Lane, which will bring London within 1hr 22min of the city. With five platforms, this will eventually provide the city with more platform capacity (22) than it had in the heyday of steam (20). The final result will be quite a success story.

The history of the Leeds stations is different from the others we have considered in detail. They were certainly the result of the way the railways around Leeds developed piecemeal, but they were not really the product of competition in quite the same way as the two principal Birmingham stations or the bitter rivalries that created two stations at either end of Princes Street in Edinburgh. Indeed, they were both joint stations shared by all the companies whose lines fed into them, and two railways, the NER and LNWR, had a share in both Central and New stations. At such an important interchange point, it was certainly an inconvenience having two stations requiring additional interchange time, even though they were quite close together. As an added complication, trains from Leeds to Harrogate left from both stations.

Again, the lesson is that capacity is easy to destroy and very costly to recreate. In Leeds the outcome has been a happy one – a joint station forming a hub for all local, regional and long-distance services, with good facilities and relatively easy interchange.

ART DECO DELIGHT
The LMS concourse at Leeds has been well restored by Network Rail and is on the site of the earlier Wellington station. It is now linked to the newer concourse behind the photographer. *Chris Austin*

Redevelopment of the Leeds Central site has been a long time coming, but at the time of writing good-quality offices and restaurants were starting to cover the site, leaving just one of the wagon hoists and the approach viaduct as a memorial to the past age. This development is on such a scale as to secure Leeds's place as the principal administrative as well as retail focus in Yorkshire and Humberside, providing a large and coherent central business district that can only be effectively served by rail. Central's loss has effectively secured the future of the railway in Leeds.

Gloucester, Cheltenham and Worcester
These are interesting examples in two neighbouring cities and the major town between them, where different solutions were chosen, each with some disadvantages for the communities served.

Gloucester
Railway history and the pressures of competition between the Midland and Great Western railways resulted in two stations in the city, Central (GWR) and Eastgate (MR).

The first railway to reach the city was the Birmingham & Gloucester Railway, which arrived in 1840, built as a standard gauge line. This was followed in July 1844 by the Bristol & Gloucester, planned as a standard gauge line, but the company was persuaded by Brunel to change this to the broad gauge. The Cheltenham & Great

CROSS COUNTRY CONNECTION
'Jubilee' 4-6-0 No 45622 *Nyasaland* awaits departure from Gloucester Eastgate with a train for the north. Beyond the station the line crosses the Great Western at Tramway Junction. In the background is the ex-GWR engine shed at Horton Road. *Chris Austin*

Western Union Railway, a broad gauge line linking Cheltenham and Gloucester to Swindon, opened in October of the same year. All three railways used stations on or near the present station site.

The city thus formed the frontier between the two gauges, and the disruption and delay caused by the exchange of passengers and parcels was a key factor in the decision of the Parliamentary Commission of 1845 to recommend the choice of the standard gauge and made inevitable the end of the broad gauge in 1892.

The break of gauge might have been of less significance had the two companies been taken over by the Great Western as had been agreed in 1843. The Midland Railway made a better offer, however, and effectively snatched the Bristol-Birmingham route[241] from under the noses of the Great Western directors. Its amalgamation with the Midland Railway was authorised by Act of Parliament in August 1846.

The need for transfer at Gloucester was seen as a straightforward affair, 'as passengers from Birmingham could simply step across the platform from one train to another.'[242] For the visit of the Parliamentary Gauge commissioners in 1845, however, J. D. Payne, the goods manager of the Birmingham & Gloucester Railway, arranged a piece of theatre by having two goods trains that had already been dealt with unloaded again to add to the work.[243] The commissioners were duly appalled at the disorganised confusion on their visit, and the Gloucester break-of-gauge 'chaos' has become part of railway folklore. The problem was finally solved in May 1872 with the conversion of the broad gauge lines in the Gloucester area to standard gauge.

Ironically, the Great Western's Central station is on the site of the original Birmingham & Gloucester terminus, although the Midland's Birmingham trains moved across to Eastgate when it was opened in 1896. Central became a through station when the Gloucester & Dean Forest Railway opened in 1851 to Grange Court, where it linked with the South Wales Railway, which opened on the same day.

Central station is closer to the city centre and serves both the route to South Wales and the routes north to Birmingham and south to Bristol and London. A triangular junction just to the east of the station allows trains from the north via Birmingham to serve Gloucester Central, then to reverse and head south to Bristol and the South West. The station originally had two long through platforms, and two through centre roads, with crossovers allowing both up and down platforms to be used by two short trains simultaneously. A bay platform at the eastern end on the up side was provided for the Chalford auto-trains, and one at the west end on the down side for the Hereford and Ledbury trains as well as local trains to Cardiff.

Eastgate station was on a loop built from the original line from Bristol at Tuffley Junction to the south of the city, and connecting back into the main line to Birmingham just to the north of the stations at Tramway Junction, a distance of 1 mile 49 chains. It was linked to Central station by a covered footbridge 250 yards long, and had three long through platforms, an up (northbound) platform and a down island platform, as well as a bay platform on the up side facing towards Birmingham.

Both stations were busy with local and express trains, but the former gradually disappeared with the Ledbury branch closing in 1959, the Chalford auto-trains being withdrawn in 1964, the line to Ross and Hereford closing the same year, and the local stations on the Bristol route closing in 1965. A number of local stations between Gloucester and Chepstow had closed at various dates between 1954 and 1964. Almost all the through trains used Eastgate at this stage, whether they were running via the Midland or Great Western routes. So, by the summer 1965 timetable the number of train departures each weekday were:

Gloucester Central	
Up trains (towards Swindon/Paddington)	2
Down trains (towards Cardiff or Cheltenham or beyond)	29
Gloucester Eastgate	
Up trains (towards Cheltenham or Birmingham)	14
Down trains (towards Bristol)	15
Down trains (towards Swindon/Paddington)	10
Total for both stations	**70**

For comparison, the total number of trains using Gloucester today is 102.

Clearly, this total of 70 trains daily would be capable of being dealt with at a single station. That station could only be Gloucester Central, given the location of the station on the route to South Wales, and its links to the Bristol-Birmingham line at Barnwood Junction going north and Gloucester Yard Junction heading south.

Removal of Eastgate station would release a large city-centre site for development and for part of an inner relief road for the city (a road that, incidentally, now severs Central station from the city centre). It would also remove five level crossings where traffic congestion was then of more concern to the council than the city's position on the rail network.

The process was not simple. BR had done a good job in convincing the city council of the merits of a single modern station, but to make the scheme work financially it needed prior outline planning permission for the development of the Eastgate site. The appeal route for this lay to the Secretary of State for the Environment, Peter Walker[244]. Planning consent could not be given without seeming to pre-judge the closure decision, which would have to be made ultimately by the same man. The plans were inconsistent with the County Council's structure plan and a formal 'departure' from the plan would also need to be approved by … Peter Walker. An added complication was that part of the site was earmarked for a primary school, and the local MP, Mrs Sally Oppenheim[245], wanted to bring a local delegation to lobby the Secretary of State for an early release of the site. Finally, the County Borough of Gloucester was due to be abolished on 6 April 1974 as part of the major reorganisation of local government that year, and BR was keen to complete the deal and consents before the new authority took over.

The Department was cross. 'The Board has put the cart before the horse,' declared Edward Osmotherly[246] in an internal memo[247]. With agreement from the City, and the Transport Users' Consultative Committee on side, the Department did not want to upset the latter by seeming to prejudice the issue, or to encourage 'railway enthusiasts' or others to lodge further objections against closure. Looking back,

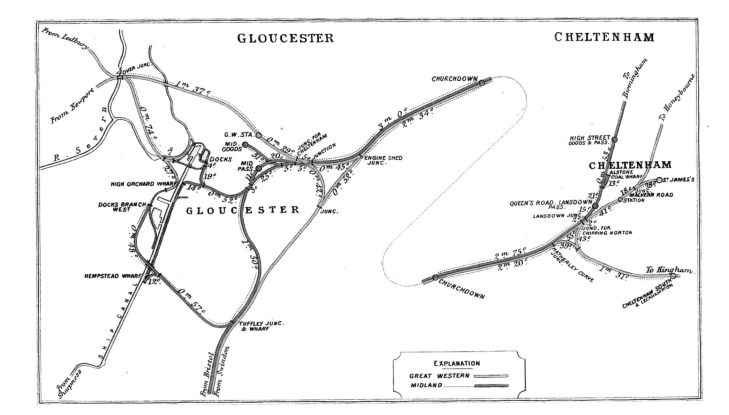

it is hard to appreciate how little the Department was prepared to work proactively towards a positive outcome, despite being involved in every stage of decision-making through the tight hold it kept on all the Board's investment (or in this case, disinvestment) proposals.

After a slow process, permission to advertise the closure was given on 1 May 1974, helped by the fact that outline planning consent for the site had by then been given. Mrs Oppenheim was persuaded not to bring her delegation, and in the event there were few objectors, and the TUCC found no evidence of hardship, other than that created by the loss of the last train from Bristol at night.[248] The station and its approach lines were closed in January 1975.

The Western Region promoted the scheme as an opportunity to rebuild and extend Central station, and the public notice relating to the closure of Eastgate set out a bright prospectus: 'This scheme, which was developed in conjunction with the former council of the County Borough of Gloucester, will provide a modern passenger station, reduce road traffic problems by the removal of five level crossings, and release land for redevelopment.' But it was not the same as Leeds, described above, and while the station was rebuilt to a reasonable specification it started to look dated and shabby within a decade. The long down platform, extended in 1977 to handle trains in both directions, with a central crossover, was convenient in providing level access, but involved a long walk. Worse than that, while much of the platform canopy was retained to protect passengers from the rain, the back wall supporting a

long section of it was declared unsafe and demolished, leaving a long gap open to the elements for all passengers going to and from the new platform extension.

The down bay platform remained for local trains to Newport and Cardiff, but the up platforms were closed to passengers, the up main platform remaining to handle parcels trains. Thus, within the space of 12 months Gloucester had gone from two stations and ten platforms to one station and three platforms. Subsequently, in 1984 the up platform at Central was reinstated for passenger use.

While trains from South Wales to Birmingham could operate normally, those from Bristol, Swindon or London heading to Cheltenham or Birmingham had to reverse at Central. This had always been the case for the Great Western's services from Paddington or Swindon to Cheltenham, but for South West to North East inter-city services the reversal was a new requirement with a time penalty of more than 10 minutes, including 5 minutes for the locomotive to run round its train, in the days before HSTs were deployed on the route. This reversal also resulted in conflicting moves at all three junctions on the triangle, which in turn became a timing constraint as the number of train services increased during the 1990s.

This meant that the faster trains ran direct and served Cheltenham Spa in preference to Gloucester. From the outset this meant a loss of four cross-country trains in each direction for Gloucester, although BR claimed that this was in response to changing demand rather than to the closure of Eastgate. It came to a head in 2002 when the requirements of the Virgin Cross Country franchise meant a much more intensive service of trains between Birmingham and Bristol as well as a service running via the Stroud Valley to and from Paddington. Codenamed 'Operation Princess', the proposals provided an ambitious and imaginative new range of journey opportunities for passengers, but the train plan did not work. The rail network as a whole was still reeling from the effect of the Hatfield accident, and the newly formed Strategic Rail Authority was under strong public and political pressure to restore performance and public confidence in the railway. Urgent action was required, and one of the key changes was to remove the Gloucester stops from the cross-country services. Co-author Chris Austin, as the SRA's External Relations Director, was the man chosen to break the bad news to Gloucester councillors. The evening meeting took place in the grim mediaeval Parliament Room in the city, and the proposals were not well received. The cross-country service from the West Country to Birmingham and beyond (now run by Arriva) still avoids Gloucester, and the change did lead to consideration of a new station on the main line at Barnwood as an alternative, to restore Gloucester's access to this route.

There is no doubt that Gloucester lost out in giving priority to the development of Eastgate and removing the traffic constraints of the level crossings in preference to securing the city's place on the cross-country network. Retention of Eastgate would have allowed cross-country trains to call at Gloucester without significant time penalty and would have avoided many of the timing constraints that are a consequence of the current station layout. It would still have allowed the release of a lot of land in the Gloucester area for redevelopment, as the requirement would have only been for a two-platform station.

The good news for the city, though, has been the development of the route from Cardiff through Gloucester to Birmingham and Nottingham, now hourly, and the huge growth in the number of its through trains to London. In 1975 the frequency was roughly 2-hourly with a change at Swindon except on three trains that ran through from Cheltenham Spa to Paddington. Now there are nine through trains a day and an hourly service to Swindon.

Cheltenham Spa

The first railway to reach Cheltenham was the Birmingham & Gloucester in 1840, with a station about a mile to the west of the city at Lansdown. Five years later the Cheltenham & Great Western Union railway reached the town from Swindon and established stations at both Lansdown and

The site of Gloucester Eastgate today. *Chris Austin*

END OF AN ERA
The 2.50pm train for Kingham awaits departure from Cheltenham Spa St James behind 2-6-2T No 5173 of Horton Road shed, Gloucester, on 23 June 1962. The locomotive was withdrawn two months later and the line to Kingham closed two months after that. On the left, the 12.15pm train from Cardiff has just arrived behind taper-boilered pannier tank No 8487, also from Gloucester shed, which has just run round its train. *Leslie Sandler*

a central one at St James, a short walk from the Royal Crescent and the Promenade. Later, in 1908, a station at Malvern Road replaced Lansdown for the GWR when a cut-off line from Cheltenham to Honeybourne was opened, providing the Great Western with its own route between Cardiff, Gloucester and Birmingham via Stratford-upon-Avon. (For the story of this line, see Chapter 3.)

St James was a four-platform terminus, but the other two stations had two through platforms each, Malvern Road having a short bay in addition where the Honeybourne auto-trains reversed.

Apart from the express trains on these main lines, stopping services ran to Birmingham, Honeybourne, Kingham, Southampton via Marlborough, and Gloucester. Three stations did result in some confusion so that, for example, a passenger for Birmingham would

need to decide whether to head to Lansdown for the train to New Street, or Malvern Road for the train to Snow Hill. For Bristol, most trains left from Lansdown, but 'The Cornishman' ran from Malvern Road. In most other cases, the station required was predicated by the destination chosen.

In 1959 there was a total of 65 daily departures from Cheltenham's three stations, but by 1968 the branch lines and stopping services had gone, as had the auto-train on the Honeybourne route; the number of trains remaining was 32, and the question of combining stations became inescapable.

The closure of the Cheltenham-Kingham branch deprived the town of its shortest and most direct route to London – 109¾ miles via Oxford, as against 121½ via the Stroud Valley and Swindon. Even as late as 1961, at many times of the day it was quicker to take the Cotswold Line and change at Kingham: the 10.45am from Paddington gave a Cheltenham arrival of 1.40pm, whereas the through train leaving London at 11.15am didn't get there until 2.25pm. If we go back to 1911, the 'Cheltenham, Worcester, Malvern and Hereford Express', which departed from Paddington at 1.40pm and ran non-stop to Worcester, had a through carriage for Cheltenham that was slipped at Kingham and joined to a local train that arrived at St James at 4.12pm, 2hr 32min after leaving London.

The presence of Lansdown on the through route between Bristol and Birmingham meant that it had to be kept and the decision was made to route the London and Swindon trains to Lansdown and close both Malvern Road and St James, and services were withdrawn on 3 January 1966. The residual service of two trains each way daily between Leamington Spa and Gloucester continued until withdrawn on 25 March 1968; for the last two years they had not called at Cheltenham at all.

In Gloucester the most central station had been kept and the one on the through route from Bristol to Birmingham was abandoned. In Cheltenham the opposite choices were made, and the central station was closed. A supermarket was built on the site of St James and its sidings, while the railway from Malvern Road has been kept as an attractive cycleway and footpath; today it is the most pleasant way to get from the railway station to the town centre, involving a 20-minute walk. A frequent bus service also links the station with the town centre and drops passengers a few minutes' walk from the bus station at Royal Well, which, ironically, is within a stone's throw of the former station at St James.

Sadly, the Honeybourne line is blocked just to the north of Malvern Road by an office block and ring road. A tunnel has sensibly been provided for the cycle route, but unfortunately not large enough for even a single line of railway. Trains do run from a second station at Cheltenham Racecourse, however, northwards to Toddington on the Gloucestershire & Warwickshire Railway heritage line. They are steam trains and offer a great day out from Toddington, and on race days provide a park and ride service to the racecourse.

Cheltenham, sadly, has missed out and is nothing like as accessible for tourists by rail as Bath, for example, with its centrally located railway station and adjacent bus station. Thousands of racegoers have to transfer to coach to rumble along the town's ancient streets to the racecourse on busy race days, and the town struggles with cars whose drivers might have used regional trains if they did not involve the mile trek from the station. The town has done better than

Gloucester following the loss of two of its stations, but it is not quite what it could have been.

Worcester

Unusually for a city of its size, Worcester has retained the two central stations – Shrub Hill and Foregate Street – located in it since 1860. They are connected by a long curve on a viaduct high above the flood plain, worked as a bi-directional single line. A second (also bi-directional) single line takes trains from Foregate Street north to Droitwich and Birmingham, and west to Malvern and Hereford.

Had the Birmingham & Gloucester Railway not decided to route its line to the east, and instead taken it through Worcester, rather than serve the city with branches from Abbotswood Junction to Shrub Hill (1850), and from Shrub Hill to Droitwich and Stoke Works (1852), Worcester would have become a railway junction of major importance.

The Oxford, Worcester & Wolverhampton's Cotswold line arrived in June 1853, and the line through Foregate Street was opened in May 1860.

Demand for rail travel in the area is high and growing. There is pressure for the present hourly fast service to Birmingham New Street via Bromsgrove to become half-hourly, the trains to Snow Hill via Kidderminster are relatively frequent and popular, and so too are those to Malvern and Hereford. Services south to Cheltenham and Gloucester are less satisfactory, with the frequency never better than 2-hourly. The Cotswold Line has seen a transformation, from a threat of closure in the 1970s to the introduction of an almost hourly timetable in both directions, following the reinstatement of double track between Evesham and Charlbury. A particular problem is the journey time to London: too many people from Worcester and the surrounding area prefer to drive to Birmingham International or Warwick Parkway, and pick up fast London trains there.

A long-running issue (over almost 40 years) is whether it makes sense to build a 'Worcestershire Parkway' station close to Norton Junction, with high-level (Cotswold Line) and low-level (cross-country) platforms. At the time of writing prospects for its construction appear brighter, with money offered by Worcestershire County Council and the Department for Transport, with revenue anticipated as being provided from car parking charges. The Cotswold Line Promotion Group – which deserves immense credit for the part it has played since the late 1970s in popularising the railway – is clear that the Parkway station must not lead to any increase in journey times, nor threaten the future of either of Worcester's two city-centre stations.

So, Gloucester kept its city-centre station but lost out on cross-country services. Cheltenham became the principal calling point between Bristol and Birmingham on the cross-country network at the expense of its city-centre station. Worcester has kept both its city-centre stations, and is inching its way towards achieving a stop on the cross-country line from the North and Midlands to the South West – the railway's 'M5'.

11
NOT ON THE NETWORK – ISOLATED TOWNS

'The railway has taken its place in the landscape with all the other
artificial elements that man has put there: fields, hedges, farms, roads, canals.
It has taken its place because it has fitted in – it rarely dominates any view – and because,
unlike the airfield which must obliterate existing features to create its shaven emptiness,
the railway etches in fresh detail to the scene.'

MICHAEL ROBBINS, *THE RAILWAY AGE*, 1962

In this chapter we look at some significant towns that were isolated from the rail network as well as those parts of the country where a whole network of lines was swept away, adding to social isolation.

Brecon

Each closure brought with it a degree of isolation, but the cumulative effect of closures was particularly acute in parts of Scotland, Wales, East Anglia and the South West. Nowhere was this more apparent than in mid-Wales.

Brecon had been linked by canal to Abergavenny and Newport from 1800, but was relatively late on the railway scene. The Brecon & Merthyr Railway was first to arrive in 1863, followed by the Mid Wales Railway the following year, while the Neath & Brecon arrived from the west in 1867. The Hereford, Hay & Brecon Railway joined the Mid Wales at the picturesquely named Three Cocks Junction[249] so Brecon was now the focus of four lines, while the junction at Talyllyn, 4 miles to the east, was a significant staging post for passengers and goods traffic between South and Mid Wales and beyond.

Apart from local services to Brecon, which was both a market town and the largest centre for 20 miles around, in their heyday the lines saw through trains in the summer from South Wales to Aberystwyth and from Barry to Llandrindod Wells, running direct via the east curve at Talyllyn. The Midland Railway (which bought the Hereford, Hay & Brecon) also ran daily trains between Birmingham New Street and Swansea St Thomas via Brecon. Local goods traffic was relatively light, but the lines were important during the First World War in carrying coal for bunkering warships from South Wales to Birkenhead and to Thurso for Scapa Flow. Later on, with the closure of the Merthyr, Tredegar and Abergavenny line in 1958, a regular train of chemical tanks from Teesside for the ICI chemical works at Dowlais was diverted to run via the Talyllyn east curve and was hauled by two pannier tanks.

The section of the B&M between Pontsticill Junction and Merthyr Tydfil had lost its minimal passenger service in November 1961, and rumours were circulating of widespread closures throughout Wales. In February 1962 the political temperature was raised when, following a conference of interested parties in Cardiff, the Lord Mayor sent a telegram to Ernest Marples seeking suspension of the closure programme in Wales. This was followed by a meeting at the Ministry on the 16 April when the papers reveal that the temperature was reduced by smooth reassuring words from the Minister about the process to be followed and the safeguard of the TUCC's consideration of hardship, even though he made it clear that the juggernaut was going to roll on. The gulf between the views of the two sides is evident from the file. The civil servants briefing for Marples reiterated their belief that closures were 'really the result of consumer choice', and that 'wholesale subsidy to the railways as they are now is not realistic economics.'[250] It went on to point out that the trains on the eastern and western valleys lines[251] out of Newport accounted for only 7% of the public transport users in the corridor, and that there were 13 bus passengers for every rail passenger. The memo went well beyond the normal impartial briefing that might be expected, by feeding the Minister the line that, of the 300 people attending the Cardiff conference in February, only 30 had come by train.

The local and opposing view was encapsulated in a letter from the Clerk of the Urban District Council of New Quay in Ceredigion[252]:

'This branch railway is first and foremost a public utility, and the matter of profitability should not be allowed to enter into the question of its continued existence as a vital feature in the life of a sparsely populated rural area, where the roads are totally inadequate for heavy goods traffic.'

Before the Beeching Report the Western Region had closed the Neath and Brecon line in October 1962, followed by the other three lines to Brecon from Newport, Hereford and Moat Lane Junction,

AT THE FOOT OF THE BEACONS
The 8.03am Newport to Brecon train enters Talybont on Usk behind pannier
tank No 3661 of Ebbw Junction shed in 1961. The start of the Seven Mile
Bank to Torpantau can be seen climbing at 1 in 37 behind the last coach.
Chris Austin

near Newtown, at the end of December of that year. Not only did
they lose their passenger services, but also goods trains, leaving just
the line from Merthyr open for goods and parcels traffic to the
county town until this last link, too, closed in May 1964. The
Beeching Report also proposed closure of the LNWR's Central Wales
line (now the Heart of Wales line) from Swansea (Victoria) to
Craven Arms, south of Shrewsbury, including the connecting line
from Carmarthen to Llandeilo, as well as those from Carmarthen to
Aberystwyth, and the Ruabon to Barmouth line.

Had the Central Wales line also closed, there would have been no
railways in mid-Wales between Merthyr in the south and Newtown in
the north, from Aberystwyth (and Devil's Bridge) in the west to
Hereford in the east. For many people in Mid Wales this threatened
unacceptable hardship and an unprecedented degree of isolation, with
people living in Brecon having to travel 20 miles to their nearest
railhead at Abergavenny, while the people of Llandrindod Wells would
have been 27 miles away from their nearest station at Newtown.

In the event the Central Wales line was reprieved, but the Brecon
closures at the end of 1962 isolated most of Breconshire and
Radnorshire, and this was dramatically illustrated the day following
the last trains. On the night of Saturday 30 December 1962 heavy
snow fell across the country and by the morning all roads to Brecon

were blocked. While there was no public train service on the Sunday,
a special train to mark the closure of the lines did run. On to this
train were loaded the newspapers and milk that could not be
delivered by road, and in its last moments the railway continued to
serve the community for whom it had been built.

In retrospect it is hard to make out a case for the whole network
of lines serving Powys, but wiping out the network within a single
year was certainly too drastic. Had the Brecon & Merthyr line
survived, it would be a much valued railway for Brecon and its
hinterland and for access to the Brecon Beacons National Park. Like
the Heart of Wales line, it would have supported the local economy,
helped the development of tourism and helped to reduce traffic on
the awful A470, as well as keeping cars out of Cardiff. In operational
terms, it would simply have been an extension of the Cardiff to
Merthyr service, requiring just two additional Class 150 units for an
hourly frequency – cost effective, if not profitable, and capable of
tackling rural isolation and deprivation.

While Brecon can only be reached by bus, the narrow gauge
Brecon Mountain Railway can take you from Pant to Torpantau,
high in the Brecon Beacons. A valuable tourist asset, the line can now
offer car-free access to the Beacons.

St Andrews

'In the mid-1960s the railway to Largo had closed. It was the
worst thing that had ever happened in this part of Fife. The
end of the railway was the end of the village.'
Paul Theroux, *The Kingdom by the Sea*, 1983

LEUCHARS JUNCTION
On 22 April 1963 the 7.35am train to St Andrews waits in the bay platform for clearance of the 7.32am to Glasgow Queen Street, which has come from Dundee Tay Bridge. *Leslie Sandler*

Opened in 1852, the branch line from Leuchars Junction[253] initially provided a connection to the Edinburgh & Northern line from Burntisland to Tayport, before either the Tay or Forth bridges were open. A circuitous link via Perth connected with the rest of the Scottish network, and one from Thornton Junction via Dunfermline to Stirling was completed on the same day, but otherwise longer journeys from St Andrews initially involved a ferry crossing.

St Andrews is a former royal borough and bishopric, the University of St Andrews founded in 1410 is the oldest in Scotland, and the Royal & Ancient Golf Club was founded here as early as 1754. It is a significant tourist centre and a magnet for golfers. So, the town has an importance well beyond what its population of 16,500 might suggest.

Thirty-five years after the opening of the branch, the Anstruther & St Andrews Railway completed the coastal line around the East Neuk of Fife, connecting the fishing villages that were becoming popular holiday resorts with Leven and Thornton Junction.

Local stations between St Andrews and Anstruther disappeared[254] in the flurry of early closures implemented by the LNER on former North Eastern and North British lines on 22 September 1930.[255]

While the line round the coast from St Andrews to Leven was included in the Beeching Report and closed in 1965[256], St Andrews itself was not, nor was the line from Thornton Junction to Leven.

Indeed, St Andrews was shown as being in the highest category of annual passenger earnings (more than £25,000 per annum). The service was shown on the Beeching map as to be 'modified' and Guard Bridge and St Fort stations were duly closed on the route from St Andrews to Dundee, while the passenger service remained.

It was the opening of the Tay road bridge in August 1966 that finished it off, as it did to the line from Dundee to Tayport. Passenger numbers slumped after the bridge opened and buses started running as an alternative to the train. The buses were direct and many of the trains required a change at Leuchars Junction. In 1968 around 200 daily passengers remained on the line, and around 800 students were thought to use the line at the beginning and end of term. It was surprising, therefore, that only 23 objections were received by the Scottish TUCC.

The Heads of Information[257] did reveal that in addition to the train crew, there were two crossing keepers on the line and seven staff at St Andrews station, even though the line was a simple 'one train working' operation, and it was certainly not run as a 'basic' railway. That the decision to close came late in the day was confirmed by the station

ET IN ARCADIA EGO
The 12.13pm train from Leuchars Junction to St Andrews crosses the River Eden at Guard Bridge on 22 April 1964. The signal box controls the level crossing over a busy main road just behind the rear coach. Only the bridge piers and abutments remain from this scene. *C. C. Thornburn*

improvements carried out just four years before. The TUCC report commented, with a sense of irony, that 'St Andrews station is in good condition, having been 'face lifted' in 1964, but bears the appearance of sad gentility suited to a Victorian lady – and St Andrews.'

The St Andrews branch closed on 6 January 1969 and was followed on 6 October of that year by the branch from Thornton Junction to Leven, leaving the East Neuk of Fife without a passenger railway.

Prior to closure there had been no car park at Leuchars Junction and, with a narrow footbridge linking the approach road to the island platform, the interchange arrangements were bad. The lack of a bus stop near the station meant that interchange was impractical. With hindsight, these issues might have been met head-on by coordinated transport planning, but this would have gone well beyond BR's remit and it had no resources to invest in such facilities. In the event, though, a replacement bus service was required, but it was to be many years before a proper interchange was provided by sensible cooperation between the parties involved (see later).

OLD COURSE
The formation of the line follows the road, and the sacred turf of the Old Course is on the right. The Jigger Inn is now part of the hotel (built by BR in 1968) and was originally the station master's house of the original St Andrews station, before the extension to Anstruther. *Chris Austin*

LAST TRAIN FROM LARGO
The last regular goods train from Crail crosses the viaduct at Largo returning to Thornton Junction on 30 May 1966. The locomotive is 'B1' Class 4-6-0 No 61308 from Thornton Junction. After this, the demolition train.
C. W. R. Bowman

If the line were reinstated it could provide a valuable service to Edinburgh as well as local connections and make a great contribution to the town's success as a holiday resort. It would be particularly valuable for bringing passengers to major events such as the Open golf championship, as well as the influx of students at the start and finish of each academic term.

But any proposal for reopening would have to overcome a number of practical problems. Housing covers the route of the railway at Guard Bridge and it is unlikely that the return of the rails would be welcomed where it runs between the Old Course and its magnificent hotel (built by British Rail in 1968, months before the line closed). The former station site would be convenient for the bus station, but is now a road and a car park.

It has to be admitted that, even without its railway, access to St Andrews by public transport is good. A bus links the town with Leuchars and Dundee stations every 10 minutes, and during the day no fewer than nine buses an hour connect Leuchars station with St Andrews. Through ticketing is available and the bus station at St Andrews sells national rail tickets. A busy taxi rank and a large car park with a ramped footbridge at Leuchars have transformed the inadequate position at the time of closure. The station has now been renamed Leuchars for St Andrews and the bus connections are shown in the railway timetable.

A better prospect for early reopening is that of Leven further south, where a freight route remains for much of the distance and there is not the same problem of encroachment on the solum of the former railway, or of the sensitivity of the area through which the line would have to pass.

Gosport

Gosport is one the largest towns in Britain without a station. Not only that, but it lost its passenger service as early as 1953, despite then having a population of 58,000. Today, its population is more than 82,000 and it is perhaps something of a mystery as to why rail connections in the area were all a dead loss.

The railway arrived early in Gosport – before Portsmouth was rail-connected – in 1841 by means of a branch from Bishopstoke (later renamed Eastleigh). The unstable Knowle Tunnel caused the line to be closed again within four days, and it reopened again in 1842. Portsmouth was not reached by rail until 1847, and the Portsmouth Direct line from Waterloo was not opened until 1859.

The other railways around Gosport were also spectacularly unsuccessful. The Stokes Bay branch was opened in 1865 to a pier station from which steamers plied to Ryde. In 1915 the line closed for the duration of the war but never reopened; in 1922 it was sold to the Royal Navy and, together with the pier, formed part of the torpedo testing facility set up by the land-based HMS *Vernon*. The track was removed, but replaced by narrow gauge lines by the Navy.

The other branch, from Fort Brockhurst to Lee-on-the-Solent, also had a short history, opening as an independent light railway in 1894, and closed by the Southern Railway, which had taken it over in 1923, as early as 1931.

Gosport itself had a magnificent station building by William Tite with a row of Etruscan columns on the front, which has been restored today and is Grade II* listed. From 1903 a more direct route to Gosport was created with the opening of the Meon Valley line from Alton to Fareham, but this did not produce the increase in traffic expected, either to Gosport or via the Stokes Bay branch and pier to the Isle of Wight.

Three years later, in 1906, the tramway from Gosport to Fort Brockhurst was extended to Fareham and electrified in direct competition with the railway. The tramway closed in 1929, but the bus route remained, operated by Provincial, which ran a network of services fanning out from the Gosport ferry terminal.

The ferry was frequent, quick and cheap, and linked to Portsmouth Harbour station, opened in 1876, which was in practice the principal station for Gosport with its wide range of connections to London, along the South Coast and to Bristol.

Like other lines covered in this book, the railway was busy with troops, sailors, stores and munitions during both world wars, but passenger demand was not great in peacetime and the line was singled in 1934. Passenger numbers dwindled after the Second World War, and the branch from Fareham lost its passenger service in June 1953. The line remained open for goods traffic until 1969, and the section from Fareham to the Royal Naval stores depot at Bedenham was used until 1991.

Since then proposals have been canvassed to reopen the line at various stages, and an ambitious project, the South Hampshire Rapid Transit scheme, was promoted by Hampshire County Council and Portsmouth City Council, and consortia interested included Stagecoach as well as major players in railway engineering. Phase 1 of the scheme would have run from Fareham to Gosport, then via an immersed tube tunnel under Portsmouth Harbour to Portsmouth & Southsea. Phase 2 would have taken it on from Fareham to Southampton, while Phase 3 would have taken it north from Portsmouth to Waterlooville, serving a corridor that was linked by an electric tramway, closed in 1935. Waterlooville now has a population of 64,000 and is also without a rail connection.

However, the scheme failed to gain Government approval as it was above the cost approved, and under Secretary of State Alastair Darling the view was that light rail schemes generally were poor value for money. A Transport & Works Act Order had been secured

'A' containers from the Royal Naval stores depot at Gosport are pulled out by Standard Class 4 2-6-4T No 80037. *Chris Austin*

in 2001 and funding of £170 million approved. However, costs rose, and by November 2004 Darling had declined to approve the new outlay and asked the councils to reduce the costs. They did this, but the result still remained 50% higher than the amount earmarked by DfT. It remained for Parliamentary Under-Secretary of State, Derek Twigg[258], finally to turn down the scheme on 29 November 2005.[259]

Today, Gosport station has been well restored and forms part of a housing and office development. The line to Fort Brockhurst is a

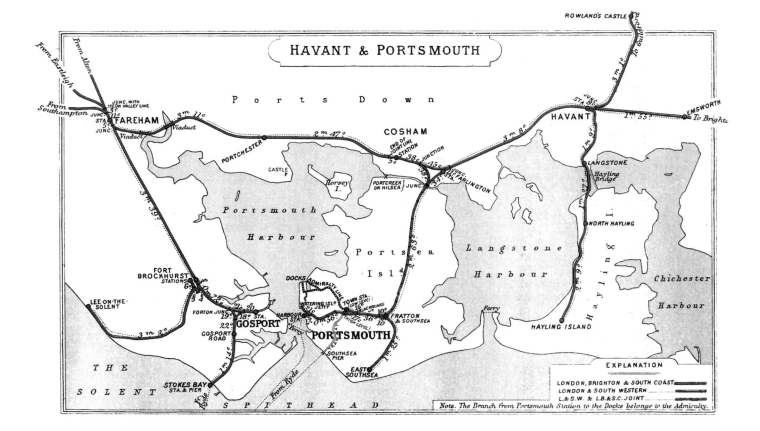

cycle path, while beyond, to Fareham, is part of a busway. The bus service operated by First Group goes way beyond anything offered by the railway, even in its heyday, linking Fareham's railway station with Gosport's ferry terminal. Comfortable buses with leather seats, Wi-Fi and real-time information online, run every 6 minutes. Only on journey time would the railway have scored; in 1914, the 5-mile journey took 11 minutes, while today's bus takes 26.

Given the history outlined above, the line would not be on our list of those to be reopened as a heavy rail branch from Fareham. It would, however, be surprising if it did not have some role as part of a light rail system in serving the transport and economic needs of the developing 'Solent city' that will one day link those two former rivals, Portsmouth and Southampton.

Keswick

One of the more controversial closures that resulted from the Beeching Report was that from Penrith on the West Coast Main Line to Keswick, a market town of around 5,000 souls in the English Lake District. The railway had arrived in 1865, with services that linked Penrith with Cockermouth and Whitehaven on the Cumbrian coast.

In the summer of 1938 there were eight trains a day from Penrith through Keswick to Workington, with most going on to Whitehaven; one was a through service that left Euston at noon ('The Southport, Blackpool, and Lakes Express' – it had coaches for both those seaside towns, and Windermere, as well as Workington via Keswick). There were also trains on Sunday to Keswick from Newcastle and Glasgow.

By the early 1960s the long-distance through services and those on Sundays had disappeared, but the pattern of eight trains a day persisted, with many of them starting or finishing at Carlisle.

Beeching proposed the closure of the entire route, but this did not happen all at once; the service from Keswick to Cockermouth and Workington was withdrawn in April 1966, but there was a concerted effort to keep open Keswick to Penrith. In December 1969, in a written parliamentary answer[260], the Minister, Fred Mulley, announced that a grant of £95,000 would be paid to British Rail in 1970 to run the service from Keswick to Carlisle (via Penrith).

That proved to be a short-lived reprieve as in January 1972 Mulley's Conservative successor, John Peyton, announced that the line would close 'subject to conditions'[261], and close it did, three months later.

Most people assumed that was that. There was no serious interest in taking over the line as a heritage railway, and there seemed to be little enthusiasm locally for bringing the railway back to Keswick. However, in 1995 an individual named Cedric Martindale, described in the local press as a 'railway engineer', drew up plans for reopening based on an unusual business model. It would be achieved, Martindale said, 'as a cooperative venture for local authorities, businesses and railway organisations in response to concerns about future traffic problems in the Lake District.'

In 1996 Cumbria County Council carried out a 'pre-feasibility' study to test Martindale's ideas about reinstating the railway. Its conclusions were very negative, with even the 'best case' model showing operating costs exceeding revenue by £1.26 million a year. 'In summary the line is unlikely to be viable unless operated as a tourist attraction and high fares are charged.'[262]

Martindale was not deterred and formed a company – CKP Railways Ltd – becoming its Managing Director. The rationale was:

'Because the Local Authorities in Cumbria have various roles to play in managing and supporting transport, but they do not have the resources to tackle reopening projects. This reopening was suggested to them as a joint project as long ago as 1996, but they chose not to take up the challenge. Some do, however, provide varying degrees of support and encouragement, but not funding.

Because lots of people have talked about the need for the Railway to "return to Keswick", but nobody else has seriously tackled the issue.

Because we, CKP Railways plc and our Project Team, have the skills and experience, from Railway design and development projects in the UK and overseas, we are local, we understand the issues, and we want to put back this "missing link" for everyone's benefit.

Somebody had to do it – nobody else volunteered!'[263]

Martindale wrote a book, *Return to Keswick – the Case for a New Railway*[264], and has pressed on relentlessly for the reopening, opposing any planning application that would compromise the line's infrastructure.

The CKP company set about raising funds, and did so by selling bonds in denominations of between £100 and £2,500. Martindale claimed that by 2001 £155,000 had been raised in this way, and a third issue was opened. They were reported as earning a 4 per cent rate of return.

Despite this energy and enthusiasm, the project received little official support. The Strategic Rail Authority turned it down in 2002. The local authorities in the area varied between being lukewarm and hostile, with the exception of Keswick Town Council, which was reported as being willing in 2008 to be its 'champion' in the public sector. In 2010 Cumbria County Council produced a new version of its local transport plan, but failed to include any reference to the line.

It is hard to see how this project could come to fruition. While much of the trackbed remains free from development – although there have been some incursions – it is popular with cyclists and walkers whose needs would have to be catered for if the trains returned. The operating economics still look very difficult: if Keswick to Penrith were to rejoin the national network and run as a conventional railway, it would almost certainly need an operating subsidy, notwithstanding the huge growth in demand for rail travel nationally. There is considerable concern locally that unless it were part of a franchise operation, that subsidy would have to come from that part of the county council's transport budget that it spends on supporting bus services.

If it had survived the Beeching cuts, there would be no question of closing it now. But that is sadly not the same as justifying its reinstatement.

A train for Workington on the line from Penrith. *Ian Allan Library*

12

MISJUDGING THE MARKET FOR SLEEPING CAR SERVICES

'Sleep the night and gain a day.'

HEADLINE OF BR ADVERTISEMENT 1972

Built for the Paddington-New Milford boat train in 1897, Dean clerestory
sleeping car No 3058 has been restored and can be seen on the West Somerset Railway.
Here it is attached to the 'Quantock Belle' for a public trip in October 2012. *Chris Austin*

A Mark 3 sleeper on the 'Night Riviera' at Paddington. *Peter Skuce*

Compared with the damage inflicted on the network by the Beeching closures and the subsequent attempts to 'rationalise' the railway through the short-sighted 'Network for Development' approach, which allowed numerous lines that were not on that list to wither and in some cases disappear altogether, the story of what happened to Britain's sleeping car services may appear a bit peripheral.

It does, however, offer a remarkable object lesson of how a well-intentioned policy can go wrong as a result of misjudging the market.

Sleeping cars have been operating on Britain's railways since Victorian times. They offered comfortable, though not luxurious, overnight accommodation on long- and some medium-distance journeys, allowing passengers to leave their home stations in the early and late evening and arrive at their destination at a civilised time the next morning. Often the trains to which they were attached would convey restaurant cars, so that dinner could be enjoyed before retiring, and, on longer journeys, breakfast in the morning. The comfort of the accommodation depended on the class of travel, and varied between six-berth compartments that offered passengers little more than the opportunity to lie down under a blanket, to single- and double-berth cabins with a wash basin and – until the 1970s – a chamber pot.

Paul Theroux wrote in *The Great Railway Bazaar* (1975), 'The romance associated with the sleeping car derives from its extreme privacy, combining the best features of a cupboard with forward movement.'

(As an aside, one of the authors vividly remembers a journey as a child from London to Morar – the penultimate station on the West Highland line extension from Fort William to Mallaig – in 1956. He and three members of his family left King's Cross on the 7.30pm 'Night Aberdonian', which had through coaches for both Aberdeen and Mallaig. The night was spent in a former LNER six-berth compartment, and arrival at Morar was just before noon the next day.)

During the days of British Railways operation there were two major investments in the sleeping car fleet. The first occurred between 1957 and 1964, when 380 Mark 1 vehicles were built to replace the fleets inherited from the LMS, the GWR and the LNER (the Southern Railway never ran any sleeping car services, although it did provide track access and haulage for the wagons-lits cars of the 'Night Ferry').

The second major build of new sleeping cars came about in the early 1980s, when 208 air-conditioned vehicles were built to the Mark 3A specification at Derby Carriage & Wagon Works by British Rail Engineering. The BR Board's original intentions, were, however a great deal more ambitious than this, as an examination of some fascinating documents in the National Archives reveals.

As early as 1973 David Bowick (Chief Executive, Railways) had submitted a recommendation to the Board's investment committee for the construction of three prototype sleeping cars based on 'a review of policy' that stated:

'Sleeping car services form an important part of the Inter-City passenger business. Even during a period when daytime services have radically improved they have continued to expand and make a substantial contribution to earnings.'

Accompanying this was a table headed 'Sleeper Services: 1971 Results'.

	Earnings (£000s)	Direct expenses (£000s)	Margin (£000s)
Full train services			
Euston to Carlisle/Glasgow	1,843	784	1,059
Euston to Perth/Inverness	1,010	481	529
King's Cross to Edinburgh	1,400	599	801
King's Cross to Aberdeen	1,269	498	771
King's Cross to Tees/Tyne	471	249	222
Paddington to West of England	558	364	194
Birmingham to Glasgow/Edinburgh	242	147	95
Total: primary services	**6,793**	**3,122**	**3,671**
Other services			
King's Cross to Fort William	139	98	61
Euston to Preston/Barrow	177	183	[6]
Euston to Manchester	124	83	41
Euston to Liverpool	116	82	34
Paddington to South Wales	134	138	[4]
King's Cross to Leeds	69	50	19
Glasgow/Edinburgh to Inverness	43	52	[9]
Euston to Stranraer	104	79	25
Euston to Scotland via Midland routes	105	120	[15]
Newcastle to Bristol	35	28	7
Total: secondary services	**1,046**	**913**	**133**
Total: all services	**7,839**	**4,035**	**3,804**

This list of services covered virtually all those operated by British Railways in the post-war period. There had been some relatively minor withdrawal of services in the 1960s and '70s, including the ending of the Friday-night sleeper to Oban. This had been attached to the 7.15pm sleeping car train from Euston to Perth, and detached at Stirling. It returned to London on the 5.15pm train from Oban to Glasgow and Edinburgh on Sunday afternoons. In the early 1960s there were also services between Paddington and Birkenhead, Manchester to Plymouth, and the extension of the Barrow sleeper to Whitehaven, all of which had disappeared by the time of BR's investment review.

In 1975 the range of destinations served by sleeper remained very extensive:

• King's Cross to Leeds, Newcastle (both via Darlington and via Sunderland), Edinburgh, Fort William and Aberdeen
• Euston to Liverpool, Manchester, Holyhead, Preston, Barrow, Carlisle, Stranraer, Glasgow (both via Dumfries and via Carstairs) and Inverness
• Paddington to Milford Haven, Exeter, Plymouth and Penzance
• Victoria to Paris/Brussels
• Bristol to Glasgow and Edinburgh
• Nottingham to Glasgow

In addition to this, sleepers were provided on a number of Motorail services, many of which were seasonal.

The remarkably positive figures in Bowick's paper provided the basis for a major investment in the sleeping car fleet. He talked about '75ft long air-conditioned coaches with improved standards of ride, sound insulation, décor and amenities generally. The marketing plan is that of a *travelling hotel* (our emphasis) which will be assisted by the provision of a bar/refreshment area in each set of three coaches with continental breakfast facilities in all compartments.'

Those intentions were admirable, and the investment decisions taken on the basis of them would have been understandable, had it not been for a series of major changes in the market for long- and medium-distance travel in Great Britain, and in the public's expectations for overnight accommodation.

Starting with the second of these, a critical error was committed by the BR Board in 1975 when it ignored the advice of the Rolling Stock Design Engineer, H. Wilcock. In a memorandum to the Chief Passenger Manager, dated 14 August 1975, he wrote:

'With regard to the compartment toilet facilities in the new Mark III design sleeping car, I note your decision that this feature should not be provided… It is true to say that there are technical problems particularly in the collection and storage of effluent from these facilities, but these problems can be overcome and as I have stated previously I would have thought that such facilities are now an established amenity in a modern sleeping car. We have gone to a great deal of trouble in association with the Director of Design to develop a much more hygienic system than which currently applies and it is my personal experience that at least a proportion of passengers appreciate this facility.'

Wilcox then commented on the proposal that tea-making facilities should be provided in the compartments of the new sleeping cars. 'I would have thought that the provision of Teasmades[265] is further justification for toilet facilities and if the facilities are not provided I am convinced that their absence would encourage much less hygienic practices at [sic] the part of at least a proportion of sleeping car passengers.'

Given that the new Mark 3 coaches were fitted with retention lavatories, the chamber pots disappeared from the individual cabins – hence Wilcox's coy comment about 'much less hygienic practices', which presumably referred to the inappropriate use of wash-basins.

Missing from this argument was any reference to the higher standards expected by the public in modern accommodation: families staying in hotels and guest houses may have been prepared to put up with the absence of 'en suite' facilities in their rooms, but by 1980 increasing numbers expected at least a shower and lavatory in their bedrooms. The railways' failure to respond to this demand was a significant reason why the sleeping car market declined in the 1980s and '90s, notwithstanding the introduction of new vehicles that were quieter, more comfortable and rode more smoothly than their Mark 1 predecessors. Other important factors that changed the market were the introduction of low-cost domestic flights from a number of regional airports – this had a particular effect on the Anglo-Irish traffic, as we saw in Chapter 5 with the decline and eventual death of 'The Paddy' (the sleeper to Stranraer), and before that sleeper services to Holyhead and Fishguard – and the very significant reduction in journey times on routes that benefited from electrification and other modernisation – examples being London to Liverpool, Manchester, Leeds, Preston, Carlisle, Newcastle and South and West Wales.

The principal issue was that the business model no longer worked. Each car carries only 12 1st or 24 Standard Class passengers and can be used only for a single trip each night. Compare this with the 76 seats of a Standard Class coach on Virgin East Coast which may operate a daily return trip between London and Edinburgh as well as one to Leeds or Newcastle. Even with the sleeper supplement the earnings per coach are small in comparison with the day coach. The acceleration of trains over the last 40 years, coupled with the extended operating day of InterCity trains, has enabled more people to travel and return home to the comfort of their own beds as an alternative to spending a night on the train.

Against these changes, John Prideaux successfully transformed the sleeper business in 1988, concentrating Anglo-Scottish services on Euston and running just two 16-car trains each night, the first to Aberdeen, Inverness and Fort William, and the second to Glasgow and Edinburgh. Lounge cars were introduced, serving simple cooked meals as well as light refreshments and drinks. The number of intermediate stops was limited, as was the disturbance of adding and detaching parcels vehicles. With a speed limit of 80mph, every effort was made to give passengers a better night's sleep. The Paddington to Penzance sleeper was similarly transformed with just one detachment of a sleeping car for Plymouth.

These trains were well patronised by Members of Parliament returning to their constituencies on a Thursday night after the 10.00pm vote. The changes were not without controversy, however, and the withdrawal of sleepers from the East Coast route was opposed by a number of MPs, who blocked the British Railways General Powers bill for that year to force a debate on the issue. Similar rows arose when the Stranraer sleeper was withdrawn.

The changes meant that the new services required only a small proportion of the number of sleeper vehicles that had been ordered and built – hence the large number to be found on heritage railways (where they are used to provide accommodation for volunteers). Ten were leased to Danish Railways.

The approach of privatisation in the 1990s brought about a further rationalisation, as it was the Government's intention that only financially viable sleeper services should come across to the new train operating companies. There was a major battle to save the West Highland service to Fort William (known as 'The Deerstalker'), which enjoyed the support of a number of influential figures, particularly in the House of Lords. 'A Sleeping Car Named Desire' was the title of an article on the threat to end the Fort William sleeper in *The Times* on 15 June 1995 by Magnus Linklater[266].

It was reprieved and remains today in the franchise for Scottish sleepers, taken over by Serco in 2015. It forms part of a service from Euston that also runs to Inverness and Aberdeen; the second Scottish sleeper serves Edinburgh and Glasgow. The Bristol to Glasgow and Edinburgh sleeper was lost at privatisation, the Department correctly judging that there would be little fuss as the service did not serve London and was not used by MPs. The only other survivor is First

The interior of a Scotrail 'Caledonian' sleeper 1st Class berth (no en suite here). *Phil Marsh*

Great Western's 'Night Riviera' sleeper to Penzance. None of these 'hotels on wheels' offers en suite facilities in the sleeping compartments.

However, Serco, the new franchise operator for the 'Caledonian' sleepers, has placed a £100 million order for 75 new cars, for delivery in 2018. These new cars will include business berths with en suite toilets and showers, and will be built by CAF.

A number of routes that carried sleeper services before 1960 were subsequently themselves closed:

- Waverley Route (Carlisle to Edinburgh)
- Dumfries-Challoch Junction, near Stranraer
- Dunblane-Crianlarich
- Stanley Junction-Kinnaber Junction
- Rock Ferry-Birkenhead Woodside
- Strathbungo-Glasgow St Enoch
- St Rollox-Glasgow Buchanan Street

13

PLANNING FOR THE FUTURE

'You cannot compete in time with airlines on trans-continental runs, but you can outstrip them in comfort, safety, dependability of service, and also show the passenger the countryside. This, we believe, is a permanent market.'

EDWARD G. BUDD JR, SPEAKING TO THE AMERICAN ASSOCIATION
OF PASSENGER TRAFFIC OFFICERS, CHICAGO, 24 APRIL 1957

The new age of the train – high speed rail and all that

The revival of the railway is the theme that runs throughout this book. To those who worked in the industry in the 1960s, '70s and '80s this seems almost miraculous. Then it was assumed that private motoring and heavy lorries would reign supreme, and the transport imperative was to build motorways on a predict and provide basis to serve them.

The railways at that time were expected to decline gracefully, with many more lines closed and services replaced by buses, capacity cut by the singling of main lines, and passengers discouraged with ever higher fares and slower services, and the rail freight business largely abolished except for heavy bulk loads and some container traffic.

As we explain elsewhere, the British public was not prepared to see its railways decline and die, and by July 2001 the distinguished City correspondent Christopher Fildes[267] was able to write in *The Spectator*: 'Railways are a growth industry. Their most sustained attempts to drive away their customers have not succeeded.'

In July 2013 Network Rail published a report entitled 'Better Connections – Options for the integration of High Speed 2':

'Over the last decade the number of journeys made by rail has increased by almost 50% and there are over a million more trains running every year. This means that the busiest parts of the network are at capacity at peak times and our biggest stations are busier than Heathrow. But demand is still increasing. By 2020 another 400 million rail journeys will be made every year.'[268]

'The railway plays a vital role in the economic life of Britain. Railways don't just move people and freight, they generate and spread prosperity by opening up new markets for businesses, creating jobs and contributing to sustainable economic growth.'[269]

Network Rail claims that it has done its best to maximise the use of remaining capacity, and has squeezed every last incremental change out of what it has got.

'But as demand continues to grow, this becomes harder and in some places impossible. Despite all the investment committed, and the additional capacity that this has provided and will deliver in the future, parts of the existing network will be unable to accommodate the forecast demand, leading to significant overcrowding; in the peak, passengers may not even be able to board a train on some routes. Further, there will be no opportunity to accommodate the expected levels of increased freight traffic on the network.'[270]

Managers who planned for decline, contraction and perhaps, ultimately, extinction 20 to 30 years ago have been replaced by modern counterparts who have been given unprecedented sums of money for investment and are getting on with the job of improving infrastructure, buying new trains, electrifying routes, and attracting ever increasing numbers of passengers and freight companies on to the rails.

One practical consequence of this growth has been significant overcrowding on a number of main routes. In the past – particularly the 1970s – this 'over-demand' was dealt with by making train travel less attractive, by such means as cutting frequency, putting up fares, and encouraging transfers of rail business to the roads. It was believed that so long as the motorway construction programme proceeded, road transport would meet Britain's needs.

While the road lobby has certainly not gone away, it is far less vocal and influential than it was. Its proponents surface from time to time in the columns of right-wing newspapers that are obsessed by the absurd notion of 'a war on motorists', and in think-tanks that receive funding from road interests and obediently put out anti-rail propaganda.[271] The political consensus has been transformed into a genuinely pro-railway stance, as demonstrated by the vote in the House of Commons on 28 April 2014 on the second reading of the High Speed Rail (London to West Midlands) Bill – 452 in favour and only 41 against.

Faced with the growing demand for rail travel, the nation is faced with four choices:

1. To try to 'choke it off' by making the rail experience sufficiently unattractive that people stop using the trains
2. To embark on a new motorway and major road construction programme

3. To patch up the existing railway

4. To embark on the construction of a new high-speed network

We have largely dealt with options 1 and 2. On road-building, it is worth remembering that the width of land required for a dual-carriageway three-lane motorway is 36 metres, compared with just 22 metres that will be needed for High Speed 2. Over the entire 330-mile route, HS2's land take will be 11.7 square kilometres (4.5 square miles), compared with 19.1 square kilometres (7.27 square miles) for the equivalent length of motorway.

And of course it is necessary to build into the calculation other consequences of more people taking to their cars, such as the need for additional town-centre and out-of-town parking, service stations and the like.

Looking at option 3 – the make-do-and-mend approach, trying to add capacity piecemeal to the West Coast and East Coast main lines – the last time the West Coast line was upgraded it was supposed to take six years, cost £2 billion and deliver 140mph trains. What actually happened was that it took nine years, cost almost £10 billion, and we still have 125mph trains – involving unimaginable disruption of existing services in the process, with seemingly endless closures and bus substitutions at weekends and sometimes longer.

If it were tried again it would, according to Network Rail, require 2,770 weekend closures, vast numbers of bus substitutions, and increased journey times over 14 years – all for a capacity increase between London and Birmingham of just 53 per cent with no increase in the current line speed, compared with HS2's 143 per cent, and dramatically reduced journey times.

The argument for HS2 is not primarily about the length of time it takes to travel from London to Birmingham, although it is obvious that if a new railway is built it will be to 21st-century standards, using technology that is tried and tested throughout Europe and Asia, rather than that of the Victorian age. It is about capacity, both that created by the new line itself and that released on the classic line by the transfer of express trains to the new route. This will enable more frequent passenger trains to be run, serving intermediate points, or more freight, or both and may also allow the journey times of freight trains to be reduced.

The essential case for building High Speed 2 is not as a separate line, physically and operationally away from the current railway, but as a crucial part of a reshaped and improved national network. In this way it will provide the capacity for the numbers of people who want to travel not only from London to Birmingham and in due course the great cities of the North of England and Scotland as well, but also between those cities and to and from the West of England and Wales.

It will also be responsible for massive economic regeneration in England's 'core cities' - Birmingham, Bristol, Leeds, Liverpool, Manchester, Newcastle, Nottingham and Sheffield.

Representatives of those cities had a letter published in the *Daily Telegraph* on 29 May 2013, in which they said:

'Research has shown that an over-reliance on the capital city is bad for national economies. England needs these eight core cities to succeed. If these cities performed at the national average, another £1.3 billion would be put into the economy every year. Unlocking growth relies on rebalancing the economy of Britain, which HS2 will help to do, bringing regeneration benefits outside the South East.

High-speed rail is not just about fast trains. Increasing capacity on the rail network is critical to our economic future. There is an important relationship between growth, jobs and HS2. High-speed rail is the best way to achieve a more sustainable economic future for the nation as a whole.'

Thus, the primary need for high speed lines, despite their name, is not for speed, but for capacity as a result of the growth in demand for rail services. The fact that some of the capacity required would have been provided by the lines we describe in this book that were closed or emaciated during the 1960s and '70s demonstrates the need to retain the infrastructure and protect it even if it has a period of disuse. But in some cases we have to ask whether it would not have been more cost-effective to have retained lines that appeared to provide some duplication of other routes, and to bear their 'losses' compared with the huge cost facing the nation of creating new capacity now.

Policy, planning and paying for restoration

The Conservative Government of John Major confidently expected the private sector to pay for the building of Britain's first high-speed line, but the private sector is notoriously risk-averse, could see the potential political and commercial problems, and did not step up to the plate. John Prescott as Deputy Prime Minister in the Labour Government of Tony Blair arranged the Government guarantee that was always going to be necessary, and the scheme was then successfully undertaken. No doubt a similar approach will form the basis of funding HS2 and its further extensions.

How are more modest line and station reopenings approved and funded? Pre-privatisation BR would have sponsored and provided the financial security and project management, even if the project were entirely funded by a local authority. Then, between 2001 and 2005, a similar role would have been undertaken by the SRA. Today, however, there is a gap and the policy has only emerged slowly. The principal method of Government funding is through the Local Sustainable Transport Fund, through purchasing outputs during the process of agreeing Network Rail's funding for each five-year control period and through franchise specification on train services. Reopening projects solely with central government funding are rare and in most cases in the English shire counties and unitary authorities, a partnership is required involving local authorities and possibly developers. In Scotland, Wales, London or the PTE areas, devolved government does provide the leadership and funding that is missing elsewhere.

'Connecting Communities' – the ATOC proposals

In 2009 the Association of Train Operating Companies published a report entitled 'Connecting Communities'. It was written by Chris Austin, one of your authors, who had worked with a small multi-disciplinary team to prepare it. It reviewed towns in England with a population in excess of 15,000 that were no longer rail-connected and considered in broad terms the feasibility and business case for putting them back on the network. Seventy-five towns were considered and a short list of 35 resulted, with several having the potential to be worth doing. Of these, 14 places were identified where a positive business case appeared possible and a further six locations where a new line might be justified on the basis of the regeneration benefits it would bring. The lines listed are shown in Appendix F.

The report revealed that some very large communities were off the network, in particular the Rossendale valley in Lancashire, and on the Ivanhoe Line between Leicester and Burton-on-Trent, both of which could potentially serve a population of around 95,000 each. If all 14 schemes with a potentially positive business case were taken forward, around a million people would be better served. The report made a strong case for safeguarding routes pending detailed studies.

One of the reasons for undertaking this study was a recognition that access to stations has become more difficult as passenger demand has grown. Car parks are full, bus links inadequate or non-existent and station entrances can become crowded. Station travel plans have helped to address these problems, but a rail connection clearly overcomes them and provides a wider range of access points to the rail network and a better service for passengers.

Widespread interest was generated by the report, although it did not result immediately in any of the proposals being taken forward. However, good progress has been made subsequently in planning for the return of the railway to Portishead near Bristol, and to Wisbech in Cambridgeshire, while the report did lead directly to proposals to reinstate Soham station on the line between Bury St Edmunds and Ely. Further work is being done on linking Heywood and Middleton in Greater Manchester, Ashington and Blyth in Northumberland, Aldridge and Brownhills in the West Midlands, and Skelmersdale in Lancashire. Most importantly, it indicated how far thinking had come since the depressing days of the 1960s and '70s, and was a very positive response by the train operators to the opportunities offered by growing demand.

Long-term planning

Throughout the period covered by this book, the railway was bedevilled by short-termism and lack of vision. At its worst, British Rail's external financing limit was sometimes not set until after the start of the financial year to which it applied, and was then revised during the autumn as a result of external financial pressures on Government. The present arrangement of franchising has improved on this, providing a contractual commitment for funding specific services for the duration of the franchise. Network Rail operates in five-year control periods with the funding approved by the Office of Rail Regulation and committed by Government for that period. The move to Route Utilisation Studies, initiated by the Strategic Rail Authority, has encouraged a more stable investment environment and a longer-term look ahead. More recently, Network Rail has initiated a long-term planning process that looks ahead for 30 years and identifies the interventions needed to meet the growth forecast over that period.

This is much better than anything that has gone before and it is perhaps not surprising that the greatest level of intervention is required in those route corridors where surplus capacity was identified by the second Beeching Report on trunk routes which was stripped out during the 1970s. Emerging options for this process include the need for more capacity on the Brighton line, more loops or track doubling between Salisbury and Exeter, more capacity on the Midland main line, particularly through Leicester, and the need for a second route between Exeter and Plymouth.

The lessons are clear: capacity is expensive to create and easy to destroy. Keep options open, and even if no requirement for capacity is foreseen in the short to medium term, make sure the land and formation are kept. The longer-term future is hard to foresee and our track record in long-term planning is not good.

Campaigning and the role of Government

'One is not accustomed to search the columns of the daily newspapers for reliable facts and figures relating to railways.'
Cecil J. Allen, 'British Locomotive Practice and Performance', *The Railway Magazine*, Vol LII, 1923

In 1963 the Government had a clear policy on the closure of a large part of the railway network identified in detail in the first Beeching Report but, as we saw earlier (Chapter 1), by 1971 it had no policy on railways. Subsequently, the policy has focussed on reducing the cost of the railway by contraction during the 1970s, and by investment and greater efficiency during the 1980s, on privatisation during the 1990s and on expanding the existing network to meet the needs of growth in the 21st century. For new lines and stations, though, the policy has been pretty opaque. The experience of OBRAC (the Oxon and Bucks Rail Action Committee), set out in some detail in Appendix D, shows just how difficult it has been to campaign for opening new lines or reopening abandoned ones, just how long it takes, and how many agencies are now involved.

The root of the problem is that throughout much of England there is no organisation charged with leading the development of new lines, and in most cases it is beyond the capability and remit of individual local authorities. The East West Rail consortium is an exception to this rule and is to be congratulated for its tenacity and strong vision in sticking with the project for so long.

In Scotland and Wales, Government agencies sponsor new lines and stations, and in England imaginative schemes have been introduced by Transport for London (the East London line) and the Passenger Transport Executives (for example the Brighouse line). Elsewhere, though, new lines have been limited to those where a determined local authority has been prepared to take the lead, as in the case of the Clitheroe line in Lancashire or the Robin Hood line, where Nottinghamshire was similarly crucial, and this helps to explain why the pace of rail development in England has more recently lagged behind. The Highways Agency and local authorities sponsor new roads, Government commissions are established to consider the case for new airports, but there is no structure to consider the need for new railways. It is not something done by the Department for Transport, while Network Rail is necessarily focussed on the current network.

In earlier years this was underscored by an unwillingness by Government to consider the case for new railway construction, until the advent of HS1. The position in 2015 is, however, different, and it has become possible to make the case for new railways, although it still requires a sponsor with a great deal of determination and money. The Government's position is that new railways can be considered in the context of a solution to an identified transport problem, and that the normal evaluation criteria can then be applied. It looks to local sponsorship of proposals. Funding, however, remains another issue, and while some Government funding may be available, match-funding is frequently beyond the means of a local authority or private developer. The other underlying problem is that of all railway investment – the timescale for implementation is long in relation to the political cycle and carries with it some uncertainty, particularly on costs. In other words, politicians can rarely enjoy the political benefits of a major rail project, which will be picked up by their successors. The formation of a Railways Division within DfT has produced a more positive response and, indeed, considerable support for the East West Rail project, but this remains an area of uncertainty, restraining the development of projects that might bring more significant benefits.

The consequence is that some areas of the country are not able to enjoy the benefits of being on the rail network, and that these may be due to subsequent development, unforeseen at the time of closure, or may simply result from the erratic way in which the Beeching Report was implemented. It is all a bit of a lottery.

Heritage railways as public transport providers

In *Holding the Line* we briefly tell the story of the heritage railway movement, and describe the scale of its operation in Great Britain.[272] Since its publication the all-party parliamentary group (APPG) on heritage rail has published an authoritative report on the contribution that this sector makes to the economies of the areas it serves, both in terms of attracting tourists and in stimulating spending on local services.[273]

Research undertaken for a number of railways indicated that for every pound that is spent on a heritage railway there is a benefit to the local economy of around £2.70. This suggests that the annual economic benefit nationally is around £250 million. The Group concludes that apart from the economic benefits, heritage railways also provide employment for more than 3,700 staff nationally and a productive outlet for 18,500 loyal volunteers. The parliamentarians observed that across the 100-plus members of the Heritage Railway Association not a single one is dependent on financial support from central or local government.

Another finding – of direct relevance to the subject matter of this book – related to the heritage railways' potential for providing regular public transport services. The APPG said this:

'We consider that more should be done to develop the potential of heritage railways to offer public transport on their lines as well as the experience of a steam train ride. This should be supported by local authority grant or franchise payment where justified, in the same way as applies to National Rail operators.'[274]

What the group had in mind here was not necessarily about providing a 'commuter' service to take people to work – although a few lines have the scope to do this – but offering a 'tourist transport' service to take people, without their cars, into sensitive areas such as national parks, areas of outstanding natural beauty or small coastal towns that are gridlocked with traffic.

The lines that may be able to offer such services would need to be connected directly to the national rail network, or at least have a station adjacent to it, and the intention would be for the public transport services to be additional to, not in place of, the heritage operation.

Whenever this has been suggested in the past numerous practical objections have been raised, covering such matters as the level of fares (heritage rail fares per mile are far higher than conventional rail fares), the employment of paid staff (either full or part time) and their terms and conditions, the hours and dates of operation, the requirement for public subsidy, and so on. But in principle it seems to make excellent sense to offer a rail service where there is a demand for it, particularly if wider social and environmental objectives are met by doing so, such as getting people out of their cars and off the roads, and providing a popular alternative to unreliable bus services.

Standard gauge heritage railways that could offer a public transport service might include:

Bodmin & Wenford Railway from Bodmin Parkway to Bodmin General
Churnet Valley Railway (Alton Towers)
Dartmoor Railway (Okehampton)
East Lancashire Railway from Heywood to Rawtenstall
Ecclesbourne Valley Railway to Wirksworth
Embsay & Bolton Abbey Steam Railway from Skipton
Ffestiniog and Welsh Highland Railways
Gloucestershire & Warwickshire Railway from Honeybourne to Cheltenham
Great Central Railway from south Nottingham to north Leicester
Keighley & Worth Valley Railway from Keighley to Oxenhope
Keith & Dufftown Railway
Mid Hants Railway to Alresford
North Norfolk Railway from Sheringham to Holt
North Yorkshire Moors Railway from Pickering to Whitby[275w]
Paignton & Dartmouth Railway
Peak Rail to Matlock to Bakewell
Severn Valley Railway from Bewdley to Kidderminster
South Devon Railway
Spa Valley Railway Eridge to Tunbridge Wells
Strathspey Railway to Grantown
Swanage Railway from Wareham
Weardale Railway
Wensleydale Railway
West Somerset Railway from Taunton to Minehead

Operating a public transport service on lines such as these, probably using low-cost diesel multiple units[276], need not detract from the provision of steam-hauled heritage trains; indeed, a properly planned timetable could bring substantial numbers of new passengers on to the heritage lines.

Some of the standard gauge lines on which heritage railways currently operate are described elsewhere in this book as routes that should not have closed, and we imagine that the volunteers who work on them will agree. A very small number would be affected if our proposals for reopening them as part of the national network were to come about – the Lavender Line, which occupies part of the Lewes to Uckfield route, is an obvious example – but we do not believe that this should preclude the restoration of services needed to provide essential capacity as the demand for rail travel continues to grow.

14

PLUGGING THE GAPS – A POSTSCRIPT

Hindsight is the only guarantee of accuracy in forecasting, so it is now clear for the first time that the retrenchment planned by the Macmillan Government of 1960 and its successors, together with the British Railways Board, went too far and too fast and that more damage was done by the 'Trunk Routes' report of 1965 than the 'Reshaping' report of 1963.

The initial proof of this is that 370 stations have been opened or reopened since Beeching left BR in 1965, together with 233 miles of new or reopened lines. Some of these lines reopened very quickly indeed. We have already mentioned the closure of Snow Hill station in Birmingham, where plans to reopen were first put forward by the new West Midlands PTE in 1973, the year following closure, but Peterborough-Spalding was even quicker and reopened within eight months of closure.

Secondary proof is offered in the development of HS2 and its extensions, whose primary function is to create additional capacity and, incidentally, to reduce journey time.

The third point is in the context of the many billions of pounds required to rebuild and expand Britain's road network to cater for the traffic growth from the 1950s that continued until it levelled off after 2006. It is accepted that much of this investment would have been required anyway to make the road system fit for purpose and, in particular, to improve the appalling road safety record of that era. The impact (and cost) of this is graphically described in Chapter 7, describing the huge investment required for the A34 once the Didcot, Newbury & Southampton line had been destroyed. It also illustrates that the growth in road freight and the rise in the weight and size of the juggernauts needed to carry it were significant factors in driving this investment.

VALLEY LINES
The Aberdare line is one successfully restored by BR in 1988 and is now an essential part of life in the valleys. Before the initial closure of the line in 1964, a train from Abercynon to Aberdare Low Level calls at Mountain Ash Oxford Street, the former Taff Vale station. *Chris Austin*

The fourth point is the unprecedented interest in new lines in addition to the high-speed network, including some significant investments such as Crossrail, the Borders Railway, East West Rail, and many more modest schemes that are being developed through Network Rail's long-term planning process.

While Scotland has been effective in planning new lines and stations, as has Wales, London and the PTE areas, the picture elsewhere in England has been patchy. Some counties like Devon and Lancashire have supported a number of line reopening projects, others like Somerset and Northamptonshire have not. There is no overall plan and in these parts of England no strong agency that can sponsor such major projects.

The Department for Transport does not see this as its job, and no part of the rail industry has the comprehensive authority to take the lead. The authors hope that the Department would, at least, take the strategic lead here and coordinate local initiatives and provide an overarching framework to explain the basis of funding and evaluation and to support sponsors of individual projects.

Despite this, the major change over the last half-century has been the change of attitude and approach by the Department and the Treasury. Indeed, the whole view of railways by opinion formers and the 'chattering classes' has been transformed. In the 1960s the 'informed' view was that railways were in terminal decline and that the future was motorways and the jet aircraft. Today, the railways are seen as an essential part of the solution to the intractable problems of road congestion, airport capacity, pollution and economic development. In the 1960s there was an agenda to shrink the rail network and a conspiracy between Government and the road lobby to shift investment from rail to road. Today, the agenda is one of expansion of the capacity and extent of the network and there are record investment levels to help rail achieve its

HOW IT SHOULD WORK
St Andrews bus station is well connected with the main line at Leuchars with nine buses an hour, and rail tickets can be bought at the bus station, which also contains a real-time departure board for Leuchars. *Chris Austin*

proper role in meeting the country's transport needs. Infrastructure investment is seen as a good thing, and rail investment is no longer referred to as 'subsidy'. There is an acceptance that the demographic trends and the drivers of economic success require good infrastructure and that this includes a major role for rail.

We are hugely encouraged by the developments of the last decade and would hope that this book will encourage further development towards extending the reach of Britain's amazingly useful railway.

OVER THE ALPS

The route from Winchester to Alton and Pirbright Junction near
Brookwood was a useful diversionary route until the line was closed in 1973.
On 8 January 1967 Class 33 No D6533 passes Itchen Abbas with the diverted
08.56 Bournemouth-Waterloo train, calling at the local stations on the way.
The main line was closed for electrification works. From the next station
at Alresford to Alton has been lovingly restored by the Mid Hants Railway.
John H. Bird

Appendix A
List of lines that would be valuable today

1. Through routes and link lines capable of restoration
Alton-Winchester
Bourne End-High Wycombe
Bristol-Avonmouth via Henbury
Exeter-Okehampton-Plymouth
Harrogate-Ripon-Northallerton
Leicester-Burton
Lewes-Uckfield
Malton-Pickering-Grosmont (Whitby)
Matlock-Buxton/Chinley – completes Derby-Manchester route
Newcastle-Ashington/Morpeth
Oxford/Aylesbury-Cambridge (East West Rail)
Skipton-Colne
Spalding-Boston and Firsby-Louth-Grimsby
Stansted Airport-Braintree (using formation of Dunmow line)
Waverley Route
Willingdon chord (Eastbourne) – direct link Brighton-Hastings
Woodhead route (Glossop-Sheffield via Stocksbridge)
Yeovil Junction-Yeovil Pen Mill

2. Branch lines or extensions capable of restoration
Barnstaple-Bideford
Bodmin Parkway-Bodmin General-Wadebridge
Bristol-Portishead
Brockenhurst-Ringwood
Edinburgh-Leith (extension of tram along Leith Walk)
Edinburgh-Glencorse (Penicuik)
Guildford-Cranleigh
Kidderminster-Bridgnorth
Kirkby-Skelmersdale
March-Wisbech
Oxford-Cowley
Penrith-Keswick
Poulton-Fleetwood
St Andrews-Leuchars (new junction for direct route to Edinburgh)
Southall-Brentford
Taunton-Minehead
Thornton Junction-Leven
Totton-Hythe
Tweedbank-Longtown for Carlisle
Wareham-Swanage
Wymondham-Dereham-Fakenham

3. Through routes or link lines that would be more difficult or impractical to restore
Accrington-Stubbins Junction
Bury (Knowsley Street) to Bolton
Bangor-Caernarfon-Afon Wen
Bridgnorth-Shrewsbury
Cheltenham/Honeybourne-Stratford-upon-Avon
Cambridge-St Ives-March
Cambridge (Shelford Junction)-Sudbury
Carmarthen-Aberystwyth
Cowdenbeath-Kinross-Perth
Didcot, Newbury & Southampton (freight)
Great Central (Calvert to Nottingham and Sheffield)
Horsham-Brighton
March-Spalding
Northampton–Peterborough
Princes Risborough-Cowley
Ringwood-Wimborne-Poole/Hamworthy Junction
Ruabon-Morfa Mawddach (Barmouth Junction)
Southport-Preston
York-Market Weighton-Beverley

4. Branch lines that would be more difficult or impractical to restore
Aberdeen-Fraserburgh
Barnstaple-Ilfracombe
Brecon-Merthyr
King's Lynn-Hunstanton
Leeds-Wetherby
Ryde-Newport
Shanklin-Ventnor
West Drayton-Uxbridge (linked to Crossrail)
Yatton-Clevedon

5. Lines reopened
Restored lines only are shown below, and short spurs are omitted, as are new lines like HS1.
Abercynon-Aberdare
Airdrie-Bathgate-Edinburgh (Newbridge Junction)
Argyle line (Finnieston Junction-Rutherglen)
Aylesbury-Aylesbury Vale Parkway (to Oxford from 2016)
Barassie-Kilmarnock

Barry-Bridgend
Birmingham Moor St-Snow Hill-Smethwick Junction
Birmingham Snow Hill-Wolverhampton (light rail)
Blackburn-Clitheroe
Blackfriars-Farringdon (Thameslink)
Blaydon-Newcastle via Dunston
Borders Railway (Newcraighall-Tweedbank)
Bridgend-Maesteg
Burnley-Todmorden
Cardiff City Line (Canton-Radyr)
Chippenham-Trowbridge
Coventry-Nuneaton
Dalston-Stratford
Dalston-Shoreditch
Deansgate-Salford Crescent
Eastleigh-Romsey
Ebbw Vale line
Halifax-Huddersfield
Heathrow Airport
Heysham-Morecambe
Kensington Olympia-Willesden Junction

Kettering-Corby-Manton Junction
Ladybank-Perth
Larkhall-Hamilton (Haughhead Junction)
Leamington Spa-Coventry
Linlithgow-Dalmeny
Manchester Airport
Maryhill-Glasgow (Cowlairs West Junction)
Motherwell-Coatbridge-Greenhill Lower Junction
Northallerton-Eaglescliffe
Oxford-Bicester
Penistone-Barnsley
Peterborough-Spalding
Robin Hood line (Nottingham-Mansfield-Worksop)
Rutherglen-Whifflet
Shields Junction-Paisley Canal
Stansted Airport
Stirling-Alloa (to Kincardine for freight)
Timperley-Stockport
Vale of Glamorgan
Wakefield (Crofton West Junction)-Pontefract Monkhill
Walsall-Hednesford

Appendix B
List of lines and stations opened under the 'Speller' Act

Date	Station/route/service	Facility	Date closed
16/05/1983	Station	Pinhoe	
16/05/1983	Route	Penistone-Barnsley	
03/10/1983	Station	Templecombe	
21/11/1983	Station	Moss Side	
14/05/1984	Station	Lostock Hall	
09/07/1984	Station	Sherburn-in-Elmet	
15/09/1984	Station	Dyce	
23/03/1985	Station	Mill Hill	
01/05/1985	Station	South Gyle	
01/05/1985	Station	Loch Awe	
06/05/1985	Station	Loch Eil Outward Bound	
11/05/1985	Route	Cardiff City Line	
13/05/1985	Station	Flowery Field	
13/05/1985	Station	Bridge of Allan	
17/05/1985	Station	Portlethen	
18/08/1985	Station	Smithy Bridge	
30/08/1985	Station	Derker[277]	
04/11/1985	Station	Ryder Brow	
24/03/1986	Route	Edinburgh-Bathgate	
24/03/1986	Station	Bathgate	
24/03/1986	Station	Livingston North	
24/03/1986	Station	Uphall	
29/09/1986	Station	Hall i' th' Wood	
29/09/1986	Station	Burnley Manchester Road	
19/01/1987	Station	Ardrossan Town	
13/04/1987	Station	Blackpool Pleasure Beach	
13/04/1987	Route	Kettering-Corby	04/06/1990 (Reopened 23/02/2009)
13/04/1987	Station	Corby	04/06/1990 (Reopened 23/02/2009)
29/04/1987	Station	Ty Glas	
09/05/1987	Route	Oxford-Bicester Town	
09/05/1987	Station	Bicester Town	
11/05/1987	Station	Wester Hailes	
11/05/1987	Station	Hag Fold	
11/05/1987	Route	Coventry-Nuneaton	
11/05/1987	Route	Heysham Port-Morecambe[278]	
11/05/1987	Station	Heysham Port	
21/06/1987	Station	Sugar Loaf	
27/06/1987	Station	Conwy	
03/08/1987	Station	Gateshead Metro Centre	
04/10/1987	Station	Danescourt	
04/10/1987	Station	Fairwater	
04/10/1987	Station	Ninian Park	
05/10/1987	Station	Curriehill	
02/11/1987	Station	Waun-Gron Park	
14/05/1988	Station	Bedworth	
16/05/1988	Route	Didcot West Curve Junction-Foxhall Junction	18/05/2003
28/11/1988	Route	Lichfield City-Lichfield Trent Valley High Level	
08/04/1989	Route	Walsall-Hednesford	
08/04/1989	Station	Hednesford	
08/04/1989	Station	Cannock	
08/04/1989	Station	Ladywood	
15/05/1989	Route	Timperley-Stockport	

Date	Station/route/service	Facility	Date closed
25/05/1988	Route	Bishop Auckland-Stanhope[279]	
25/05/1988	Station	Stanhope	
30/07/1990	Station	Corkerhill	
30/07/1990	Station	Crookston	
30/07/1990	Station	Drumbreck	
30/07/1990	Station	Mosspark	
30/07/1990	Station	Paisley Canal	
02/10/1990	Station	Bloxwich North	
12/04/1991	Station	Hawkhead	
11/05/1992	Station	Featherstone	
11/05/1992	Station	Pontefract Tanshelf	
11/05/1992	Station	Streethouse	
08/05/1993	Station	Newstead	
08/05/1993	Station	Hucknall	
29/05/1994	Station	Ivybridge	
29/05/1994	Route	Willesden High Level Junction-Mitre Bridge Junction	
06/05/1994	Station	West Brompton	
29/05/1994	Station	Cam & Dursley	
29/05/1994	Station	Digby & Sowton	
29/05/1994	Station	Bulwell	
29/05/1994	Station	Sileby	
29/05/1994	Station	Syston	
29/05/1994	Station	Barrow-upon-Soar	
29/05/1994	Station	Ramsgreave & Wilpshire	
29/05/1994	Station	Langho	
29/05/1994	Station	Whalley	
29/05/1994	Route	Earlestown Liverpool Curve	
29/05/1994	Route	Additional platforms at Earlestown	
29/05/1994	Route	North Somerset Junction-Dr Day's Junction	
29/05/1994	Station	Llansamlet	
29/05/1994	Station	Skewen	
29/05/1994	Station	Pyle	
29/05/1994	Station	Briton Ferry	
24/09/1994	Station	Camelon	
05/09/1994	Station	Prestwick International Airport	
10/11/1995	Route	Newstead-Mansfield Woodhouse	
12/11/1995	Station	Kirkby-in-Ashfield	
10/11/1995	Station	Sutton Parkway	
10/11/1995	Station	Mansfield	
10/11/1995	Station	Mansfield Woodhouse	
12/11/1995	Route	Heald Green West Junction-Heald Green South Junction	
28/05/1995	Route	New Beckenham-Beckenham Junction	29/05/2000
28/05/1995	Station	Willington	
28/05/1995	Station	Chafford Hundred	
17/02/1996	Station	Yarm	
11/03/1996	Station	Filton Abbey Wood	
01/06/1996	Route	Dalmeny Junction-Winchburgh Junction	
01/06/1996	Station	Baglan	
24/05/1997	Route	Crediton-Okehampton (see overleaf)	
24/05/1997	Station	Okehampton (see overleaf)	
01/06/1997	Route	Hednesford-Rugeley Town	
01/06/1997	Station	Rugeley Town	

Date	Station/route/service	Facility	Date closed
27/07/1997	Route	Maindee North Junction-East Usk Junction	
15/12/1997	Station	Euxton Balshaw Lane	
24/05/1998	Route	Crayford-Slade Green	
19/01/1998	Route	London Paddington-Heathrow Junction Station	Spur into temporary station closed 25/05/1998
19/01/1998	Station	Heathrow Junction Station	Temporary station closed 25/05/1998
01/03/1998	Station	Dalgety Bay	
24/05/1998	Station	Shirebrook	
24/05/1998	Station	Langwith Whaley Thorns	
24/05/1998	Station	Cresswell	
24/05/1998	Station	Whitwell	
24/05/1998	Route	Doncaster-South Milford	
24/05/1998	Route	Crayford-Slade Green	
24/05/1998	Route	Rugeley Town-Rugeley Trent Valley	
17/04/1998	Route	Crediton-Okehampton	
17/04/1998	Station	Okehampton[280]	
29/05/1999	Route	Romsey-Eastleigh via Chandler's Ford	
25/01/2000	Station	Dunfermline Queen Margaret	
28/05/2000	Route	South Acton Junction-Old Kew Junction	29/09/2002
28/05/2000	Route	Graham Road Curve	29/09/2002
01/02/2002	Station	Beauly	
21/06/2002	Route	Swansea District Line	
01/05/2003	Route	Dore South curve	10/09/2004
22/05/2011	Route	Hawkeridge Junction-Westbury East Loop Junction	
08/07/2011	Station	Southend Airport	

Source: Phil Deaves

Appendix C
Lines with a 'Parliamentary service' of trains in February 2015

Stockport-Stalybridge (one train a week in one direction)

Gainsborough-Barnetby (three trains on Saturdays only)

Minster-Sandwich (two trains from Minster to Sandwich daily, one return)

Morecambe-Carnforth direct (one train each way daily)

Morecambe-Heysham (one train each way daily)

Paddington-South Ruislip (one train each way daily)

Wigan North Western-Liverpool Lime Street via Golborne Junction and Newton le Willows Junction

Chester to Runcorn via Halton Curve (one train in one direction, summer Saturdays only)

Teesside Airport station has one train each way a week on Sundays.

Stations that have not been closed, but have no train service:

Wedgwood

Barlaston

Norton Bridge

Newhaven Marine

Appendix D
East-West Rail project diary compiled by the Oxon and Bucks Rail Action Committee (OBRAC)

In 1973, the Milton Keynes Development Corporation commissioned Freeman Fox 'to identify what potential these lines have for Milton Keynes' and found 'the case for immediate reintroduction of services between Bletchley and Oxford is doubtful' but 'an economic case for an Oxford-Bicester service in the immediate future would be relatively far more attractive.' A further review was to be carried out in 1979.

In 1974, Milton Keynes Transport Users Group pressed for the retention of the route for passenger use. Bucks County Council said in 1975: 'Future Transport for Bucks recognised the need to investigate the possibility of rail services from Milton Keynes to Aylesbury and Oxford and the undesirability of the need to travel into London to make northbound journeys from Aylesbury.'

In 1979 the Aylesbury and Milton Keynes Community Health Council saw a need for 'a rail service linking all the major towns in Buckinghamshire with perhaps a train running from Northampton through Milton Keynes to Aylesbury.' BR responded by saying there was no way of costing the proposal, whilst Bucks CC claimed not have considered the option. Meanwhile, a petition in Winslow attracted 1,400 signatures and saw rail as a way of cutting car use. Milton Keynes Development Corporation responded by claiming that the growth of the new town would see the line reopen eventually, but in 1980 their review concluded that there was 'no immediate prospect of reopening to passenger services'. In 1981, the MK Green Party joined the efforts to seek reopening.

The Railway Development Society proposed a Didcot to East Anglia service in 1983, and included the idea in their book *Bring Back the Trains*. Bicester Labour Party sought the views of BR on a Bicester to Oxford service, which BR costed at £1m. Aylesbury and District Rail Passengers Association, in the campaign to save Marylebone station, suggested services should be extended to Milton Keynes. The London Regional Passengers Committee supported this view. Special trains operated in 1984 and were well supported.

In 1985, in response to representations from a Bicester Rail Promotion Group, BR announced a low-cost proposal for Oxford-Bicester services. In 1986, Oxfordshire County Council, Cherwell District Council and Bicester Town Council added their support to the plan and later funding.

One year later, the Bedford-Bletchley Rail Users Association (BBRUA) published an appeal for activists to set up a group to campaign for the reopening of the Oxford-Bletchley rail link to passengers. BBRUA was formed in 1980 to promote the route and as a secondary aspiration recognised the value of the Oxford link. A public meeting was organised for 7 December 1986, coinciding with well-supported Christmas Specials to Milton Keynes from Oxford and Aylesbury.

On 7 March 1987 the meeting was reconvened and it was decided that a coordinating group of the Railway Development Society (later renamed Rail Future) and the user groups would advance the case for MK-Oxford/Aylesbury passenger rail services. Thus, OBRAC was born.

The Bucks County Structure Plan confirmed that 'with Milton Keynes expanding to 200k people by the turn of the century, it is important that existing and potential rail routes to and from the city be kept under review.' Bucks CC noted a new round of campaigning was under way and asked BR for their views. BR quoted £1.3m capital costs for reopening and £200k pa revenue support, which was felt to be not feasible. BR put Winslow station up for sale. Winslow Town Council and OBRAC launched a fierce fight to halt the sale, including a tree preservation order on the trees on the site. BR agreed to preserve access to the platforms and a parking area. One of the group attended the sale to advise buyers of the TPO. OBRAC hoped that with the interest of councils, the success of special trains, the growth of Milton Keynes and the prospect of Bicester-Oxford services, the campaign would be brief.

Oxford-Bicester Rail Users Group (OBRUG) was formed to represent users of the new service, which was to start in May. BR noted that success could see extension to Milton Keynes. Bucks CC Christmas shopper specials ran again and also an OBRUG service from Swindon and Oxford to MK. OBRAC gained support from MPs and councils and was surprised to find that whilst the DfT had a road network programme, there was no such rail plan and BR was left to decide what was needed.

In 1988 Milton Keynes Council decided to seek revised costings from BR and £2,375,000 was quoted and an annual operating deficit of £50k forecast. The Christmas shopper specials were used by 1,252 people, and demonstrated how much public interest there was in the line.

In 1989 an officers' special traversed the lines and councils agreed to fund a full feasibility study by Kennedy Henderson. In April BR ran a test train to consider the feasibility of a Peterborough to Swindon service to start in 1991 using Class 158 units. Capital costs of £3-4m were expected plus a new platform at Bletchley. No subsidy was expected. The proposal was widely welcomed. OBRAC, meanwhile, published their *Perspective for A New Vision to Link Major Towns*. The Christmas shopper specials carried 812 people including Maeve Kennedy from *The Guardian* who ran a feature on her day with OBRAC.

In 1990 the Kennedy Henderson report was published suggesting that capital expenditure of £2.3 to £5.9m was required above that for the BR Peterborough-Swindon proposals to provide a local service along the route and to Aylesbury. OBRAC attended a public inquiry into the Aylesbury Vale Local Plan and secured reference to rail services north of Aylesbury in the Plan. OBRAC organised a 140th celebration of the opening of Winslow station, publishing a history, running a public meeting and unveiling a model of a reopened station. The Leighton Buzzard Youth Theatre presented a musical play *Re-open the Line*. BBRUA published a book *Oxford-Cambridge – Then and Now* and ran a special train to Bristol, calling at Winslow, Bicester Town and Islip. At the year end, BR reported that the case for their proposal was 'not as good as originally thought' and it would be reviewed in 1993/94. There was also a rolling stock shortage. Christmas shopper specials attracted 730 users, including 100 on a trip from MK to Aylesbury.

In 1991 OBRAC organised a special train from Oxford to Bedford – 'The Oxford Mail' – for the River Festival, and BBRUA used the train for a Bedford-Oxford Special. Both ran full. A meeting with Roger Freeman[281], the rail minister, was positive but on his return to the DfT he felt the proposals were 'premature' and OBRAC was 'overzealous' and BR needed 'to identify worthwhile new services'. OBRAC helped the Open University produce a video *Railway Revival* as part of training course. OBRAC also undertook talks 'Bring Back the Trains' and wrote an article for the *Local Council Review* highlighting the role for councils in developing new rail links. Christmas shopper specials failed to run due to increased costs, stock and crew issues. Transport 2000 (Beds) ran talks on east of Bedford.

In 1992 Milton Keynes Development Corporation, in the run-up to their wind-down, recommended the New Towns Commission re-examine the potential for rail services to Oxford and Aylesbury. (OBRAC felt MKDC had failed to be proactive in pressing the case and seemed to favour roads and bridleways.) Wiltshire County Council pressed the EWRL [East West Rail Link] case and sought a further study. Oxon CC, Beds CC and Aylesbury Vale DC expressed support for EWRL. The TUCC (West) published *The Mid West Network* and highlighted the role of EWRL. OBRAC organised special trains to Spalding (for Flower Festival) and Nottingham (for Goose Fair) and both ran to capacity. Bill Simpson produced a video of the EWRL. The Government published *New Opportunities for Rail*, which proposed rail privatisation and suggested that new services could develop. John Patten[282], MP for Oxford West, sought assurances that the government could still support new rail links. Local MPs continued in their support.

In 1993 OBRAC started the year with an invite to a Kilroy television debate on rail privatisation where public concern was forcefully expressed and prophesied the future failings of privatisation. BR announced a Westbury-Oxford-Nottingham service was being examined. Oxon CC and Wilts CC funded a study of an Oxford-Swindon-Chippenham service. Bucks CC and Beds CC supported EWRL in their structure plans. MK Council funded a study into coach links. Winslow station was demolished in March but OBRAC gained assurances that the platforms would be retained. BR announced the closure of the Claydon Junction to Bletchley freight line from 31 May. OBRAC took up the closure with the minister who confirmed the route was mothballed for possible future use and the Peterborough-MK-Swindon service was the type of initiative that he hoped would be introduced by rail privatisation. He had no intention of being 'a son of Beeching'. He assured Bucks CC that nothing would be done to hamper reopening. In the run-up to closure several special trains ran, including another OBRAC special to Spalding and Lincoln, a Herts HST Rail Tour to Matlock and a 'Mothball Special'. Worse followed as the Avon-Calvert 'bin liners' were to be diverted via Wycombe so the Bicester Town to Calvert section could be closed. OBRAC decided to raise the profile of EWRL and built a 66-foot-long model of part of the route to exhibit in Winslow and at a rail day in Bicester. This gained national coverage in the model press. David Bowker, a rail artist, painted a picture of Bicester Town with a train to Milton Keynes, and OBRAC organised talks on the EWRL.

In 1994 the de-mothballing of Bicester to Calvert for 'bin liner' trains was encouraging but BR removed the crossover to Bletchley flyover and installed a gate across the tracks at Claydon Junction. The *Daily Telegraph* picked up on the OBRAC campaign and ran a feature on rail reopenings with the Swanbourne station topiary as the photo. Transport 2000 (Beds) ran a conference on EWRL. The Franchise Director (OPRAF) confirmed to OBRAC that he had power to help fund reopenings. The *Re-Open the Line* musical had another run, sponsored by OBRAC and BBRUA. OBRAC met the Chiltern Line director, Adrian Shooter, who confirmed he was in contact with councils and 'was keen to see the line reach its full potential'. A report by Oxford Brookes University *Promoting Rail Use in the M40 Corridor* identified the potential for the EWRL. The Oxon and Wilts CC study into Oxford-Swindon and Chippenham confirmed the case whilst the MK Council study found a demand for an east-west coach link. Railway Development Society (East) published an EWRL leaflet and contacted councils in the Standing Conference of East Anglian Local Authorities to seek support for a new study.

In 1995 Ipswich Borough Council with MK Council sought support to establish a consortium to promote the EWRL. OBRAC successfully urged councils in Oxon and Bucks to join. Twenty-five councils joined the East West Rail Consortium (EWRC). Steer Davies Gleave was commissioned to study the options. Stagecoach started the X5 Oxford-Cambridge coach service.[283]

In 1996 the East West Rail Study was published and recommended a detailed study of Norwich/Ipswich-Cambridge-Bedford-MK-Oxford-Swindon. Phase 1 could cost £40-90m. Interest was high and funding was raised to develop the case, including a link to Aylesbury. Oxon CC resolved to progress work on an Oxford-Swindon link. The Bicester-Oxford service in the Thames Rail franchise was cut to six trains a day and the Sunday service withdrawn. A meeting with the rail minister, John Watts, confirmed that DfT could help fund new lines if a case was proved.

In 1997 Phase 2 of the East West Rail Study was published and a £150m scheme of a 90mph route was proposed and the link to Aylesbury included. Freight would further enhance the proposals. Subject to funding, services could open in 2000. A BR Bristol-Oxford service was announced for 1998. Railtrack included the scheme in their network statement. The EWRL was raised with candidates at the general election and OBRAC thought the election of New Labour meant new rails. Chiltern Railways won the Chiltern Line franchise but did not plan a service north of Aylesbury due to the capital cost.

In 1998 the EWRC met Glenda Jackson[284], the new rail minister, and Railtrack. The scheme was felt to be viable, subject to funding, and could open in 2001. The regional benefits were recognised. Bedford Council, however, were concerned about how the EWRL would be routed through the town. An EWRC study from Berkeley Hanover reported 10k jobs could be created along the EWRL. The Oxford-Bristol service started in June. North London Railways won the franchise for services to MK and felt the link to Oxford offered 'exciting possibilities'. OBRAC continued to work with Phyllis Starkey[285], MP for MK SW, who gained the support of other MPs and raised the issue in Parliament. Rail Future published 'A-Z of Re-Openings' and included the EWRL. *Railway World* published an OBRAC article on EWRL.

In 1999 the EWRC made a bid to the new Rail Passenger Partnership (RPP) Fund. Routing through Bedford remained an issue. Patrick Hall[286], the Bedford MP, raised EWRL at Prime Minister's Questions and Tony Blair[287] felt a phased approach was appropriate. Local transport plans continued to include EWRL and the support of the new development agencies. Chiltern Railways included an option for services to MK in their franchise bid renewal and ran three successful Aylesbury to Oxford special trains. OBRAC used the service to entertain some councillors to explain the EWRL.

In 2000 the year began with the news that £5m was to be spent on restoring the access to Bletchley flyover and track towards Swanbourne sidings for use as part of the main-line upgrade. The OBRAC AGM was upbeat as the EWRC hoped to gain funds for an Oxford-MK service with 60mph single track. Anglia Railways signed an agreement to develop the EWRL plans. Chiltern Railways won their franchise renewal and aspired to provide services from MK to Oxford and Aylesbury as well as an Oxford-Marylebone service. The new government transport strategy noted 'the potential of the Cambridge-Oxford line (if approved) to provide a greatly increased range of east-west services avoiding London. This is of economic importance to the strategic development of the rapidly expanding towns and cities to the north of London.' OBRAC organised talks about '100 Years of Railways' in Winslow and Bicester Town to promote EWRL.

In 2001 there was still no news on the RPP funding bid and Anglia Railways wanted to start the service in June. Skanska, meanwhile, was appointed to develop and fund plans for east of Bedford. Bill Simpson published a new book, *Oxford-Cambridge Railway 1960-2000*, which brought public focus on to the route. The re-election of a Labour government brought news that the RPP bid had been rejected after over £1m had been spent on preparing and revising the bid. Chiltern Railways was expected to consider an MK-Aylesbury service in 2005. Anglia Railways, however, won £9.2m to introduce a Norwich to Cambridge service, which was seen as Phase 1 of the EWRL. MPs, Dr Starkey and Patrick Hall raised the issue of the RPP in the Commons. The EWRC reopened discussions on funding with the Strategic Rail Authority (SRA), which OBRAC never found very strategic on EWRL. The SRA asked that freight options be included in a bid after previously refusing to include them. The rail passenger committee published a report on the potential for reopenings including Felixstowe to the West.

In 2002 the EWRC had gained the support of 36 bodies and planned ongoing study work with SRA assistance. The SRA in their 10-year strategy suggested the Bletchley-Claydon Junction section could reopen within 2-3 years for freight. A new Winslow station site was identified off Furze Lane, and Greenway Homes proposed a highly controversial housing development at Little Horwood and offered £6.5m towards the EWRL.

In 2003 the SRA axed the Bristol-Oxford rail service in May in spite of suggesting, in 2002, this form part of the EWRL case. There was no progress on an MK-Aylesbury link and the Government ordered work to stop on the Skanska studies for east of Bedford. OBRAC began to question its very existence and launched a campaign 'No Population without Rail Transportation', which seemed to grab the public imagination. The publication of the London to South Midlands multi-modal transport study provided a major boost to the decision to continue. The report found that the Oxford-MK rail link could be implemented relatively quickly and recommended the SRA should advance construction. A Bristol to Bedford service was proposed and further work to look at the options beyond Bedford to Cambridge (possibly using the A428 corridor). An Oxford-Bicester Rail Action Group (OBRAG) was re-formed to fight for their service as the line faced cuts. OBRAC attended the inaugural meeting and met local MP, Tony Baldry. Meanwhile, the EWRL Phase 1 service from Norwich to Cambridge was a huge success, attracting 500k passenger journeys per annum and 1,000 passenger journeys per day – 30% above expectations. Forty-four per cent of users had a car.

In 2004, after five years of studies and over £1m spent, the SRA remained unconvinced of the value of EWRL and had no funds for the scheme. The EWRC latest business case suggested the service could start in 2007 if funded. OBRAC raised the call again that there should be no population without rail transportation. Former BR Chairman, Sir Bob Reid[288], became chair of MK Partnership which was overseeing the MK growth plan. OBRAC briefed him on the chaotic years of EWRL campaigning and he pledged to seek to make fast progress (possibly not realising how slow and expensive decisions are made on a privatised railway). Meanwhile, local MPs (John Bercow[289], Tony Baldry[290], Phyllis Starkey, Brian White[291], and Patrick Hall) were also stressing the need for infrastructure (including EWRL) before housing growth.

In 2005 Jeff Rooker[292], the regional development minister, announced funding for two new studies for the Office of the Deputy Prime Minister, to cover East West Links and a proposed Aylesbury Vale Parkway station. AVP was to be 3 miles north of the town and would open a small part of the EWRL to passengers. Further OBRAC meetings with Sir Bob Reid confirmed the EWRL study that he felt was critical to the growth of MK. Funding for a bay platform for EWRL trains at MK Central had been sought as part of the main-line upgrade. The SRA proposed that the Bicester-Oxford service be cut to one train a day. A 500-signature petition was laid before the Commons by Tony Baldry and in an early day motion it was noted that before the general election the government was discussing a EWRL to connect Oxford to MK '…only for this new franchise to move Bicester back rather than forward'. East of Bedford, proposals for a rowing lake at Willington were threatening to block restoration of the route to Sandy if that was required for EWRL.

In 2006 OBRAG welcomed the Bicester-Oxford service becoming seven trains per day. The Office of the Deputy Prime Minister published the EWRL study which looked at transport options for the corridor, the growth of housing, employment and the economy and the EWRL. It validated the EWRC findings and concluded that 'improved EWRL are at the heart of the growth strategy for the MKSM region'. Twelve hundred trips a day were forecast for 2011. A capital cost of £65m was quoted. The case for the Aylesbury link was also positive. Finance options were reviewed and contributions from development suggested. A further £300k study was to be undertaken to look at growth, transport and land values as a funding source. Laing Rail was to revisit the operational aspects of the EWRL. Aylesbury Vale Parkway was to be funded by the ODPM community infrastructure fund, Chiltern Railways and Bucks CC.

In 2007 the £300k Steer Davies Gleave GRIP2 report was published. It suggested a £134m scheme of two trains an hour between MK and Oxford and funding by developer contributions. An Aylesbury to MK service was feasible and increased capital costs by £64m. In the long term services could be extended to Swindon and Cambridge. The general election campaign saw Tory candidates, including Iain Stewart[293], who became a key supporter for EWRL, gather at Swanbourne station to promote rail reopenings. EWRC agreed to fund further development work to develop the final specification and identify funding and to seek entry to the next government high-level output specification for the rail industry. This was due to cost £1.5m. OBRAG, with Oxon CC, had succeeded in securing the service level on the Bicester-Oxford line. Meanwhile, busway proposals in Cambridge would see loss of some of former track bed to Bedford at Trumpington.

At the end of the year, the Commons saw MPs Patrick Hall, Evan Harris[294], John Bercow and Phyllis Starkey, emphasising the need for the EWRL to cope with planned population growth. The rail minister responded that government priority was capacity on the existing network. It would consider proposals for reopening disused lines where there was a sound case. The issue was raised in the Lords by Lord Faulkner of Worcester[295], who found that the Government had not studied reopening lines and had no specific funds to reopen lines. They would consider reopenings where a case existed.

In 2008 EWRC received the GRIP level three report from Steer Davies Gleave. This considered over 50 options with capital costs between £190m to £232m. If funding were found, 2012 was seen an opening date. It was agreed to pursue to the next study stage of GRIP4 and identify funding options. The potential for freight and inter-regional services was to be explored. Planning authorities were to be briefed to identify developer funding. Further work on options for east of Bedford were to be explored.

Sir Bob Reid left MK Partnership and a key achievement of his was seen to be the progress on the EWRL.

Aylesbury Vale Parkway was opened by Lord Adonis in December. MK Central upgrade work was also under way including the new platform for EWRL services.

Network Rail published a new business plan (to 2014) and saw Oxford-MK as a reasonable aspiration and MK to Aylesbury and Wycombe could achieve multiple aspirations. Manchester to Reading services (saving 40 minutes) and freight could use the EWRL.

In 2009 Chiltern Railways went to public consultation on proposals for an Oxford-Bicester Town-Marylebone service with a journey time of 66 minutes. This would secure them a seven-year franchise extension. Oxford-Bicester timing would be cut to 14 minutes. They agreed to work with the EWRC so that upgrade work was compatible and reduce the cost of the EWRL. DfT agreed to fund £18m of work at Wolvercote Tunnel (near Oxford) to accommodate possible future freight container traffic.

'The Phase 1, Norwich-Cambridge service was carrying 700k passengers per annum, showing a growth rate of 70 per cent in six years. The Ipswich-Cambridge service became hourly. The EWRC published the Steer Davies Gleave study into options east of Bedford and a new option via Luton and Stevenage emerged.

EWRC had a positive meeting with Lord Adonis[296], the Secretary of State for Transport, who recommended a funding bid to the DfT for 2014. Network Rail and DfT were interested in exploring freight and Manchester-Bournemouth services using the route.

The new bay platform for EWRL services was completed at MK Central and Lord Adonis, at the end of the year, opened Aylesbury Vale Parkway.

ATOC (Association of Train Operating Companies) published the report 'Connecting Communities' identifying potential towns for rail reopening. The EWRL was seen to offer the opportunity to link several towns in a growth area. In response, the Government felt it was up to councils to bring forward viable proposals. Bill Simpson published a new book, *Oxford and Cambridge in Profile*, which again brought public interest in the EWRL. An OBRAC article was published in *Today's Railways*.

In 2010 Atkin provided the EWRC with the GRIP4 business case, and engineering design work studies were published in July and revealed an exceptional business case and benefit cost ratio for the EWRL. The proposals were now costed at £178m for the core scheme and the services were expected to generate a surplus over the operating costs. EWRC planned to review the option of extending services to Reading and the Aylesbury service to High Wycombe and Marylebone. Private sector funding was to be further examined to improve the cost benefit even further. A 2017 opening date was now suggested. The EWRC and MK MPs (Iain Stewart and Mark Lancaster[297]) met the new rail minister, Theresa Villiers[298], and agreed a bid for DfT funding be made for the next spending round of 2014-19.

Meanwhile, the Bicester Link service (Oxford-Bicester) service reported a 74 per cent increase in on/offs at Bicester Town and a 40 per cent increase at Islip in 2009/10. This was due to an improved service of 11 trains a day and a Sunday service, improved marketing and an increase in use by Bicester Village visitors. Extra weekday car parking had been arranged at Bicester Village. The TWA Order Inquiry for the Oxford-Bicester line opened in November. The EWRC presented their case and Railfuture (Thames) made an oral presentation. OBRAC had made a written representation.

In 2011 the Public Inquiry into Chiltern Railways TWA Order to upgrade the Oxford-Bicester line closed after 33 days of evidence. At the end of the year it was recommended that the order should not be granted until Natural England and Chiltern Railways had resolved the issue of the protection of a bat colony in Wolvercote Tunnel (near Oxford). This was expected to be resolved. Chiltern Railways took over the Bicester Link service as a prelude to their operation of the line and the upgrade work.

EWRC published a prospectus for the EWRL highlighting the benefits of the EWRL and the results of an economic appraisal by Oxford Economics which suggest that 12k jobs will be created and the economy will benefit annually by £38m.

OBRAC met Iain Stewart, MK SW MP, and found he was in discussions with the EWRC. He took up the cause in Parliament by setting up an all-party parliamentary group to press the EWRL case and organising a debate which included a mention of OBRAC. MPs from the east (and from Northern Ireland) voiced their support. Andrew Smith[299] from Oxford was the only Labour MP present. Theresa Villiers responded by saying how impressed she was by the EWRL case. The Chancellor's statement saw the surprise announcement that £270m of funding was to be available for EWRL subject to a satisfactory business case and some private sector funding from EWRC. An opening date of 2017 was still expected. After the news, the rail minister visited Bicester Town at an event attended by OBRAC. The EWRC expect to meet the conditions imposed. DfT had asked ATOC to examine the feasibility of inter-regional services along the EWRL, which will improve the cost benefit ratio further.

In 2012 the 25th anniversary of OBRAC saw the Chiltern Railways Oxford-Bicester upgrade approved, EWRL funding agreed and further planning work. DfT were also showing interest in examining, with the EWRC, the feasibility of the EWRL section east of Bedford. At some stage DfT will need to identify a train operating company and if inter-regional services are feasible. OBRAC will continue to monitor progress and be ready to respond to any problems that may arise.

On 16 July 2012 the East West Rail Consortium made the following announcement:

'The Secretary of State for Transport, the Rt. Hon Justine Greening MP[300], today announced that the Western section of East West Rail (EWR) will be part of the Government's strategy for rail transport, confirming not only funding for the project but also for electrification of the Oxford to Bedford part of the route. EWR will provide an electric link between the electrified Great Western, West Coast and Midland main lines. This further investment in the project upgrades it to form a key part of the new "Electric Spine" passenger and freight route between the South Coast, the East Midlands and Yorkshire.'

Appendix E
Extracts from the secret notebook of Cabinet Secretary Sir Burke Trend [301] on Cabinet discussions, 11 March 1965

Item 4 RAIL CLOSURES c (65) 41

MT [Minister of Transport, Tom Fraser]:
As in memo[302]. Real opposition is from unions, on loss of jobs, but this is being looked after. Decline in passenger mileage offset by increase in freight mileage. In last 2 years Rail Board's deficit reduced by £30m, and wage increase of £40m absorbed, therefore must maintain policy; block Spearman Bill[303], and don't appear to abandon modernisation.

PM [Prime Minister, Harold Wilson[304]]:
Adopt device of blocking proposals before TUCC stage – and be seen to do it.[305] Also invoke Regional Boards' comments before final ministerial decision.

FSofS [First Secretary of State, George Brown[306]]:
DEA [Department of Economic Affairs] have had very full cooperation from MT but I don't object to PM's proposal.

MHLG [Minister of Housing and Local Government, Richard Crossman[307]]:
We too have had full co-operation – but note that freight service decisions (on which no consultations have taken place) can appear to 'prejudice' consultations on passenger service.

MTech [Minister of Technology, Frank Cousins[308]]:
No real improvements in railway services as a whole. All the improvement has been achieved by sacking. Unions won't be satisfied until there is a co-ordinated transport policy[309] before closures can take place.

S/SW [Secretary of State for Wales, James Griffiths[310]]:
I agree on Wales. More co-ordination of bus and rail services essential.

PBT [President of Board of Trade, Douglas Jay[311]]:
I endorse support for consultation with regional planning authorities.

MT [Tom Fraser]:
Railways Board not very anxious to co-operate on early sift procedure, but will do their best. I take MHLG's ([Crossman's] point, but I can't intervene in subsidisation of freight services, since this would prevent railways from retaining such traffic as they have. Must allow railways to carry freight as efficiently as they can, and this means an industry of maximum labour intensity. Some redundancy – don't interfere with Board's managerial independence. On regional consultation, I would accept consultation on every case if required (if regional councils were all in agreement) but preferably before the TUCCs see, since economic considerations should have priority over passenger hardship.

PM [Harold Wilson]:
I agree on improvement.

MTech [Frank Cousins]:
But not really an economic problem. If it were, outcome is to confine to main services. Otherwise must have a co-ordinated road-rail policy. No point – if not an economic problem – in putting to economic regional councils alone. And unions should participate in management decisions.

MT [Tom Fraser]:
I am not taking decisions on economic grounds alone. I have said railways, and commuter services, will never really pay if social considerations are taken into account.

Ch.Duchy [Chancellor of the Duchy of Lancaster, Douglas Houghton[312]]:
I agree cabinet committee to take all considerations into account including regional ones. We would consult with regional councils – be far more effective than consultation with DEA [Department of Economic Affairs]. Only new factor is Hinton enquiry[313], and few closures would be affected by this. Therefore CHSL[314] should examine proposals in relation to Hinton, and if no link, consider on merits. If a link, defer closures until Hinton reports. But this would make little difference, and no further change would be justified.

Ch.Exchq [Chancellor of the Exchequer, James Callaghan[315]]:
Don't under-estimate party dissatisfaction[316] on grounds of:
(a) Refusal to halt all closures pending Hinton report
(b) Disposal of railway land to private developers rather than the local authorities
(c) Transfer of work from railway workshops to private undertakings
(d) Lack of means to compete with 'C' licence holders.

PM [Harold Wilson]:
All departments and regional councils should be invited to find work for railway workshops, and overseas aid might help in kind.

[Exit FS/S (George Brown)]

MT [Tom Fraser]:
Railway workshops to be considered by EDC. On land, I have encouraged offers to local authorities, but they can acquire compulsorily if they want it. But if suitable for commercial development, [Railways] Board can't be expected to lose profit. But will certainly do all I can within limits of our land policy – since can't deal with railway land in isolation from other publicly owned land.

S/Sc [Secretary of State for Scotland, William Ross[317]]:
A closure, not major at outset, may become so in light of Buchanan[318] – and should councils have a decisive voice?

MT [Tom Fraser]:
No, their views must be put to me via FS/S [George Brown]. On Hinton, a misunderstanding – H's job is mainly to advise me from time to time on various aspects of transport policy – this will never be a published report. Better to rely on regional councils.

PM [Harold Wilson]:
Endorse report, on basis that early sift procedures should be expedited. Regional councils should be consulted before TUCC stage, relevance to Hinton enquiry should be considered at outset.

On railway workshops, wait for EDC – but consult regional councils here too.

On railway land, MT [Fraser] and MHLG [Crossman] should put proposals to EDC, who should be considering policy on surplus land disposal as a whole.

In light of above MT [Fraser] to make parliamentary statement as soon as possible.[319]

Appendix F
Lines listed in ATOC's 'Connecting Communities' report

Evaluation of links ranked by benefit/cost ratio (Appendix One of the report):

Hythe, Brixham, Bordon, Fleetwood, Rawtenstall, Aldridge, Brownhills, Cranleigh, Ringwood, Washington, Leicester/Burton*, Skelmersdale, Ashington/Blyth, Wisbech, Madeley, Stourport, Ripon*, Norton Radstock*, Portishead*, Witney, Annfield Plain (1), Biddulph, Spennymoor, Dereham, Thornbury, Leek (2), Haverhill*, Guisborough, Leek (3), Bideford, Daventry, Ripley, Anston, Louth*, Annfield Plain (4)

Notes:
(1) via Washington, (2) from Stoke, (3) from Macclesfield, (4) via ECML

Other potential links lines (Appendix Three of the report):

Bishops Stortford-Braintree-Colchester
Burscough curves (Lancashire)*
Chessington South-Leatherhead
Glazebrook-Partington (Manchester)
Lewes-Uckfield*
Matlock-Buxton*
March-Spalding*
Oxford-Bletchley* (and Manton curve)
Northampton-Bedford
Rugby-Peterborough
Skipton-Colne*
Stafford-Wellington
Stourbridge-Walsall
Whelley Lines (Wigan)
Willingdon chord (Eastbourne)*
Woodhead route*

* included in this book

Appendix G
Bibliography

Atthill, Robin *The Somerset & Dorset Railway* (David & Charles, 1967)

Baker, S. K. *Rail Atlas Great Britain and Ireland* (Oxford Publishing Company, 2015)

Baxter, Ian and Harper, Richard *Birmingham Snow Hill: A Great Station* (2002)

Britain's Growing Railway (Railfuture, 2010)

British Railways Pre-grouping Atlas and Gazetteer (Ian Allan, 1980)

Daniels, Gerald and Dench, L. A. *Passengers No More*, 2nd ed (Ian Allan Publishing, 1973)

Dendy Marshall, C. F. *History of the Southern Railway*, revised by R. W. Kidner (Ian Allan, 1963)

Dow, Andrew *Dow's Dictionary of Railway Quotations* (John Hopkins University Press, 2006)

Dow, George *Great Central* (1962)

Faulkner, Richard and Austin, Chris *Holding the Line* (Oxford Publishing Company, 2012)

Gourvish, T. R. *British Railways 1948-1973* (Cambridge University Press, 1986)

Grinling, Charles H. *History of the Great Northern Railway 1845-1902* (Methuen & Co, London, 1903)

Hamilton Ellis, C. *British Railway History*, Vol 1 (George Allen and Unwin Ltd, 1954)

MacDermott, E. T. *History of the Great Western Railway*, Vol 1, revised by C. R. Clinker (Ian Allan, 1964)

Maggs, Colin G. *Bristol Railway Panorama* (Millstream Books, 1990)

Martin, Don and Maclean, A. A. *Edinburgh & Glasgow Railway Handbook* (Strathkelvin District Libraries and Museums, 1992)

Simmons, Jack and Biddle, Gordon (eds) *The Oxford Companion to British Railway History* (Oxford University Press, 1997)

Suggitt, Gordon *Lost Railways of Lancashire* (Countryside Books, 2003)

The Reshaping of British Railways (British Railways Board, 1963)

Thomas, John and Turnock, David *A Regional History of the Railways of Great Britain, Vol 15, The North of Scotland* (David & Charles, 1989)

Appendix H
Acknowledgements

Martin Bairstow
Richard Burningham MBE
Neil Buxton
Adrian Caltieri
Simon Clarke
Phil Deaves
David Faulkner CB
Richard Hope OBE
Prof Paul Salveson MBE
Theo Steel
John Yellowlees

Association of Community Rail Partnerships
National Records of Scotland
National Railway Museum
Network Rail archives
OBRAG
Railfuture
The National Archives

Notes

Preface

[1] *Holding the Line: How Britain's Railways Were Saved* (Oxford Publishing Company, 2012)

Introduction

[2] John Kenneth Galbraith (1898-2006) 'was America's most famous economist for good reason. A witty commentator on America's political follies and a versatile author of bestselling books that warn prophetically of the dangers of deregulated markets, corporate greed, and inattention to the costs of our military power (among them *The Great Crash: 1929, The Affluent Society,* and *The New Industrial State*), Galbraith always made economics relevant to the crises of the day.' (Extract from publicity for *John Kenneth Galbraith: His Life, His Politics, His Economics* by Richard Parker, University of Chicago Press, 2005.) Born in Canada, Galbraith spent most of his career in the USA writing, teaching and advising presidents, including John F. Kennedy, who made him the ambassador to India.

[3] Dr Richard Beeching (1913-85), ennobled as Baron Beeching in 1965. Member of the Stedeford Committee, 1959-61. Chairman of the British Railways Board 1961-65, on secondment from ICI, to which he returned after the Labour Government, elected in 1964, declined to renew his appointment to the BRB.

[4] Office of Rail Regulation annual report for 2013/14 on rail infrastructure, assets and environment.

[5] Passenger Transport Executives were local government bodies established under the Transport Act to operate public transport in the major conurbations outside London.

Chapter 1

[6] Michael Bonavia (1909-99), railwayman, historian and author. His varied career started with the LNER in 1945 and finished as Director, Channel Tunnel, in 1972-74 (when the project was cancelled by the Labour Government). He had written a best-selling textbook on *The Economics of Transport* in his 20s, which was widely used by students for more than 30 years. In 1971 *The Organisation of British Railways* was published, based on a University of London PhD thesis, which he completed in 1968. Other publications included *The Four Great Railways* (1980) and *The Nationalisation of British Transport: The early history of the British Transport Commission, 1948-53,* written in 1987.

[7] Frederick Chilton Margetts (1905-89), Asst Operating Supt, LNER Scotland, 1946; BR Scotland, 1949; Chief Operating Supt, BR Scotland, 1955; Chief Traffic Manager, 1958; Asst General Manager, 1959; General Manager, 1961, BR York; Member BR Committee, 1962; Operating Member, BR Board, 1962-67. CBE 1966. Later in retirement to support conversion of railways into roads (see Terry Gourvish's book *British Rail 1974-1997: From Integration to Privatisation*).

[8] Gerry Fiennes, *I Tried to Run a Railway* (Ian Allan, 1967)

[9] 'Organising the Railway as a Business', F. C. Margetts. National Archives, ZLIB 29/709

[10] Memorandum to J. M. Moore. MT 124/1448

[11] See *Holding the Line,* Chapter VII

[12] Joe Peeler served in both the Home Office and Ministry of Transport. He later came into prominence in 1978 when revealed in a leak to the *Guardian* as the author of the notorious 'Peeler Memorandum', which proposed a 'presentational' public inquiry that would lead to the introduction of heavier lorries. He was then Under-Secretary in charge of the freight directorate at the Department of Transport. This remarkable story is described in detail in pp108 and 109 of *Holding the Line.*

[13] Memorandum from Peeler dated 23 June 1971. T 124/1439

[14] 'The Future Role of the Railways', October 1971. MT 124/1448

[15] John Peyton (1919-2006), Conservative MP for Yeovil 1951-83, Minister for Transport, 1970-74. Became Lord Peyton of Yeovil in 1983; ten years later in the Lords he forced and won a vote on an amendment to the Railways Bill, which would have enabled BR to bid for franchises. Had this become law – and BR had shown any enthusiasm for using the powers – it may have changed the nature of privatisation. The 'Peyton amendment' was reversed when the Bill returned to the Commons for consideration of Lords amendments. Twenty years on, the Labour Party in opposition proposed that the state-owned train operating company – Directly Operated Railways – should be given to right to compete for franchises, given the perceived success of DOR operating the East Coast Main Line, following the earlier failure of National Express in running the service.

[16] Rt Hon Anthony Crosland (1918-77), Labour politician who served as Secretary of State for the Environment, March 1974-April 1976, then Foreign Secretary for the last ten months of his life. MP for South Gloucestershire, 1950-55, and for Grimsby, 1959-77. He was a minister throughout the 1964-70 Labour Government. In 1956, during his spell out of Parliament, Crosland had published *The Future of Socialism,* a seminal work that set the agenda for the Labour Party's debate on revisionism.

[17] Sidney Weighell (1922-2002), railwayman, professional footballer and trade union general secretary. Joined LNER in 1938, following his father, grandfather and brother on to the railway. Was initially a fireman, became an engine driver in 1943, left the railway to play professional football for Sunderland in 1945, but returned to the railway in 1947. Became a full-time NUR official in 1954.

[18] William Rodgers (b1928), Labour and later SDP/Liberal Democrat politician who served as MP for Stockton-on-Tees, 1962-83. He was Secretary of State for Transport, 1976-79. A passionate pro-European, Rodgers joined Roy Jenkins, Shirley Williams and David Owen in the 'Gang of Four' in 1981. Ennobled as Lord Rodgers of Quarry Bank in 1987, he was leader of the Liberal Democrats in the House of Lords, 1997-2001. 'My two clearest memories were saving the Tyneside Metro in the first three months of my Department of Transport career: I am proud of that. And resisting the tachograph to avoid a T&G national strike: I am not proud of that although it was a necessary political response.' (From a personal letter to the authors, dated 4 March 2012).

[19] 'An Appreciation of Unremunerative Rail Passenger Services', MT 188/1 by Joe Peeler.

[20] Ian McDonald Campbell, CVO, BSc, CEng, FICE, FCIT, 1922-94. Formerly with the LMS, then an LNER traffic apprentice, he rose to become General Manager, Eastern Region, Executive Director, Systems and Operations, BRB, Chief Executive and Vice Chairman. He also chaired the Scottish Board, and was a colonel in the TA. His

father was Chief Civil Engineer of the Eastern Region and had been responsible for the construction of the new Woodhead Tunnel.

[21] Memo from Ian Campbell to the LMR Management Committee, 9 June 1969. National Archives, AN 155/121.

[22] Tom Fraser (1911-88), Labour MP for Hamilton, was Minister of Transport for little more than a year (October 1964 to December 1965). In *Holding the Line* (pp40-41) the authors reveal the minutes of the fateful Cabinet meeting on 11 March 1965, when ministers accepted a paper from Fraser in which he recommended they 'stand firm' on closures, thus condemning scores of lines and hundreds of stations to be closed in the following five years.

[23] Alfred Ernest Marples (1907-78), Conservative politician who served as Postmaster-General and Minister of Transport. MP for Wallasey, 1945-74, when he was ennobled as Lord Marples. He was an immensely controversial figure for the reasons explained at length in *Holding the Line*.

[24] Memo from H. Woodhouse, Legal (Transport) Branch of the Department of the Environment, to Mr R. D. Crompton, 20 May 1974. National Archives.

[25] Fred Mulley (1918-95), Labour politician who served as Minister of Transport for the last six months of the 1966-70 Government, and again as Minister of State for Transport, March 1974 to March 1975. He was MP for Sheffield Park, 1950-83. He also served as Minister of Aviation, and Minister for Disarmament in the 1966 Government, and after 1975 as Secretary of State for Education, and Secretary of State for Defence. He was a prisoner of war in France from 1940, using his time in the PoW camp to study voraciously, which enabled him to go up to Christ Church Oxford after the war, where he got a first class honours degree after two years' study. For many years he was a member of Labour's national executive committee. He was ennobled as Lord Mulley in 1985.

[26] Richard Marsh (1928-2011) was Labour MP for Greenwich, 1959-71. Succeeded Barbara Castle as Minister of Transport in 1968, serving until 1970. Appointed by the Conservative Government as Chairman of British Rail in 1971, serving until 1976. Ennobled as Lord Marsh in 1981, he sat on the cross-benches in the House of Lords. In his obituary in the *Guardian* on 2 August 2011, Julia Langdon wrote: 'His early posts in government after the 1964 election were as a junior minister at the Ministry of Labour for one year and then at Technology for another. He then became Minister of Power for two years, closing 100 pits during that time, until in 1968 Wilson promoted him to succeed Barbara Castle as the Minister of Transport, with a seat in the Cabinet. He celebrated his new job, he admitted privately, by driving at 90mph on the M4. His appointment was not a success, not least with Castle, who regarded him as a dilettante, not really interested in pursuing his policies and proposed legislation. She pleaded with Wilson to sack him on one occasion, claiming that he was 'cynical, superficial and lazy', and the Prime Minister did indeed subsequently sack him after just a year in the post.'

[27] David Marshall Bowick (1923-95), CBE 1977. Served with the Fleet Air Arm, 1942-46. Movements Supt, King's Cross, 1962; Planning Officer, British Railways Board Headquarters, 1963; Asst General Manager, London Midland Region, BR, 1965; Executive Director, Personnel, BRB Headquarters, 1969; General Manager, London Midland Region, BR, 1971; Chief Executive (Railways), BR, 1971-78; Vice-Chairman (Rail), BRB, 1978-80. President, Group of

Nine EEC Railways, 1978-80. Member of Council, Manchester Business School.

[28] Robert Basil Reid (1925-93), Kt 1985, CBE 1980, was a career railwayman who joined the LNER in 1947, after war service as a captain in the Royal Tank Regiment. He was Chairman of British Rail, 1983-90, having previously been Chief Executive (Railways), responsible for the highly successful sector management reorganisation. He re-established trust with ministers on BR's ability to manage its resources and in return for meeting cash limits secured investment in East Coast Main Line electrification, completed in 1991. Traffic Apprentice, LNER, 1947; Goods Agent, York, 1958; Asst District Goods Manager, Glasgow, 1960; District Passenger Manager, 1961; Divisional Commercial Manager, 1963; Planning Manager, Scottish Region, 1967; Divisional Manager, Doncaster, 1968; Deputy General Manager, Eastern Region, York, 1972; General Manager, Southern Region, BR, 1974-76; British Railways Board: Executive Member for Marketing, 1977-80; Chief Executive (Railways), 1980-83; Vice-Chairman, 1983. Director, British Transport Hotels Ltd, 1977-83; Docklands Light Rly, 1991-93; Chairman, Freightliner Co Ltd, 1978-80. Chairman, National Industries Chairmen's Group, 1987-88; President, European Community Rlys Directors General, 1988-89. President, CIT, 1982-83.

[29] (John) Michael (Worthington) Bosworth (1921-2007), CBE 1972. Deputy Chairman, British Railways Board, 1972-83 (Vice-Chairman, 1968-72). Served Royal Artillery, 1939-46. Peat, Marwick, Mitchell & Co, 1949-68, Partner, 1960; Chairman: British Rail Engineering Ltd, 1969-71; British Rail Property Board, 1971-72; British Rail Shipping and International Services Ltd, later Sealink UK Ltd, 1976-84; BR Hovercraft Ltd, 1976-81; British Transport Hotels, 1978-83; British Rail Investments Ltd, 1981-84; British Rail Trustee Co, 1984-86; Director: Hoverspeed (UK) Ltd, 1981-89; British Ferries, 1984-90.

[30] Peter Parker (1924-2002), Chairman of British Railways Board, 1976-83. Knighted 1978. Described by Prue Leith as a 'prodigiously energetic polymath who pioneered modern management methods at British Rail. Interested in education, the arts, sport, politics, to all of which he brought knowledge, enthusiasm, charm and prodigious energy; he could have been a soldier, a politician or an actor.' (*Guardian*, 30 April 2002). Labour parliamentary candidate in 1951, later a member of the SDP. First Great Western Trains named Class 43 HST power car No 43127 *Sir Peter Parker 1924-2002 – Cotswold Line 150*. See Chapter 12 of *Holding the Line* for a longer appraisal of his career.

[31] Public Service Obligation grant. Introduced as a block grant replacing the individual line grants made under the Transport Act, 1968, by the Railways Act, 1974. This Act also required the Board to maintain services at a level broadly comparable to that operating on 31 December 1973, thus protecting the network size for the next 20 years.

[32] The 'contract' was a concept invented by Peter Parker as a means of describing the payments made by central and local government to the British Railways Board to operate socially-necessary rail services. He was keen to replace the word 'subsidy', on the basis – as he put it – 'subsidies are sickening, contracts are quickening'.

[33] Derek Fowler (1929-2006), CBE 1979. Joined BRB as internal audit manager in 1964 after a number of appointments in local government. Rose to Deputy Chairman of BRB in 1990.

[34] Clifford Rose (1929-83), Member for Operations and Deputy Chief Executive, British Railways Board, at the time of his death,

previously member for personnel, 1977-83. Joined GWR as booking clerk, 1944; served in London area, West Country and South Wales; Divisional Movements Manager, Cardiff, 1966; Asst Divisional Manager, 1968. Movements Manager, Southern Region, 1968; Divisional Manager, first of South Western, then South Eastern Division, 1970; Chief Personnel Officer of Southern Region, 1972; Executive Director, Personnel, 1975-77. He remained a member of the Transport Salaried Staffs Association for the whole of his railway career. CBE 1983.

[35] James Urquhart (b1925). Served in RAF, 1941-44. Management Trainee, BR Eastern Region, 1949-52; Chief Controller, Fenchurch Street, 1956-59; District Traffic Supt, Perth, 1960-62; Divisional Operating Supt, Glasgow, 1962-64; Divisional Manager, Glasgow and SW Scotland, 1964-67; Asst General Manager, Eastern Region, 1967-69; BR Board HQ: Chief Operations Manager, 1969-72; Executive Director, Personnel, 1972-75; General Manager, London Midland Region, 1975-76; BR Board: Executive Member, Operations and Productivity, 1977-83; Member, Exports, 1983-85; Chairman: British Transport Police, 1977-86; BRE-Metro, 1978-86; BR Engineering Ltd, 1979-85; Freightliner, 1983-85; Transmark, 1983-86. CVO 1983.

[36] John Palmer CB (b1928). Career civil servant who entered the Ministry of Housing and Local Government in 1952; he served in the Cabinet Office, 1963-65, then joined the Department of the Environment in 1965, and was latterly Deputy Secretary in the Department of Transport, 1982-89. On his retirement he joined the British Railways Board and served as Chairman, European Passenger Services, 1990-94.

[37] Paper from the Provincial sector to the Serpell Inquiry dated 10 September 1982. AN 170/488.

[38] Report by Sir David Serpell of 1983 setting out various options for reducing the cost and size of the rail network. The most extreme option would have seen the network reduced to a rump of only 1,630 route miles. Comprehensively leaked and roundly rubbished by the press prior to publication, it marked the end of serious attempts by Government to tackle the cost of the railway through any dramatic cut in the size of the network. It demonstrated that there was no 'profitable core' that would be acceptable to the British public.

[39] AN 170/488.

[40] 'Reshaping' report. p22.

[41] Barbara Castle (1910-2002), Labour politician who was Minister of Transport from December 1965 to April 1968. MP for Blackburn, 1945-79, member of the European Parliament, 1979-89, ennobled as Baroness Castle of Blackburn, 1990. Described in *Guardian* obituary (4 May 2002) as 'Labour's Red Queen, the woman Michael Foot called 'the best socialist minister we've ever had'. However, the author Anne Perkins also said: 'Her career foundered on an inability to master the key political skill of building support where it counted, in the parliamentary party. She claimed to find making political alliances demeaning; her critics found her wearisomely egocentric. Even her friends distrusted her temper.' Her record as transport minister is disputed: her admirers draw attention to her success in establishing the passenger transport authorities in Britain's conurbations, which kept open scores of local urban rail services that had been listed for closure in the Beeching Report, and for setting up the system of government grants to support loss-making

services generally. Castle's detractors claim that she took too little notice of the Labour Party's policy to halt the implementation of the Beeching closure programme.

[42] Memorandum on Railway Transport in the Isle of Wight, November 1951. National Archives, AN 177/84.

[43] The Hillman Minx was a popular medium-sized family car built by the Rootes Group between 1932 and 1970. It disappeared following the American Chrysler Corporation takeover of the business.

[44] National Archives, AN 177/83.

Chapter 2

[45] Quoted in *Our Iron Roads: Their History, Construction and Administration*, Chapter XVI, by Frederick S. Williams (Routledge, 1852).

[46] John Bright (1811-89) was one of the greatest parliamentary orators, radicals and reformers of the Victorian age.

[47] *Holding the Line*, pp58-62

[48] *Off the Rails: An Autobiography* by Richard Marsh (Weidenfeld & Nicolson, 1978), p170.

[49] Richard Hope (b1934), OBE (1989), chartered electrical and mechanical engineer who joined British Rail in 1959 to work on the electrification of commuter lines east of London. Member of board of Talyllyn Railway Trust for 45 years to 2013. Joined the staff of *The Railway Gazette* in 1964, becoming Editor in 1970. Since retiring in 1991, he has continued to write as consultant editor for *Railway Gazette International* and also for its UK newsletter, *Rail Business Intelligence*.

[50] Dr Stewart Joy (d1998), Australian academic who worked for Barbara Castle as a consultant on railway policy and later for three years as chief economist for the British Railways Board. He was the author of *The Train That Ran Away: A Business History of British Railways 1948-68* (Ian Allan, 1973), and was subsequently in the 1980s deputy director general of transport in the Australian state of Victoria.

[51] Sir David Serpell (1911-2008) joined the Ministry of Transport in 1960 as Deputy Secretary responsible for railways and roads. In this position, he was secretary to the Stedeford Committee. He became its Permanent Secretary in 1968 and retired in 1972, becoming a member of the British Railways Board, 1974-82. In 1982 the notorious Serpell Report was published setting out some stark options for future network size. See Chapter 2.

[52] Leslie Huckfield (b1942), Labour MP for Nuneaton, 1967-83 (he succeeded Frank Cousins – qv), and MEP for Merseyside East, 1984-89. Junior industry minister, 1976-79. Latterly represented ASLEF in House of Commons.

[53] Sir Roy McNulty CBE (b1937), Chairman of the Rail Value for Money Study sponsored by the Department of Transport and the Office Rail Regulation, 2010-11, Deputy Chairman of the Olympic Delivery Authority, Chair of Advantage West Midlands, 2009-12. Previously he was Chairman of the Civil Aviation Authority (CAA) (2001-09), Chairman of National Air Traffic Services (NATS) (1999-01) and, prior to that, Chief Executive and Chairman of Shorts Brothers plc.

[54] *Holding the Line*, p66.

[55] Harold Evans (b1928), distinguished author and journalist who edited both the *Sunday Times* (1967-81) and *The Times* (1981-82). Knighted 2004.

[56] *Holding the Line*, pp73-76.

57 Transport Policy, Her Majesty's Stationery Office, June 1977, Cmnd 6836.

58 *The Times*, 11 January 1978, p19.

59 *The Times*, 12 January 1978, p18.

60 *The Times*, 17 January 1978, p20.

61 National Archives, AN 215, Papers of Sir Peter Parker, Chairman of British Rail, 1976-1983.

62 Sir Peter Fry (1931-2015), Conservative MP for Wellingborough 1969-97. Former Buckinghamshire County Councillor and county rugby player. From 1974 to 1997 he was joint chairman of the all-party roads study group, and of the road passenger group (1992-97). He was seen as the roads lobby's strongest supporter in Parliament. After losing his seat in 1997 (to Labour, by 187 votes), he served as Chairman of the Bingo Association for 10 years, and has been president of EUBingo from 2006.

63 Hansard, Col 439, 1 February 1978.

64 *The Times*, 23 February 1978, p19.

65 Alan Mattingley (b1949), Director of the Ramblers' Association from 1974 to 1998. A member of the Outdoor Writers' Guild, he received that organisation's Golden Eagle Award in 1998. His previous publications include *Tackle Rambling* (1981), *Walking in the National Parks* (1982) and *Walking in the Cathar Region* (Cicerone, 2005).

66 Norman Fowler (b1938), MP for Nottingham South, 1970-74, and Sutton Coldfield, 1974-2001. Ennobled as Lord Fowler, 2001. Correspondent on *The Times*, 1961-70. Held a succession of ministerial offices, 1979-90, including Minister of Transport and Secretary of State for Transport.

67 David Howell (b1936), Conservative MP for Guildford, 1966-97, and Secretary of State for Transport, 1981-83. He also served as Secretary of State for Energy, 1979-81, and Junior Minister, 1970-74, becoming Chairman of the Foreign Affairs Select Committee in 1987. He is an author and journalist, ennobled as Lord Howell of Guildford in 1997, and returned to Government as Minister of State in the Foreign and Commonwealth Office with the 2010 coalition government. Howell is also the father-in-law of George Osborne, Chancellor of the Exchequer since 2010.

68 *Holding the Line*, pp90-91.

69 Alan Williams (b1943) is a regular writer and commentator on political and safety issues surrounding transport, including a much-admired monthly column in *Modern Railways*. Before retirement in 2003 he held a succession of senior public relations posts with the Post Office and, previously, the Department of Trade and Industry and HM Treasury. Chairman of Esk Valley Railway Development Company since 2003. President of Railway Study Association, 1998-99. Author of *Railway Signalling* (editions since 1963), *Not the Age of the Train* (1983), and *Two Centuries of Railway Signalling* (2008).

70 Dr John Denys Charles Anstice Prideaux CBE (b1944) was head of the British Rail Policy Unit and later Managing Director of BR's InterCity. After privatisation he bought, with a venture capital group, one of the three new train leasing companies, Angel Trains, selling it on to the Royal Bank of Scotland for £395million, making a personal fortune of £15 million in the process. Since 2006 he has been Chairman of the Festiniog Railway Company and the Festiniog Railway Trust.

Chapter 3

71 Edward Pease (1767-1858) was the main promoter of the Stockton & Darlington Railway, and came from a Quaker woollen manufacturing family in Darlington.

72 The 'Big Four' railway companies – the Great Western, London & North Eastern, London Midland & Scottish, and Southern – were created in 1923 following the passage of the Railways Act, 1921.

73 Sir Edward William Watkin (1819-1901), 1st Baronet, created 1880. Liberal MP for Great Yarmouth, 1857-58; for Stockport, 1864-68; for Hythe, 1874-86; Liberal Unionist MP for Hythe, 1886-95; formerly a Manchester merchant. Knight of the Order of the Redeemer, Greece, and of Leopold, Belgium.

74 Sir Lawrence Alma-Tadema (1836-1912), Knighted 1899, OM 1905, RA 1879. Popular artist at the time who specialised in scenes from ancient Rome, meticulously researched, many depicting scenes of luxury and decadence and languorous figures painted with a remarkable delicacy of touch. Amongst his many works were *The Roses of Heliogabalus* (1888) and *The Finding of Moses* (1904). His home was in Grove End Road, St John's Wood, London NW.

75 Quoted in *Great Central*, Vol Two, by George Dow (1962).

76 The hotel was built speculatively by Frank Crocker, a local entrepreneur.

77 Sir Sam Fay (1856-1953), Knighted 1912. Entered LSWR service as clerk, 1872; General Manager, Midland & South Western Junction Railway, 1892; Superintendent of the Line, LSWR, 1899; General Manager, Great Central Railway, 1902-22. Member of Railway Executive Committee and of Ports and Transit Executive Committee, 1913-21; Director of Movements, War Office, 1 January 1917-21 March 1918; Director-General of Movements and Railways, War Office, and Member of Army Council, 1918-19. Member of Committee on Post Office Wages, 1904; Member of Departmental Committee on Inshore Fisheries, 1913; President, Institute of Transport, 1922-23; Chairman of Royal Commission on New South Wales Government Railways and Tramways, 1924; reported to New Zealand Government on working of New Zealand Railways, 1925.

78 The changing role of the Great Central main line', LMR, East Midlands Division pamphlet, December 1959. National Archives, AN 111/657.

79 Paper by F. C. Margetts to BRB dated 11 December 1963. National Archives, AN 111/657.

80 National Archives, MT 124/175.

81 Lance William Cripps Ibbotson (1909-98), CBE 1971, subsequently became General Manager, Southern Region, and later of the Western Region, where he pursued a programme of retrenchment, including the closure of the down side of Swindon station, a major timetable constraint and source of delay on the Great Western main line until the Strategic Rail Authority (SRA) sponsored the construction of a new down platform on 2 June 2003. On his retirement, he became an active member of the Railway Conversion League, dedicated to concreting over railway lines.

82 Meeting of 14 July 1964, papers in National Archives, AN 111/657.

83 National Archives, MT 124/175.

84 David Clarke (d1999), President and benefactor of the Great Central Railway, a former racing driver and commercial film-maker.

85 Adrian Shooter (b1948), a career railwayman who joined British Railways in 1970 as an engineering graduate trainee. Area Manager, St Pancras, 1984-87; Managing Director, Red Star Parcels, 1987-89;

Director, Parcels Business, 1989-93; Managing Director, Chiltern Railways, 1993-2001, Chairman 2002-11. Credited with the foresight to reinstate double track on the Chiltern main line, and to create new Oxford to London service via the new curve at Bicester. Chairman, Oxon Local Enterprise Partnership, 2012-. Chairman, West Midlands Regional Council, CBI, 2011-.

86 From *Coming Up Trumps: A Memoir* by Jean Trumpington (Macmillan, 2014), p43. 'There' was Bletchley Park, the Government's top-secret defence establishment responsible for decoding German secrets during the Second World War, at which Baroness Trumpington worked as a secretary for much of the war's duration.

87 Joseph Paxton (1803-65), architect, gardener and Member of Parliament, representing Coventry as a Liberal from 1864 until his death. The Crystal Palace was his crowning glory, for which he was knighted by Queen Victoria, but he also designed numerous glass houses, greenhouses and gardens, and among other jobs he held was that of head gardener at Chatsworth House. He was a director of the Midland Railway and became wealthy through investing successfully during the 'railway mania'.

88 Harry Verney (1801-94), Liberal MP for Buckingham, 1832-41, for Bedford, 1847-52, and Buckingham again, 1857-74 and 1880-85. He was born Harry Calvert and changed his name to Verney on inheriting his father's baronetcy, so that he could inherit the Verney family estates. He was uniquely responsible for the naming of two railway stations – Calvert being the other – neither of which originally served a community bearing its name.

89 John Betjeman (1906-84), Poet Laureate, 1972-84, CBE 1960, Knight Bachelor, 1969. Founder of the Victorian Society. Passionate supporter of the railway and its Victorian architecture, about which he wrote numerous poems and broadcast extensively. He was instrumental in saving St Pancras station from demolition in the 1960s, and is honoured by a statue of him on the concourse of the international station. Uniquely he had three railway locomotives named after him: a Class 90 electric locomotive that operated mainly out of Liverpool Street on the former Great Eastern main line, a pier locomotive on Southend pier, and an English Electric Class 20, which operates on the London Underground system.

90 This was The Six Counties Limited, which travelled over a number of lines that had already closed to passenger services, such as the Princes Risborough-Watlington branch, and others which would succumb in the 1960s (Bourne End-High Wycombe, Princes Risborough-Oxford, Bicester-Bletchley, Leighton Buzzard-Dunstable-Luton-Welwyn Garden City and Dalston to Broad Street). It was hauled out of Paddington by 92220 *Evening Star*, the last steam locomotive built by BR, on its first run in passenger service.

91 Hansard, House of Commons Debate, 19 December 1963, cc1593-1604.

92 Frank Markham (1897-1975), politician who sat in the House of Commons representing three different parties. He was Labour MP for Chatham, 1929-31, defecting with Ramsay MacDonald just before the 1931 election, when he stood down and became National Labour, and was elected for that party in Nottingham South in 1935. He then became Conservative candidate for Buckingham in 1950, elected in 1951, winning Buckingham by 54 votes. Retired from Parliament in 1964. Knighted 1953. Author of acclaimed *A History of Milton Keynes and District*, 1973.

93 Thomas ('Tam') Galbraith (1917-82), Conservative MP for Glasgow Hillhead, 1948-82, and junior transport minister, 1963-64. He predeceased his father, the first Lord Strathclyde, and the title passed to his son, also Thomas Galbraith (b1960), who served as a junior minister, chief whip and leader of the House of Lords, 2010-13.

94 Robert Maxwell (1923-91) was born Ján Ludvík Hyman Binyamin Hoch in what was then Czechoslovakia. He was a media proprietor and Labour MP for Buckingham, 1964-70. Founder of Pergamon Press after the Second World War (in which he received the Military Cross for gallantry) and owner of the Mirror Group of newspapers, he was one of the most colourful characters of the second half of the 20th century. For a time he and his family were involved with three Football League clubs – Oxford United, Reading and Derby County. He had close links with eastern European dictatorships, and was honoured by Israel, which gave him a state funeral, following his unexplained death caused by falling off his yacht cruising near the Canary Islands. Subsequently it was discovered that Maxwell had stolen hundreds of millions of pounds from his companies' pension funds.

95 Hansard, House of Commons Debate, 3 November 1964, Vol 701, c89.

96 In *Holding the Line* (p54) the authors report a conversation that Richard Faulkner had with Barbara Castle when as an Oxford undergraduate (and occasional user of the service to Cambridge) he challenged her about it at an Oxford University Labour Club meeting on 28 May 1965. Her response was testy and rude: 'You can't possibly expect me to comment on something so trivial,' was the gist of it. Within seven months (December 1965) Castle had become the minister responsible for rail closures.

97 Reginald Eyre (b1924), Conservative MP for Birmingham Hall Green, 1965-87. Government whip and later junior transport minister in the Thatcher and Major Governments. Knighted, 1984, Freeman of City of Birmingham, 1991, the city in which he worked as a solicitor from 1951.

98 William Benyon (1930-2014), Conservative MP for Buckingham, 1970-83, Milton Keynes, 1983-92. Vice Lord Lieutenant of Berkshire, 1994-2005. Landowner. His son Richard became Conservative MP for Newbury in 2005.

99 Hansard, House of Commons Debate, 23 November 1972, Vol 846, cc1735-1742.

100 Ibid.

101 Quoted in *Bletchley's Railway Heritage*, published online by the Milton Keynes Heritage Association.

102 From an email sent by Caryl Jones, communications manager, East West Rail Consortium, to members of the East West Rail All Party Parliamentary Group, 4 October 2014.

103 From press statement posted online by the Liberal Democrats, 6 October 2014.

104 Quoted by Peter Burman in *Railway Architecture*, 1979.

105 Isambard Kingdom Brunel (1806-59) was arguably the greatest English civil and mechanical engineer of all time. He built the Great Western Railway, dockyards and steamships, and many bridges and tunnels. His designs revolutionised public transport and modern engineering.

106 West of Exeter Route Resilience Study, Network Rail, Summer 2014.

107 Named after Charles Castleman, a Wimborne solicitor and original proponent of this sinuous line.

[108] The name comes from Thomas Hardy's eponymous short story.

[109] Tom Hanks (b1956) is a phenomenally successful US actor, producer, director and writer. By 2014 his films had grossed more than $8.4 billion worldwide. A passionate supporter of progressive causes such as same-sex marriage, electric cars and the US Democrat Party.

[110] West of Exeter Route Resilience Study, Network Rail, Summer 2014.

[111] Gerard Francis Gisborne Twistleton-Wykeham-Fiennes OBE, MA (1906-85) was a career railwayman who started as Assistant Yardmaster at Whitemoor, moving to Chief Controller at Cambridge. He became General Manager of BR's Eastern Region and later Chief Operating Manager at BRB. He was fired from British Rail in 1967 for publishing the book *I Tried to Run a Railway*, which was outspoken about the management of British Rail and particularly critical of the frequent management reorganisations it had gone through since nationalisation.

[112] *I Tried to Run a Railway* (Ian Allan, 1967).

[113] Papers of the Board's Corporate Rail Planning Officer. National Archives, AN 199/110.

[114] National Archives, AN/199/112.

[115] Chief Civil Engineer (of the Western Region).

[116] Nicholas Ridley (1929-93), Conservative MP for Cirencester & Tewkesbury, 1959-92, and Secretary of State for Transport, 1983-86. Ennobled as Baron Ridley of Riddesdale in 1992, he spoke in the House of Lords against railway privatisation. His positive working relationship with Robert Reid as BR Chairman was key to restoring Government confidence in the Board to manage its own affairs and led directly to approval of East Coast Main Line electrification.

[117] Letter from TUCC for Scotland to the Minister of Transport, 16 December 1965. Scottish Records Office, RCC6/72/1.

Chapter 4

[118] Memorandum of North Eastern Region consultation meeting held on 11 September 1963. National Archives, AN 168/89.

[119] Letter of 15 September 1966, which also gave consent for Harrogate-Northallerton. National Archives, AN 168/89.

[120] Memorandum of meeting held of 11 September 1963. National Archives, AN 168/89.

[121] Letter from Ministry of Transport dated 25 March 1969. National Archives, AN 177/192.

[122] Access and Connections: East Sussex (report by Jonathan Roberts Consulting). Jonathan Roberts (b 1950) is a transport policy consultant of over 40 years' standing. He set up his own practice in 2009, and had previously worked for the leading public affairs consultancies in this field. He was a work colleague of the authors in the 1980s and '90s.

[123] Ashby de la Zouch Castle features in Scott's novel *Ivanhoe*.

[124] *I Tried to Run a Railway* (Ian Allan, 1967).

[125] Letter from Harold Few, at Liverpool Street, to Charles Haygreen at BR's Central Planning Unit, dated 20 November 1963. National Archives, AN 121/287.

[126] Letter from R. G. Smith (Assistant Director of Costings, BRB) to Eastern Region, 22 January 1965. National Archives, AN 121/287.

[127] There was a siding connection at Radstock, a short-lived wartime connection near Bruton, and wagons could be exchanged at Highbridge. At Wells, the S&D even had its own station at Priory Road, separate from the GWR one at Tucker Street until closure in 1951.

Chapter 5

[128] *Holding the Line*, pp38-41.

[129] Today it is 80 minutes via Stirling on the 'Highland Chieftain' from King's Cross, but ScotRail trains cover it in 75 minutes via Ladybank.

[130] Hansard, House of Commons Debate, 15 November 1968, Vol 773, cc172-180W.

[131] Letter from DfT dated 27 July 1964. Scottish Records Office, RCC6/19/2.

[132] It was later reopened for coal traffic in 1988.

[133] John Brewis (1920-89), Conservative MP for Galloway, April 1959-September 1974, Lord-Lieutenant of Wigtownshire, Chairman of Scottish Select Committee, pro-European farmer and businessman.

[134] Hansard, House of Commons Debate, 29 January 1970, Vol 794, cc1869-78.

[135] Bob Brown (1921-76), Labour MP for Newcastle-upon-Tyne West, 1966–83, Newcastle-upon-Tyne North, 1983-87. Parliamentary Secretary, Ministry of Transport, 1968-70. Lord Mayor of Newcastle, 1994-95. Apprenticed plumber and gasfitter, Newcastle & Gateshead Gas Co, 1937; plumber, 1946; Inspector, 1949; in service of Northern Gas Board until 1966.

[136] Cecil Parkinson (b1931) was Secretary of State for Transport, 1989-90. Conservative MP for Enfield West, 1970-74, Hertfordshire South, 1974-83, Hertsmere, 1983-92. He was appointed as a minister in Margaret Thatcher's first Government in 1979, rising to Secretary of State for Trade and Industry in 1983. He was forced to resign when his former secretary, Sarah Keays, announced that she was pregnant with his child. He returned to office as Energy Secretary, 1987-89, before going to Transport, eventually resigning on the same day as Thatcher. Ennobled as Lord Parkinson in 1992. A chartered accountant by profession, he has been a director of numerous companies.

[137] Reported in the *Glasgow Herald*, 3 August 1978.

[138] *Memoirs of a Station Master* (1879), by Ernest J. Simmonds, edited by Jack Simmonds (Adams & Dart, 1974)

Chapter 6

[139] Sir Alfred Sherman (1919-2006), former Communist who fought on the Republican side in the Spanish Civil War. Founded the right-wing think-tank the Centre for Policy Studies with Margaret Thatcher and Sir Keith Joseph in 1974. Contributed to Thatcher's speeches, and used to send her memos almost daily, which he typed himself on an old typewriter. Leader writer on the *Daily Telegraph* until fired in 1986.

[140] *Holding the Line*, p98 et passim.

[141] Hansard, Vol 973, c379.

[142] Antony Kirby Speller (1927-2013), Conservative MP for North Devon. Entrepreneur who set up his own chain of photocopying shops in South West England. Exeter city councillor, 1963-74.

[143] Jeremy Thorpe (1929-2014), Liberal MP for North Devon, 1959-79, and leader of the Liberal Party, 1967-76. A colourful and flamboyant politician, his political career came to an end over a sex scandal involving Norman Scott, who claimed to have had a homosexual affair with him in the early 1960s. Scott's dog ('Rinka') was shot by a hired gunman, and Thorpe was charged, with three others, with conspiracy to murder Scott. At the trial, which was delayed until after the 1979 election at which Thorpe lost his seat to

Tony Speller (qv), all four were acquitted.

[144] 'This is the age of the train' was the strapline in a highly successful series of BR InterCity advertisements at the time.

[145] Peter Mills (1921-93), Conservative MP for Torrington, 1964-74, Devon West, 1974-83, Torridge and West Devon, 1983-87. Junior minister, 1972-74. Farmer.

[146] Hansard, 15 May 1981, Vol 4, cc1049-64.

[147] Kenneth Clarke (b1940), Conservative MP for Rushcliffe in Nottinghamshire since 1970. Fifth longest-serving minister in recent times, having been a member of the governments led by Margaret Thatcher, John Major and David Cameron for a total of 20 years. He has been Chancellor of the Exchequer, Home Secretary, Lord Chancellor and Justice Secretary, Education Secretary, Health Secretary and Minister without Portfolio; the two jobs denied him were Foreign Secretary and Prime Minister. He contested the Conservative Party leadership three times – in 1997, 2001 and 2005. He was awarded the CH (Companion of Honour) when he finally resigned as a minister in 2014.

[148] Hansard, 15 May 1981, Vol 4, cc1049-64.

[149] Hansard, 16 January 1987, Vol 108, cc325-6W.

[150] Malcolm Bruce (b1944), Liberal Democrat MP for Gordon, 1983-2015. Deputy leader of the party since January 2014. Knighted in 2012.

[151] Michael Denzil Xavier Portillo (b1953), former Conservative MP for Enfield Southgate (1984-97) and Kensington and Chelsea, 1999-2005. Minister of State for Transport, 1988-90, and subsequently Chief Secretary to the Treasury, and Secretary of State for Employment, then Defence. Since leaving Parliament Portillo has forged a brilliantly successful career as a broadcaster and after-dinner speaker; his *Great Railway Journeys* programmes for the BBC have added significantly to the public's affection for its railways and rail travel.

[152] Hansard, 5 December 1989, Vol 163, c185W. Bishop Auckland – Weardale subsequently lost its regular passenger service in 1992

Chapter 7

[153] Section 8 of the Railways Act, 1974.

[154] Alastair Darling (b1953), Labour MP for Edinburgh Central, 1987-2005, Edinburgh South West 2005 – 15, Chief Secretary to HM Treasury, 1997-98, Secretary of State for Social Security, 1998-2001, for Work and Pensions, 2001-02, for Transport, 2002-06, for Scotland, 2003-06, for Trade and Industry, 2006-07; Chancellor of the Exchequer, 2007-10. Chairman, Better Together campaign, 2012-14. Advocate by profession.

[155] *Holding the Line*, pp104 et seq.

[156] See Chapter 3 for earlier skirmishing between the two railways in relation to Wessex.

[157] C. Hamilton Ellis, *British Railway History*, Vol 2, p120 (George Allen & Unwin, 1959).

[158] Sir John Fowler KCMG, LLD (1817-98), eminent Victorian railway engineer, whose many lines included the Metropolitan Railway (1863) and the Oxford, Worcester & Wolverhampton Railway. He was retained by the GWR as a consultant following Brunel's death in 1859.

[159] James Staats Forbes, Chairman of the London, Chatham & Dover and Metropolitan District railways. A well-respected railway manager, he was brought in to broker a deal with the approval of both the GWR and LSWR. His name is today commemorated by

Network Rail in a suite of offices at the old Ewer Street depot in Southwark, near London Bridge station.

[160] T. B. Sands, *The Didcot, Newbury & Southampton Railway* (Oakwood Press, 1971).

[161] E. L. Ahrons, *Locomotive and Train Working in the Latter Half of the Nineteenth Century* (Heffers, Cambridge, 1953). Suakin was the headquarters of the Egyptian and British troops operating in the eastern Sudan against the dervishes under Osman Digna in 1884. When these operations were begun a project for linking Suakin to Berber by railway was revived and a few miles of rails were laid in 1884. Then the Sudan was abandoned and the railway remained in abeyance until 1905-06, when it was finally built.

[162] *The Didcot, Newbury & Southampton Railway* by Paul Karau, Mike Parsons and Kevin Robertson (Wild Swan Publications, 1981).

[163] Location for the filming of the popular TV series *Downton Abbey*.

[164] The camp was at Morn Hill.

[165] Letter of 16 November 1918 in National Archives, RAIL 1057/845. Cheesehill was the original name of Winchester Chesil station.

[166] Papers in the National Archives, AN/2/246/42.

[167] See *Holding the Line*, pp104-108.

[168] At this time the A30 was the principal trunk road between London and Devon and Cornwall, before the development of the A303.

[169] Ministry of Transport files. National Archives, MT 120/110.

[170] Paper of December 1977 filed in the National Archives, AN 176/257.

[171] The first two took place during the English Civil War. In September 1643 the parliamentary forces led by the Earl of Essex won a decisive victory over Charles I, and the second, in October 1644, was indecisive.

[172] Ministry of Transport press notice, 3 September 1963.

[173] Brian Mawhinney (b1940), Conservative MP for Peterborough, 1979-97, and for North West Cambridgeshire, 1997-2005; Secretary of State for Transport, 1994-95; Chairman of Conservative Party, 1995-97; ennobled 2005; Chairman of Football League, 2003-10. Although he was at Transport for only 12 months, and was one of nine Secretaries of State during the 1990s, he is remembered for launching the great transport debate in 1995. Seen cynically by some as an alternative to taking political decisions, the debate was a milestone in the development of transport policy in Britain. It marked the point of realisation by the Treasury, reflecting research by Professor Phil Goodwin, that traffic would continue to grow to fill the road space available, and that it was not possible to build your way out of congestion. It marked the reversal of Roads to Prosperity, launched by Mawhinney's predecessor, John MacGregor, as 'the biggest road programme since the Romans', and eventually to a change in the approach to rail policy.

[174] Daniel Hooper (b1973), environmental campaigner and activist.

[175] C. Hamilton Ellis, *British Railway History*, Vol 2 (George Allen and Unwin, 1959).

[176] Gerry Fiennes, *I Tried to Run a Railway* (Ian Allan, 1967)

[177] Frank Paterson MBE (b1930) is a career railwayman who joined the LNER in 1946 and rose to be General Manager of BR Eastern Region, 1978-85. Member of the Friends of the National Railway Museum since 1988, Chairman, 2002-12. One of the most able and respected railwaymen of his generation. Had been Board's chief freight manager during the row over the Didcot distribution depot

in 1978, and was responsible for hard-hitting 'Highway Robbery' press advertising that we describe on pp108-109 of *Holding the Line*.

[178] Letter of 7 July 1980 in National Archives, AN 176/360.

[179] Now called Railfuture.

[180] Letter from Department of Transport to BR dated 19 August 1982. National Archives, AN 176/360.

[181] Henry Johnson (1906-88) was the first career railwayman to become Chairman of the British Railways Board. Joined LNER as traffic apprentice in 1923, rising through the ranks to become General Manager, BR Eastern Region, 1958, and London Midland Region, 1962. Vice-Chairman of BRB, 1967. Knighted 1968. BRB Chairman, 1968-71. Class 86 electric locomotive No 86227 was named after him.

[182] John Ruskin, *Praeterita*, 1871-77. Quoted in *Holding the Line*, p7.

[183] *The Woodhead Route*, Alan Whitehouse (Ian Allan Publishing, 2014).

Chapter 8

[184] One of the authors recalls Parker using the onion analogy in a conversation with senior railway managers – he added 'and it all ends in tears'.

[185] Colonel Holman Fred Stephens (1868-1931) was a civil engineer and manager involved in 16 light railways in all parts of England and Wales, including the Ffestiniog and Kent & East Sussex railways. The son of pre-Raphaelite artist and critic Frederic George Stephens, he was first apprenticed in the workshops of the Metropolitan Railway and later attained the rank of colonel in the Territorial Army during the First World War. Material from the railways with which he was associated can be viewed at the award-winning Colonel Stephens Railway Museum at Tenterden station, on the Kent & East Sussex Railway.

[186] Letter to the Minister, 24 May 1965. National Archives, MT 124/751.

[187] Letter to the Ministry, 27 April 1965. Ibid.

[188] Ibid.

[189] BR Heads of Information. National Archives, MT 124/751.

[190] Letter from General Manager Western Region (Gerry Fiennes) to F. C. Margetts, 11 August 1964. National Archives, AN 121/287.

[191] File note dated 17 August 1964. National Archives, AN 121/287.

[192] Minutes of meeting of 27 January 1966. National Archives, MT 124/751.

[193] Internal MoT memo from A. E. Thomasson to J. H. Baxter, 14 April 1966. National Archives, MT 124/751.

[194] Owen Humberstone Prosser (1923-2004) was one of the pioneers on the Talyllyn Railway in 1951 and was a tireless campaigner to protect or reopen railways. A Royal Naval cadet during the Second World War, he saw service on D-Day and after demobilisation joined the civil service. A master of circumlocution, he also had great patience and insight and retained a vision of the railway's potential, even during the darkest days.

[195] Letter of 12 March 1966. National Archives, MT 124/751.

[196] Letter from Ministry of Transport to British Railways Board, 23 July 1965. National Archives, MT 124/1194.

[197] Letter from Clerk to Isle of Wight Council to Minister, 17 February 1967. Ibid.

[198] Memorandum from Stewart Joy to Peter Lazarus, 5 July 1968. Ibid.

[199] Correspondence. Ibid.

Chapter 9

[200] Formal closure was on 1 January 1968. In common with most Edinburgh services, no Sunday service ran, and the last train was on the Saturday, 30 December 1967.

[201] John Morris (b1931), Labour politician who served as parliamentary secretary responsible for railways, 1966-68, when Barbara Castle was Minister of Transport. He served continuously on the Labour front bench from 1964 until 1999, in a variety of senior positions including Secretary of State for Wales and Attorney-General. He was MP for Aberavon, 1959-2001, when he was ennobled as Lord Morris of Aberavon. He was a Cambridge-educated QC who became a recorder, Lord Lieutenant of Dyfed and Chancellor of the University of Glamorgan. Knighted 1999, Knight of the Garter 2003.

[202] Hansard, 20 December 1967, Vol 756, c410W.

[203] Neil George Carmichael (1921-2001), Labour MP for Glasgow, Woodside 1962-74, and Kelvingrove, 1974-83, held a series of junior ministerial posts, including Ministry of Transport 1967-69. Ennobled as Lord Carmichael of Kelvingrove, 1983.

[204] Hansard, 7 December 1967, Vol 755, c379W.

[205] Ministry of Transport Working Party on Passenger Closure Proposals, 25 June 1964. National Archives, MT 124/749.

[206] Memorandum to Ministry of Transport in its files. National Archives, MT 124/749.

[207] Letter of 7 July 1966. National Archives, MT 124/749.

[208] Letter to Ministry of Transport, 15 April 1969. National Archives, MT 124/749.

[209] Papers in the National Archives, AN 168/24.

[210] One that did not was the Stockport-Stalybridge line, where, since the withdrawal of PTE support in 1989, the service was reduced to a token one train a week. Very sensibly, as the line is required for freight anyway, the line and its stations remain intact, if a little run down, and would be available to use again when required. In recent years a number of (hitherto unsuccessful) attempts have been made to run an 'open access' service up the West Coast Main Line and on across the Pennines to towns such as Huddersfield, Halifax and Bradford, which would have taken the Stockport-Stalybridge route.

[211] Memorandum from Line Manager, Manchester, to General Manager, Euston, 18 November 1964. National Archives, AN 155/201.

[212] Now Iarnrod Eireann.

[213] Memorandum from CCE Manchester, 19 November 1964. National Archives, AN 155/201.

[214] Memorandum from Line Manager, Manchester, to General Manager for use by Ministry of Transport, 26 November 1964. National Archives, AN 155/138.

[215] David Charles Waddington (b1929), Conservative MP for Nelson and Colne, 1968-September 1974, Clitheroe, March 1979-1983, Ribble Valley, 1983-90. Ennobled 1990 as Lord Waddington. Governor and Commander-in-Chief of Bermuda, 1992–97; Recorder of the Crown Court, 1972-99. Held a succession of ministerial appointments from 1979, including Government Chief Whip, Home Secretary and leader of the House of Lords.

[216] Papers in the London Midland closures file. National Archives, AN 155/138.

[217] *Reinstating a trans-Pennine route – At a Glance 2014*, published by the Skipton East Lancashire Rail Action Partnership.

218 From *YDR News*, No 90, Spring 2011.

219 'In some cases, the section of railway preserved is only part of a longer route, and has no real worthwhile public transport function to perform. While some lines go "from nowhere to nowhere", others do run in a corridor where a conventional public transport service could be offered, subject to the issues referred to above. In other cases, the railway could have a valuable "public tourist transport" role to offer, even if a conventional commuter service would be unlikely to be worthwhile.

This phrase was used by Paul Lewin (Ffestiniog Railway) in his evidence. The new Welsh Highland Railway performs this function well in providing car-free access to the Snowdonia National Park. The North York Moors Railway does the same for Whitby where summer parking is constrained and the roads approaching the town are badly congested. The Swanage Railway operates a park and ride service allowing drivers to avoid the congested A351 which severs the picturesque village of Corfe Castle.'

Chapter 10

220 Quoted by John Betjeman in *First and Last Loves* (John Murray, 1952).

221 L. T. C. Rolt, *George and Robert Stephenson* (Longman, 1960).

222 York did have a second station, Layerthorpe, built by the Derwent Valley Light Railway, but this was a late entry and an early departure from the passenger network.

223 Also served by the Selsey Tramway until 1935.

224 *The Reshaping of British Railways* (British Railways Board, 1963), p14.

225 These two railways amalgamated to form the London & North Western Railway in 1846.

226 Taken over by the Midland Railway in 1846. See Gloucester below.

227 The Midland Railway had been formed by the amalgamation of the Birmingham & Derby Junction, the North Midland and the Midland Counties railways in 1844.

228 The Department for Transport originally intended that the Birmingham terminus of HS2 would be called 'Faseley Street'. At the time that the white paper was published in March 2010, co-author Richard Faulkner was working with Lord Adonis as transport whip in the House of Lords. At a meeting of ministers and officials to review the final draft Faulkner pointed out that as the new high speed line was to finish at the Grade 1 listed Curzon Street building, that was a far more appropriate name for the HS2 station. This was agreed, and Faulkner obtained a copy of the original drawing of the 1839 Curzon Street from the National Railway Museum archive, which duly appeared on page 116 of the white paper High Speed Rail (Cmnd 7827).

229 Bought by the Great Western in 1846.

230 The best journey time from Euston to New Street today is 1hr 22min.

231 Alfred Thompson Denning (1899-1999), a grammar school boy who rose to the topmost height of the legal profession, serving as Master of the Rolls for 20 years, 1962-82. Knighted 1944, Order of Merit 1997. Became a KC in 1938, and a high court judge in 1944. Among many public appointments he was best known for the inquiry into the circumstances of the resignation of John Profumo, Secretary of State for War, in 1963. Denning had served in the British Expeditionary Force to France, 1917-19, and was awarded Chevalier, Légion d'Honneur (France) in 1998, in addition to numerous honorary degrees and doctorates from universities around the world.

232 So called because the city was constantly wreathed in smoke from coal fires, with the fuel supplied latterly by the Edinburgh & Dalkeith Railway.

233 The Caledonian became part of the LMS, while the North British went to the LNER. In more recent years this rivalry flared up again when the North British route via Arrochar was chosen as the route to Oban, and the Caledonian route via Callander was closed in 1966. The undercurrent of tension remained until relatively recently, by which time the staff who had worked on the Oban line prior to 1966 had all retired.

234 Chris Green (b1943), career railwaymen who joined British Rail as a management trainee in 1965 after graduating from Oriel College, Oxford. Held a succession of management posts including General Manager, Scottish Region, 1984-86, Director, Network SouthEast, 1986-91, and Managing Director of InterCity, 1992-94, and ScotRail, 1994-95. After privatisation he was Chief Executive of Virgin Trains and Chairman of Virgin Rail, and later a non-executive director of Network Rail, 2005-10.

235 BRB papers in National Archives, AN 111/486.

236 Donald Kaberry (1907-91), Conservative MP for Leeds North West, 1950-83. A solicitor who served for 20 years on Leeds City Council, he had a distinguished war record, twice mentioned in despatches, and was a battery commander during the Dunkirk evacuation. Baronet, 1960, ennobled, 1983.

237 Geoffrey Hirst (1904-84), Conservative MP for Shipley, 1950-74. Director of various companies in the hospitality and catering industry.

238 *The Times*, 3 January, 1962.

239 Memorandum from C. P. Scott-Malden at the Ministry to John Ratter, BRB, 18 July 1963. National Archives, MT 124/634.

240 National Archives, MT 124/634.

241 Amalgamation of the Birmingham & Gloucester and Bristol & Gloucester railways had taken place in 1845.

242 *The Bristol & Gloucester Railway*, Colin Maggs (Oakwood Press, 1969).

243 G. P. Neele, *Railway Reminiscences*, (1904).

244 Peter Walker (1932-2010), Conservative MP for Worcester, 1961-92, and Secretary of State for the Environment, 1970-72. Also served as Minister of Housing and Local Government, and Secretary of State for Trade and Industry in the 1970-74 Heath Government. When the Conservatives returned to office in 1979 Walker was successively Minister of Agriculture, Secretary of State for Energy (during the miners' strike) and Secretary of State for Wales, leaving office in 1990. He was a 'One Nation' Conservative, a prominent Young Conservative, and a businessman who had been a partner in Slater Walker, and Chairman of Kleinwort Benson. Ennobled as Lord Walker of Worcester in 1992. His son, Robin, was elected MP for Worcester in May 2010.

245 Sally Oppenheim (b1930), Conservative MP for Gloucester, 1970-87. Ennobled as Baroness Oppenheim-Barnes, 1989. Minister of State (Consumer Affairs), Department of Trade, 1979-82. Chairman, National Consumer Council, 1987-89; Council of Management, National Waterways Museums Trust, 1988-89. Non-executive Director: and Member, main board of Boots Co, 1982-93; Fleming High Income Trust, 1989-97; HFC Bank, 1989-98.

246 Edward Osmotherley (b1942), career civil servant who served as

Under-Secretary (Railways), 1982-85, and Deputy Secretary in the Public Transport and Research Department of the Department of Transport, 1989-92. Assistant Secretary, Department of the Environment, 1976-79, and seconded to BRB, 1979. Local Government Ombudsman, 1993-2001. CB 1992, knighted 2002. Head of the Machinery of Government division in the Cabinet Office, 1980-81, when so-called 'Osmotherley Rules' were formulated, which specified how ministers and civil servants should respond to requests from parliamentary select committees in the Lords and the Commons. Informally within the Department these were known as the 'O'Smotherley Rules'. They have no formal parliamentary standing and have been revised and modified in the years since 1980, the most recent version issued being 'Giving Evidence to Select Committees: Guidance for Civil Servants' in October 2014.

[247] National Archives, MT 188/76.

[248] National Archives, AN 176/42.

Chapter 11

[249] Named after a nearby inn.

[250] Memorandum from Railways 'B' Division, 13 April 1962. National Archives, MT 124/180.

[251] The lines to Blaenavon (Low Level), Brynmawr and Ebbw Vale.

[252] Served by the Aberayron branch, which had been freight-only since 1951. Letter to J. E. R. Carson of Aberystwyth. National Archives, MT 124/180.

[253] The line was engineered by Thomas Bouch, the engineer of the first Tay Bridge.

[254] Stravithie station building did not disappear but has been restored as a boutique guest house.

[255] See *Holding the Line*, pp13 and 14.

[256] Goods traffic ceased the following year.

[257] National Records of Scotland, BR/RSR/4/2006.

[258] Derek Twigg (b1959), Labour MP for Halton since 1997. Junior transport minister, 2005-06. Former civil servant.

[259] Hansard, 29 November 2005, c18WS.

[260] House of Commons Debate, 18 December 1969, Vol 793, cc395W-401W.

[261] House of Commons Debate, 18 January 1972, Vol 829, cc158-60W.

[262] Penrith Keswick Railway Pre-Feasibility Study, Cumbria County Council, 1996.

[263] Described on the website, www.keswickrailway.com.

[264] *Return to Keswick – the Case for a new Railway* (ISBN 978 1 902543 02 4).

Chapter 12

[265] Teasmade is the trademark name of an automatic tea-making device activated by an alarm clock. They were most popular in the 1970s, when they featured on many wedding present lists. They may be making a comeback as a sought-after retro item.

[266] Magnus Duncan Linklater (b1942), distinguished Scottish journalist and broadcaster. Scotland editor of *The Times*, 2007-12. CBE 2013.

Chapter 13

[267] Christopher Fildes (b1934), financial journalist since 1963 (*The Times, Spectator, Daily Mail, Euromoney, Evening News, Investors Chronicle*). Member, Railway Heritage Committee, 1999-2010. OBE 1994.

[268] 'Better Connections – Options for the integration of High Speed 2' (Network Rail), p3

[269] Ibid.

[270] Ibid, p7.

[271] See for example the so-called 'Taxpayers' Alliance', which receives significant funding from parts of the road lobby, particularly road haulage interests in the West Midlands. The Institute for Economic Affairs has published a number of virulently anti-rail papers: one – 'The High Speed Gravy Train' (August 2013) – not only rubbishes HS2, but also attacks the construction of the Jubilee Line and High Speed 1, and the author makes clear his preference for investment in road-building – a transport policy approach that is 30 years out of date. The IEA followed this up with a report in January 2015 on converting commuter rail routes into roads. These, and other IEA reports, were published as a result of grants received from the Nigel Vinson Charitable Trust, as indeed was the notorious report in January 1976 – 'Better Use of Rail Ways' by Peter Hall and Edward Smith, Department of Geography, University of Reading – which only saw the light of day thanks to Lord Vinson, as the Department of the Environment, which had commissioned the study, declined to publish it (see *Holding the Line*, p97).

[272] *Holding the Line*, pp111-13.

[273] 'Report on the Value of Heritage Railways', published by the Heritage Rail All-Party Parliamentary Group, July 2013 (copies available via the Heritage Railway Association).

[274] Ibid, p7.

[275] The North Yorkshire Moors Railway already operates into Whitby, and has itself sponsored the restoration of a disused platform at Whitby station to provide for more services.

[276] As suggested by the Embsay & Bolton Abbey Railway for its services into and out of Skipton (see chapter 9).

Appendix B

[277] Derker was opened experimentally on 30 August 1985 and closed on 3 October 2009. It was reopened as a stop on the Manchester Metrolink line to Rochdale and Oldham on 16 December 2012.

[278] Heysham Port station is still open, but served by only one train a day in each direction.

[279] Between May 1988 and September 1992 the public timetable contained details of summer weekend services. There is currently a summer service between Stanhope and Wolsingham operated by the Weardale Railway.

[280] The Crediton to Okehampton service runs on Sundays only from May to September. See Chapter 3.

Appendix D

[281] Roger Freeman (b1942), Conservative MP for Kettering, 1983-97, ennobled as Lord Freeman, 1997. Minister of State for Transport, 1990-94, Defence 1994-95, Chancellor of the Duchy of Lancaster, 1995-97. Chartered accountant.

[282] John Patten (b1945), Conservative MP for City of Oxford, 1979-83, Oxford West and Abingdon, 1983-97. Secretary of State for Education,

1992-94. Former Oxford University lecturer, 1969-79, Fellow of Hertford College, university of Oxford, 1972-94. Oxford City Councillor, 1973-76. Parliamentary Under-Secretary of State: NI Office, 1981-83; DHSS, 1983-85; Minister of State for Housing, Urban Affairs and Construction, DoE, 1985-87; Minister of State, Home Office, 1987-92.

283 The service still operates but takes 3hrs 35min for the journey between Oxford and Cambridge.

284 Glenda Jackson (b1936), Labour MP for Hampstead and Highgate, 1992-2010, Hampstead and Kilburn, 2010-15. Junior transport minister, 1997-99. Award-winning actress, 1957-92, with major parts in scores of films, TV and theatre productions.

285 Phyllis Starkey (b1947), Labour MP for Milton Keynes South West, 1997-2010. Oxford City Councillor, 1983-97 (Leader, 1990-93). Lectured in obstetrics and gynaecology at University of Oxford, 1984-93.

286 Patrick Hall (b1951), Labour MP for Bedford, 1997-2010. Former local government planning officer.

287 Tony Blair (b1953), Prime Minister, 1997-2007, Leader of the Opposition, 1994-97, Labour MP for Sedgefield, 1983-2007. Most successful election-winning Labour Party leader of modern times (1997, 2001 and 2005). Former barrister who read law at Oxford University. His subsequent reputation was marred by the decision to commit British forces to invade Iraq with the Americans in 2003.

288 Robert Paul Reid (b1934), Chairman of BRB, 1990-95. Came to the job from the oil industry, having previously been Chairman and Chief Executive of Shell. Knighted in 1990 and confusingly known as Sir Bob Reid like his immediate predecessor as BR Chairman. Had the unenviable task of preparing the railway for privatisation.

289 John Bercow (b1963), Conservative MP for Buckingham, 1997-2009, when he was elected Speaker of the House of Commons, retaining his seat in the 2010 election. Before entering Parliament he worked for Hambros Bank and as a City PR consultant.

290 Tony Baldry (b1950), Conservative MP for Banbury, 1983-2015. Held various middle-ranking ministerial jobs, 1990-97. Knighted 2012. From 2010 spoke in Parliament on behalf of the Church of England as Second Church Estates Commissioner.

291 Brian White (b1957), Labour MP for Milton Keynes East, 1997-2005. Former systems analyst.

292 Jeff Rooker (b1941), Labour MP for Birmingham Perry Barr, 1974-2001, when he joined House of Lords. Minister of state in a succession of government departments, 1997-2008. First job at 16 was as an apprentice toolmaker at an engineering firm in Birmingham.

293 Iain Stewart (b1972), Conservative MP for Milton Keynes South since 2010, which he won at the third attempt. Formerly a trainee chartered accountant, headhunter and researcher for Scottish Conservative Party. Member of Commons Transport Select Committee, 2010-13, then Parliamentary Private Secretary to Secretary of State for Transport, Patrick McLoughlin. Founded East West Rail all-party parliamentary group (APPG).

294 Evan Harris (b1965), Liberal Democrat MP for Oxford West and Abingdon, 1997-2010. Former House Officer, Radcliffe Hospital, Oxford. Associate director of Hacked Off, the campaign for a free and accountable press, formed in 2011 following the many telephone-tapping scandals involving tabloid newspapers.

295 Your co-author, also a vice-chair of East West Rail APPG.

296 Andrew Adonis (b1963), Secretary of State for Transport, 2009-10, and Minister of State at the same department, 2008-09. Widely regarded as the most pro-rail minister of recent times, Adonis was responsible for winning political and public support for High Speed 2, and other major rail investment decisions. Previously an academic, newspaper columnist and head of the Prime Minister's policy unit at 10 Downing Street.

297 Mark Lancaster (b1970), Conservative MP for Milton Keynes North since 2010, Milton Keynes North East, 2005-10. Appointed government whip 2012, former soldier and director of a fireworks company.

298 Theresa Villiers (b1968), Conservative MP for Chipping Barnet from 2005. Minister of State for Transport, 2010-12, Secretary of State for Northern Ireland from 2012. MEP for London Region, 1999-2005. Former barrister.

299 Andrew Smith (b1951), Labour MP for Oxford East since 1987. Chief Secretary to HM Treasury, 1999-2002, Secretary of State for Work and Pensions, 2002-04. Former Oxford City councillor.

300 Justine Greening (b1969), Conservative MP for Putney since 2005. Secretary of State for Transport, 2011-12, and for International Development since 2012. Former finance, and business strategy manager.

Appendix E

301 Burke St John Trend (1914-87), career civil servant who rose to Secretary of the Cabinet, 1963-73. Knighted 1962, ennobled as Lord Burke, 1974.

302 The 'memo' was Fraser's note that proposed 'standing firm' on railway closures.

303 The 'Spearman Bill' was the private member's bill introduced by the MP for Scarborough and Whitby, Alexander Spearman, which would have given the Minister of Transport the power to reverse a closure decision taken by his predecessor. It would have been crucial in the case of the Whitby closures.

304 (James) Harold Wilson (1916-95), leader of the Labour Party who won four general elections (1964, 1966, February and October 1974) out of five. MP for Ormskirk, 1945-50, and Huyton, 1950-83. Oxford don aged 21 and at 31 became youngest Cabinet Minister of 20th century when appointed President of the Board of Trade in 1947. (Resigned in 1951 over imposition of National Health Service charges.) Wilson's first thesis as an academic was a study of 19th-century commercial railway policy. Elected Labour leader following death of Hugh Gaitskell, 1963; Prime Minister, 1964-70 and 1974-76, and ennobled as Lord Wilson of Rievaulx in 1983.

305 Wilson's reference to the 'device of blocking proposals before TUCC stage' gave the green light to early ministerial intervention between the time that a closure proposal had been announced and the holding of the subsequent enquiry by the Transport Users' Consultative Committee. This was used to refuse closure of the Manchester to Bury electric service and the Edinburgh to Glasgow line via Shotts, and to delay the withdrawal of those in East Lincolnshire (though they closed later in October 1970).

306 George Brown (1914-85), Labour politician, MP for Belper, 1945-70, and deputy leader of the party, 1960-70. Defeated by Harold Wilson (see above) for leadership in 1963, and served as First Secretary of State and Secretary of State for Economic Affairs, October 1964-August 1966, and Foreign Secretary, 1966-68. Resigned abruptly, having threatened to do so on numerous previous occasions. He was a difficult colleague whose personal behaviour was not enhanced by the amount of alcohol he consumed. He went

to the House of Lords on losing his seat in 1970, and was so disenchanted with the Labour Party that he became President of the Social Democratic Alliance in 1981, presumably believing, as many others did, that the SDP would replace Labour as the political party of the centre-left.

[307] Richard Crossman (1907-74), Labour politician, academic, journalist, Second World War propagandist and MP for Coventry East, 1945-74. Passed over as a minister in 1945 Government, allegedly for being too pro-Zionist. Prominent member of Labour Party's left wing, holding a series of cabinet positions in 1964-70 administrations. Also edited *New Statesman* magazine, 1970-72, and authored three-volume *Diaries of a Cabinet Minister*.

[308] Frank Cousins (1904-86), General Secretary of Transport & General Workers Union, 1956-69, Minister of Technology in Harold Wilson's first government, 1964-66, and MP for Nuneaton (1965-66). Found the House of Commons and ministerial office uncongenial, finally returning to his old trade union job at TGWU.

[309] Cousins's reference to an 'integrated transport policy' reminded his colleagues of a long-standing but never implemented Labour Party policy, the delivery of which was made difficult because the comrades either had differing ideas of what it meant, depending on whether they came from a road or rail background, or didn't understand it at all.

[310] James Griffiths (1890-1975), veteran Labour MP for Llanelly, 1936-70, first Secretary of State for Wales, 1964-66. Came from South Wales mining background, having been miners' agent for Anthracite Mines Association, 1925-36, President of South Wales Miners' Federation, 1934-36, and member of executive committee of the Miners' Federation of Great Britain, 1934-36. Served in 1945 Attlee Government as Minister of National Insurance, 1945-50, and Secretary of State for the Colonies, 1950-51. In opposition he was deputy leader and vice-chairman of Parliamentary Labour Party, 1956-59. Privy Counsellor, 1945, and Companion of Honour, 1966.

[311] Douglas Jay (1907-96), Labour MP for Battersea North, 1946-83, President of Board of Trade, 1964-6. Had been a Treasury minister in post-war Labour Government. Dedicated opponent of British membership of Common Market, and was reputed to take his own sandwiches when travelling abroad on government business because of his dislike for foreign food. Life peer, 1987.

[312] Douglas Houghton (1898-1996), Labour MP for Sowerby, 1949-74. For 38 years was Secretary of Inland Revenue Staff Federation (1922-60), member of TUC General Council, 1952-60. Chancellor of Duchy of Lancaster, 1964-66, and Minister Without Portfolio, 1966-67. Chairman of Parliamentary Labour Party, 1967-74. Companion of Honour, 1967, and life peer, 1974.

[313] Lord Hinton of Bankside joined Ministry of Transport as special adviser on transport planning. Announcing his appointment, Fraser told House of Commons, 'The task Lord Hinton will undertake is, broadly speaking, to inquire into the means whereby and the extent to which the transport of goods and passengers in Great Britain can best be co-ordinated and developed in the national interest' (House of Commons Debate, 8 February 1965, Vol 706, c30). This, however, was somewhat at odds with what Fraser told the Cabinet at this meeting (see later comment by Fraser).

[314] It is unclear what Houghton was referring to. CHSL may have been a committee of the Cabinet.

[315] Leonard James Callaghan (1912-2005), Labour politician who rose to become Prime Minister, 1976-79, after being a Royal Navy chief petty officer, Inland Revenue tax officer, trade union official, Cardiff MP (1945-87), Chancellor of the Exchequer, Home Secretary, and Foreign Secretary. Also a Junior Transport Minister in Attlee Government and Opposition Spokesman on Transport, 1951-53. Ennobled as Lord Callaghan of Cardiff, 1987.

[316] This was by far the most perceptive political comment made at the meeting. It demonstrated how much in tune Callaghan was with grass-roots Labour Party thinking.

[317] William Ross (1911-88), Labour MP for Kilmarnock, Ayr and Bute, 1946-79, Secretary of State for Scotland, 1964-70 and 1974-76. Former schoolmaster, awarded MBE on wartime military service as major in Royal Signals. Ennobled as Lord Ross of Marnock, 1979. Lord High Commissioner, General Assembly of Church of Scotland, 1978-80.

[318] A reference to the influential report on *Traffic in Towns* published by town planner Professor Sir Colin Buchanan in 1963, which addressed issues arising from the growth of personal car ownership and its effect on life in towns and cities.

[319] Which he did on 31 March 1965 (House of Commons Debate, 31 March 1965, Vol 709, cc1650-5)

Index